ROUTLEDGE LIBRARY EDITIONS:
WILLIAM BLAKE

Volume 3

READING BLAKE'S *SONGS*

READING BLAKE'S *SONGS*

ZACHARY LEADER

Routledge
Taylor & Francis Group

LONDON AND NEW YORK

First published in 1981 by Routledge & Kegan Paul Ltd

This edition first published in 2016
by Routledge
2 Park Square, Milton Park, Abingdon, Oxon OX14 4RN

and by Routledge
711 Third Avenue, New York, NY 10017

Routledge is an imprint of the Taylor & Francis Group, an informa business

© 1981 Zachary Leader

British Library Cataloguing in Publication Data
A catalogue record for this book is available from the British Library

ISBN: 978-1-138-93813-7 (Set)
ISBN: 978-1-315-67509-1 (Set) (ebk)
ISBN: 978-1-138-93912-7 (Volume 3) (hbk)
ISBN: 978-1-138-93927-1 (Volume 3) (pbk)
ISBN: 978-1-315-67512-1 (Volume 3) (ebk)

Publisher's Note
The publisher has gone to great lengths to ensure the quality of this reprint but points out that some imperfections in the original copies may be apparent.

Disclaimer
The publisher has made every effort to trace copyright holders and would welcome correspondence from those they have been unable to trace.

READING BLAKE'S
SONGS

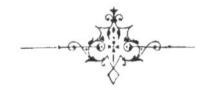

ZACHARY LEADER

ROUTLEDGE & KEGAN PAUL
Boston, London and Henley

First published in 1981
by Routledge & Kegan Paul Ltd
39 Store Street, London WC1E 7DD,
9 Park Street, Boston, Mass. 02108, USA and
Broadway House, Newtown Road,
Henley-on-Thames, Oxon RG9 1EN

Set in 10/11pt Plantin by
Computacomp (UK) Ltd
Fort William, Scotland
and printed in the United States of America by
Vail-Ballou Press, Inc.,
Binghamton, New York

British Library Cataloguing in Publication Data

Leader, Zachary
Reading Blake's 'Songs'.
1. Blake, William. Songs of innocence and
experience
I. Title
821'.7   PR4144.S63   80-41301

ISBN 0 7100 0635 7

CONTENTS

ILLUSTRATIONS

ACKNOWLEDGMENTS

This study of Blake's *Songs* began life as a doctoral dissertation presented to Harvard University in 1977. It would never have grown into a book without the far-sighted and exacting supervision of its original readers, the late Professors Isabel MacCaffrey and Reuben Brower of Harvard. Others to whom I am indebted for early criticism and encouragement are Jean Hagstrum, who first taught me to value Blake's composite art, Warner Berthoff, Heather Glen, Christopher Ricks, Theodore Redpath, and Stephen Brook of Routledge. For help at a later stage, and for reading and commenting in detail on the entire manuscript, I want especially to thank John Beer and Martin Butlin. Michael Ferber, a friend and improver of this book from its inception, also read and commented on the entire manuscript. Lastly, I want to thank my wife, who has been a perceptive critic and supporter throughout.

I am grateful to the following people for help in obtaining illustrations: Joyce Irene Whalley; Mme Véronique Goupy; Alfred and Doris Palca; T. A. J. Burnett; Aldo Cupo. The author and publishers are grateful to the following institutions for kind permission to reproduce the illustrations shown: the National Gallery, London, no. 1; the British Library, no. 2; Princeton University Library, no. 3; the Tate Gallery, London, nos 4, 16, 19; the British Museum, London, nos 5, 10, 12, 20, 21, 22, 23, 24, 25; the Victoria and Albert Museum, London, nos 6, 7, 8, 14; the Garman-Ryan Collection, Walsall Museum and Art Gallery, no. 9; Musée du Louvre, Paris, nos 11, 17; the Fitzwilliam Museum, Cambridge, no. 13; the Paul Mellon Collection, Yale Center for British Art, no. 15; the Metropolitan Museum of Art, New York, all rights reserved, no. 18.

KEY TO REFERENCES

All quotations from Blake's works, letters excluded, come from David V. Erdman, ed., *The Poetry and Prose of William Blake* (1965; rpt Garden City, NY: Doubleday, 1970). Quotes are cited within the text by the letter 'E' followed by reference to pages. An abbreviation of the work in question and arabic numerals indicating plate or page and line numbers will precede the citation from Erdman. Angle brackets within quotations from the prose <thus> enclose words or letters written to replace deletions, or as additions.

The following abbreviations and short titles are employed for those of Blake's works cited in text and footnotes:

A	America – *America a Prophecy*
ARAO	*All Religions Are One*
DC	*Descriptive Catalogue* – *A Descriptive Catalogue of Pictures*
E	*Europe* – *Europe a Prophecy*
FZ, V	*The Four Zoas* (earlier title, *Vala*)
G	*Gates* – *The Gates of Paradise* (*For Children* and *For the Sexes*)
I	*Innocence* – *Songs of Innocence*
J	*Jerusalem* – *Jerusalem the Emanation of the Giant Albion*
M	*Milton* – *Milton a Poem*
MHH	*Marriage* – *The Marriage of Heaven and Hell*
N	Notebook ('The Rossetti Manuscript')
PA	*Public Address*

Key to references

PS   *Poetical Sketches*
S   *Songs – Songs of Innocence and of Experience*
T   *Thel – The Book of Thel*
U   *Urizen – The First Book of Urizen*
VDA   *Visions – Visions of the Daughters of Albion*
VLJ   *Visions of the Last Judgement*

INTRODUCTION

Critics no longer make excuses or exceptions for Blake, even for the most difficult and rebarbative of his prophecies. The Norton and Oxford Anthologies of English Literature, key indices to and incubators of established opinion, provide ample selections from all phases of Blake's work. The third edition of the former excerpts eighteen pages from *Jerusalem* alone, the latter forty-five from the three epics together, seven more than from *The Prelude*. Blake as prophetic as well as lyric poet has not only arrived, he has become, in the words of one of the best of his modern editors, 'what Wordsworth used to be – the inescapable poet.'[1]

This faith in the importance, centrality, and ultimate intelligibility of Blake's vision, is, in F. W. Bateson's words, 'a modern discovery.' 'We now know,' writes Bateson, 'thanks to a generation of Blake scholarship, most of it trans-Atlantic, that the fantasies Housman admired because they were meaningless function in a completely rational and explicable framework.'[2] By 'trans-Atlantic scholarship' Bateson means Northrop Frye and David Erdman and the schools of lesser, though often eminently distinguished, critics and scholars who trail in their wake. Frye's followers, like Bateson, begin by assuming the ultimate consistency and coherence of Blake's 'system,' not only in individual works, but in the whole of his poetic output; so too do Erdman's, though their focus is primarily on its social or political constituent. They also have a proper (and properly grateful) appreciation of its inclusiveness and eclecticism. What Eliot found 'terrifying' about Blake, the fact that 'he was not compelled to acquire any other education in literature than he wanted, or to acquire it for any other reason than that he wanted it,'[3] turns out to have been a godsend for modern scholarship, yielding a rich and fertile harvest (including, to choose at random from the mystical strain alone, Boehme, Swedenborg, Paracelsus, the Kabbala, Thomas Taylor) for lesser toilers. Blake's omnivorous but 'untutored' reading, his assimilation of diverse disciplines and traditions (many of them quite outside Eliot's 'tradition'), together with the assumption of a single unified canon, keeps Blake studies alive and thriving.

But it also, I believe, for all the very real light it sheds, distracts us from certain crucial questions about the nature of Blake's achievement. I would frame one of the most elementary and important of these questions as follows: To what extent do Blake's individual works stand alone, apart from his corpus? This question, I realize, is likely to raise all sorts of suspicions about my own assumptions; suspicions which, for the moment at least, I hope to quiet by asking why its answer should not be of interest and importance even to those who think of Blake's works as 'contributions to the formulation of a system upon which their *full* meaning largely depends.'[4] When René Wellek tells F. R. Leavis, in the spirit of Frye and his followers, that Blake's 'Introduction' to *Experience* 'has only one possible meaning, which can be ascertained by a study of the whole of Blake's symbolical philosophy,' he receives the following response, one with which, in some respects, I agree:

> when in Blake's poetry his symbols function poetically they have, I believe, a life that is independent of his 'symbolical philosophy': for instance, 'Earth,' 'starry pole,' 'dewy grass' and 'wat'ry shore,' in the *Introduction* to *Songs of Experience*, seem to me to have a direct evocative power. Knowledge of Blake's arbitrary assignment of value to a symbol may often help to explain why he should have written as he has done here, there and elsewhere; I do not believe that it will ever turn what was before an unsuccessful poem into a good one.[5]

To object to this passage on the grounds that words and symbols are historically or culturally or socially determined – that Leavis seems to mistake tradition (however broad) for immutable fact – is right and necessary but, in the immediate context, may also be unhelpful. Though Blake borrowed from a variety of occult or non-established traditions, the audience he hoped to reach (when he considered it at all), was neither specialized nor elect. Like Wordsworth, he thought of himself as 'a man speaking to men.' This was especially true of the periods most important to this study: from 1789 to 1794, before neglect and disappointment drove him into himself, and from 1818 to 1825, during which he seems to have attained a new serenity and something of a following; though even in the intervening years it was 'the Public' rather than posterity or some fit few Blake sought to address.[6]

What meaning, moreover, can one ascribe to a phrase like 'the whole of Blake's symbolical philosophy,' when one believes, as the previous paragraph's reference to 'periods' suggests I do, that Blake changed; and not only in temperament, but in thought and practice as well. 'The Voice of the Ancient Bard,' for example, which plays a key role in the last chapter of this book, means different things at different times in Blake's career. It first appears in 1789 as one of the *Songs of Innocence*. In the 1790s, though it stays in *Innocence*, its meaning, for those who encounter it in the newly constituted *Songs of Innocence and of Experience* (first appearance, 1794), is effected not only by *Experience* as a whole, but by one's sense of the experienced Bard (of 'Introduction') in particular. Later on, when Blake transfers the plate to *Experience*, its meaning is again effected. How can it, then, have 'only one possible meaning which can be ascertained by a study of the whole of Blake's symbolical philosophy'?

Nor is it fair to argue that Leavis's criteria are inadequate to other and important questions one might well ask about Blake and his art. He never claims they are. Though characteristically provocative ('arbitrary' is carefully calculated), Leavis's reply to Wellek does not deny the existence or consistency of Blake's larger system or argument, or its relevance to an understanding of 'why he should have written as he has done.' It does, though, insist upon the independence, the 'life of its own,' of words and the symbols they form; criteria which, having first invoked Blake's Public — that broad tradition he, like Leavis, merely assumed — I shall apply in the pages that follow, extending it to the visual art as well.[7] That Blake was not always attentive to or careful of this independence, even the most partisan of his critics would agree. In the *Songs of Innocence and of Experience*, though, he was, and that controlled attentiveness helps make the book a great and justly admired work of art.

I use 'book' and 'work of art' in the above sentence (rather than 'them' and 'poems') advisedly. Chief among my aims in this study is to encourage others to approach *Songs* as a single, carefully organized volume of verbal and visual art (hence '*Songs*' rather than 'the *Songs*'), one in which almost every poem and design contributes to a larger artistic unity. This is not, I am aware, a fashionable ambition. Of late, criticism has turned, with much profit, from what fits (the richness of a work, in Coleridge's words, measured by 'the variety of parts which it holds in unity'[8]) to what one critic calls 'absences' or 'lacunae'[9]; those aspects of a text, to quote another, John Bayley, which are 'unsettled or left over to give the whole job a saving instability, to invite by reticence or irresolution participation by us in the processes of genius.'[10] Blake's works are rich in 'saving instabilities,' but they are also the creations of a life-long apostle of unity, one for whom currently unfashionable organicist criteria were gospel. Often Blake's works are literally about the tension they embody: as when too obsessive a unifying or ordering spirit threatens to crush or hide 'Minute Particulars' (*J* 91.21: E249) – Blake's term for the 'unsettled' or 'left over.'

This, I shall argue, is true of *Songs*, the nature and achievement of which, for all the popularity of its constituent lyrics, is still only imperfectly understood or appreciated. *Songs*, as has long been acknowledged, is more than a simple collection of lyric poems accompanied by decorative illustration. It is more, even, than a series of paired but antithetical plates. The relations between one poem and/or design and another are often extremely complex and subtle, even within separate volumes. Focusing exclusively or predominantly on paired plates can blind us to the larger purpose their and other more subtle relations serve.

That purpose, the governing principle or project of *Songs* as a whole, is usually sought for – by way of Swedenborg, Boehme, and the *Marriage of Heaven and Hell* – in Blake's theory of contraries.[11] This is not an approach I find particularly helpful, if only because of the cloudy or controversial nature of the dialectical progression or marriage (in Blake as well as in some of his sources and expositors) which lies at its core.[12] Nor, for reasons that will soon be apparent, am I comfortable with its more judicious rival theory: *Songs* as a merely (or maturely) objective, impartial (in a Keatsian sense) exploration of the relation between the perfect possibilities of human life, by which is meant 'Innocence,' and the confusions and imperfections of actual existence or 'Experience.'[13]

My view, introduced at the end of chapter 1, and argued in detail in chapters 3 through 7, is quite different. It is based on two assumptions, to each of which I devote chapters. The first is that Blake's immediate models for both *Innocence* and the combined *Songs* were children's books and educational treatises of the late seventeenth and eighteenth centuries.[14] The second is that the designs to *Songs* play a crucial role in disclosing its larger purpose and unity, and that they repay the closest possible attention. These are not particularly radical assumptions, but they have never in my opinion been properly applied. Though many critics have studied *Songs* in the light of children's hymns (particularly those of Bunyan, Watts, and Mrs Barbauld) most limit their discussion to similarities between individual poems. My study is the first to take note of an altogether broader and more general debt *Songs* owes to its pious predecessors. This debt is both thematic and functional: it provides a frame or context for Blake's ideas, as well as a means of exemplifying and testing them (in what I hope to show is the uniquely multi-functional manner of a children's book). Similarly, though a number of studies of individual poems have been published in the last few years which read a design closely and relate it to its accompanying text, no such approach has yet been used for the work as a whole. Erdman's invaluable commentary in *The Illuminated Blake* attends to the poetry 'only as it relates to the pictures,'[15] whereas my work also deals with aspects of the verse which have no visual referents. Moreover, as Erdman himself admits, his commentary is restricted in length by its format. As for previously published full-length studies of *Songs*, they either ignore the designs completely or give them only cursory or intermittent attention. This, in part, is why my book is the first to uncover what I believe to be the full 'story' of *Songs* – the narrative or drama that runs through and links its groupings.

A NOTE ON COPIES

Songs poses special technical or bibliographical problems to its students, the most important of which, especially to those who argue for its ultimate unity, is that Blake repeatedly altered the order and appearance of its plates. Though finally, after nineteen different arrangements, he seems to have 'settled down to'[1] a fixed order in 1815, it is impossible, no matter what the copy, to find a coherent, inevitable sequence from first plate to last. The opening plates of most copies of *Innocence* and *Experience* clearly belong in their present sequence, but many others could easily be switched around. Interpretations which assume, for instance, that a poem in the middle of a post-1815 copy constitutes a direct response to the poem immediately preceding it are likely to strike us as contrived or arbitrary. Because we can construct plausible arguments for almost any permutation (Question: 'Is there any ulterior structure to the *Dream Songs*'? Berryman's Answer: 'Ah — you mean someone can get to be an associate professor or an assistant professor by finding it out?')[2] it is best not to attribute much importance to the immediate context when dealing with later plates.

The problem of sequence is perhaps best understood by comparing *Songs* with other collections of lyric poetry, Herbert's *The Temple*, for instance, if not Berryman's *Dream Songs*. Though *The Temple*, too, opens with a series of poems obviously intended to form a sequence, this sequence quickly evaporates as we move into the main body of the work. Yet as Herbert himself says in the second of two poems on 'The H. Scriptures,' the reader frequently discovers that 'This verse marks that, and both do make a motion/ Unto a third that ten leaves off doth lie.'³ While the order in which most of its poems are set may seem random or only intermittently significant, later lyrics in *The Temple* clearly refer or allude to other lyrics. A similar process of cross-reference and allusion plays a vital part in unifying *Songs*.

Changes in the actual appearance of the plates pose even greater problems. Nearly all of Blake's writings, *Songs* included, were published in a form he called 'Illuminated Printing.' A complicated and delicate process of relief etching (largely, if not solely, of Blake's own invention)⁴ was used to transfer poem and design to copperplate; individual pages were then printed in an ordinary press and colored by hand. Blake issued copies separately, and never printed more than a few copies of any book at a time.⁵

Over twenty copies of *Innocence* and twenty-seven of the combined *Songs* are known to exist.⁶ No two copies look exactly the same. Blake varied the ground tints, sometimes used a fine pen to outline, heighten, or add details, and may even have made minor alterations to the original copperplate.⁷ The coloring, however, accounts for most of the more significant variations. Whole details from the original printing disappear, others are added. The size and shape of figures, the expressions on their faces, the contours of trees, bushes, bodies, and buildings are transformed in subtle and significant ways. What look like plants in one copy become flames in another; clear skies turn black and stormy; haloed figures lose their haloes. In most cases, our reaction to the accompanying poem is altered. Each copy, in effect, constitutes a separate text.

A further complication arises from the fact that Blake's wife seems to have helped with the illumination – like Enitharmon, her mythic *alter ego* in *Vala* or *The Four Zoas*, who 'tincturd' her husband's creations 'with beams of blushing love' (7a.90.36: E356). Keynes thinks she may have colored at least two copies of *Innocence* and two of the combined *Songs*, 'though it is impossible to identify her work with any certainty.'⁸ We can, however, be reasonably sure about some of the copies Blake colored. On a fly-leaf to copy Z, for example, the original owner tells us that he received his copy 'from Blake himself – And coloured by his own Hand.'⁹ Copy U, at least as elaborately finished as copy Z, was said to have been 'executed by the highly gifted artist expressly for his friend, Mr. Wainwright; to whom,

I am told, he was at the time under considerable pecuniary obligations.'[10]

Some copies are more carefully and thoughtfully produced than others. 'The quality of the colouring ...,' writes Keynes, 'varies as much as the method.'[11] Though Blake's style of illumination changes over time, becoming more elaborate in later years, chronology alone accounts for only some variations. Friends and important or respected patrons invariably received fine copies; titled or wealthy customers received copies appropriately heightened with gold, silver, and crimson. The character and intelligence of customers seem also to have been considered. Blake may well have reserved particularly obscure or daring ideas for 'close friends who will not laugh or will laugh the right way.'[12] Though technically, 'every version has independent authority,'[13] some colorings are clearly more inventive – more alive with visionary and artistic intelligence – than others.

I consult a number of copies in the pages that follow,[14] but use Z of the combined *Songs* as a basic 'text.' I chose Z for several reasons: it is late, bearing the marks of ample thought and care; if the fly-leaf is to be trusted, Blake colored it himself (while working on the illustrations to Dante, arguably the richest and most imaginatively colored of his creations); the original can be seen in the Lessing J. Rosenwald collection in the Library of Congress (formerly in the Alverthorpe Museum in Jenkintown, Pennsylvania); and its first owner, Henry Crabb Robinson, was, in many respects, precisely the sort of man most likely to call forth Blake's imaginative energies.

Crabb Robinson deserves a moment's attention. Born in 1775, he lived for most of his ninety-one years at the heart of literary Europe. He was a journalist (war correspondent for *The Times* in Spain) and barrister, one of the founders of University College, London, and a friend of Goethe, Schiller, Herder, Wieland, Wordsworth, Southey, the Lambs, and Coleridge. Though knowledgeable, intelligent, and an early champion of Blake's works, he was hardly a kindred spirit. 'It is strange,' writes Robinson in his 'Diary,' 'that I, who have no imagination, nor any power beyond that of a logical understanding, should yet have great respect for the mystics.'[15]

Robinson first met Blake in 1825. They never became particularly close, but in the course of several conversations (carefully recorded in Robinson's 'Diary' and later in the

'Reminiscences') they discussed, among other topics: the uses of education; the divinity of Jesus Christ; the distinction between natural and spiritual realms; Dante's religious beliefs (and those of Milton, Newton, Bacon, and Locke); Jacob Boehme; the omnipotence of God; the poetical or allegorical language of the Bible; Wordsworth's poetry; the distinction between body and soul; and the nature of evil. Robinson ordered his copy of *Songs* in the course of one of these conversations, and Blake offered what G. E. Bentley, Jr calls the 'somewhat preferential' price of five guineas, roughly half the cost he proposed for Cumberland's copy a year later.[16]

Robinson's manner when talking with 'this insane man of genius' seems to have been simultaneously respectful and patronizing, and Blake's was no less mixed. If Robinson's policy was 'to humour the mental case,' as Mona Wilson puts it, 'this was doubtless obvious to the patient.'[17] Yet Blake thought Robinson worth talking to, and by refusing to moderate his views – or to express them in a less visionary form – he may well have been paying the diarist a compliment. 'You say that I want somebody to elucidate my ideas,' writes Blake in a famous letter (August 25, 1799) to Dr J. Trusler, author of *The Way to Be Rich and Respectable* (1775) as well as several books for children, and a man even less sympathetic to 'Spiritual Sensation' than Robinson. 'But you ought to know that what is Grand is necessarily obscure to Weak men. That which can be made explicit to the Idiot is not worth my care. The wisest of the Ancients considered what is not too Explicit as the fittest Instruction because it rouzes the faculties to Act.'[18]

When conversing with freer or more sympathetic (or credulous) auditors, John Linnell or John Varley, for instance, Blake would occasionally soften or 'explain' his wilder statements;[19] to the sceptical and analytic Robinson, his manner seems to have been unyielding, a calculated attempt to prevent Robinson from lapsing into any merely passive understanding – to 'rouze the faculties to Act.' Much the same goal lies behind the best of the illuminations, and Blake must have seen Robinson's copy of *Songs* as an excellent opportunity to provide sorely needed 'fittest Instruction' to an intelligent and interested customer.

The decision to concentrate on a single late copy, and to treat all others as variants, was only in part a product of limitations of space and time. An eclectic interpretation based on a study of several copies tends to obscure the internal coherence and consistency of separate versions. Actual texts are replaced by a kind of 'Ur' or ideal coloring, the sum or best of a selection of copies. Troublesome or arresting details in one set of illuminations are avoided or explained away by reference to another. We learn a great deal about Blake's development, and about his attitude towards past work, but relatively little about the nature and extent of his achievement in any one copy. This, however, is precisely what the present study hopes to determine: hence its choice of a single text as a focus for detailed readings. To object to such an approach on the grounds that Z, a late copy, may fail to reflect Blake's intentions thirty years earlier,[20] or that opposing impressions are created in other versions, is to miss the point. Copy Z is an independent work of art (though it belongs to a group of identically ordered and elaborately illuminated late copies: T-U, W-AA). We may look to other copies for help in interpreting its designs, but only if we remember that each new coloring creates a new work.

The Blake Trust facsimiles provide a final, practical reason for concentrating on copy Z: they have made it the best known, and most accurately reproduced, of all copies. In the 1955 edition of *Songs* three or four collotype printings were used and as many as thirty-four colors for a single plate were applied by hand, through stencils. Keynes calls it 'practically indistinguishable from the original,' and Herbert Read writes of 'reproductions of extraordinary fidelity.'[21] The later, 1967 Orion Press facsimile and the 1970 Oxford University Press paperback version, produced by high-speed offset, are also exceptionally good, though I would encourage readers to use the earlier editions if possible.

My own readings of the designs are based on the original Crabb Robinson copy, which I was able to examine at first hand, comparing it with the facsimiles. Many of the color values in the facsimiles, particularly the 1967 and 1970 editions, are slightly off; the subtly modulated background washes of the original are, indeed, somewhat 'crudely managed';[22] and in all three facsimiles it is hard to distinguish between dark yellow, gold-leaf, and the orange-red of the ground tint. Otherwise, however, there are few differences. The single major discrepancy between original and reproduction occurs on 'The Divine Image' plate, where all facsimiles gown the cruet-carrying maiden above the title in green rather than yellow. More minor discrepancies, along with relevant variants from other copies, are noted in the course of the chapters which follow. The reader, it is assumed, has a 'text' (the Oxford University Press paperback is easily accessible): reproducing it here seemed unnecessary as well as impractical, like reprinting the texts upon which comparable critical studies of, say, *Paradise Lost* or *Lyrical Ballads* are based.

CHAPTER 1
CHILDREN'S BOOKS, EDUCATION, AND VISION

If I had not taught you your letters every day – you could not now have read a chapter in the Bible nor the Pilgrim's Progress nor Sandford and Merton nor the Songs of Innocence nor any of your pretty story books.

SAMUEL PALMER to his
three-year-old son,
September 14, 1845.[1]

I

By 1789, the year in which *Songs of Innocence* first appeared, books written specifically for the use of children outside of school had become, in F. J. Harvey Darton's words, 'a clear but subordinate branch of English literature.'[2] One of my aims in this book is to show how *Innocence* and the combined *Songs* grew out from that branch, and from the educational theory in which it was rooted, though neither work seems to have been intended primarily for juvenile readers. In comparing *Songs* to juvenile books of the late seventeenth, eighteenth, and early nineteenth centuries, I shall be concerned less with the style and subject matter of individual poems, designs and stories,[3] than with the larger philosophical debate they helped spark and reflected. I shall concentrate on the relation between 'Vision,' the key to Blake's larger religious, social and philosophical thought, and the underlying principles of educational theory and juvenile literature current in Blake's age. To start with, though, I want to look briefly at the sources and extent of Blake's knowledge of books for and about children.

In 1777, at the age of twenty, Blake ended his five-year apprenticeship to the engraver James Basire and was admitted as a student to the Royal Academy. There he became friends with Thomas Stothard, a fellow artist, engraver, and, in later years, illustrator of children's books by Thomas Day and Mrs Barbauld. Stothard introduced Blake to the young sculptor, John Flaxman, and Flaxman in turn introduced him to his friends and benefactors the Reverend and Mrs A. S. Mathew. It was the Mathews who arranged for *Poetical Sketches* to be set in type in 1783, sometime after Blake had been invited into their literary and artistic circle. This circle, according to J. T. Smith, one of its members, 'was ... frequented by most of the literary and talented people of the day.'[4] It fitted neatly into Laurence Stone's description of the class from which new attitudes to childhood and education were advanced in the late eighteenth century: 'professional people, wealthy merchants and the squirearchy, all of whom were economically entrepreneurial, often upwardly mobile, and united by a common literary culture.'[5]

In Mrs Mathew's drawing room, Blake may have met, among others, Mrs Barbauld, who by 1781 had already published the popular *Lessons for Children from Two to Three Years Old* (1780) and *Hymns in Prose for Children* (1781); Mrs Chapone, part-author of number 10 of *The Rambler*, poetess, and published 'improver of young minds';[6] Mrs Montague, witty and articulate defender of Shakespeare against Voltaire, and patroness of chimney sweepers or 'climbing boys'; and Hannah More, friend, like Mrs Montague and Chapone, of Johnson and Garrick, tragic playwright, and author and founder of the immensely influential 'Cheap Repository Tracts' (1795–8), a scheme to provide suitable reading matter for the poor and their children. Nor was it only Blue Stockings of the sort Mrs Mathew attracted who combined literary, artistic, and philosophical, including scientific, interests with a concern for children and education. The all-male Lunar Society of Birmingham (once thought a model, like the Mathew set, for Blake's Quid and Co. in *An Island in the Moon*),[7] numbered among its learned members not only scientists like Priestley, who was himself a school teacher, and Watt of the steam engine, but the poetical botanist, Erasmus Darwin (who had written on Rousseau's *Émile*), Dr Thomas Day, disciple of Rousseau and author of the popular children's book *Sandford and Merton* (1783–9), and Richard Lovell Edgeworth, father of Maria, and co-author with her of *Practical Education: The History of Harry and Lucy* (1780), a book urging children to teach themselves.

Though the characters in Blake's *An Island in the Moon* have never with certainty been identified, all critics agree that the work itself is a satire of Blake's early intellectual milieu. In that milieu questions of childhood and education figure prominently. In chapter 9, for example, a character named Obtuse Angle, called 'schoolmasterly' by Erdman and others,[8] praises the charitable work of Richard Sutton, founder of Charterhouse or Sutton's Hospital, the pensioner's home and school for boys. Later, in chapter 11, Obtuse Angle sings a song in praise of charity schools (eventually to become the innocent 'Holy Thursday') which is followed in turn by Mrs Nannicantipot's 'Nurse's Song,' with its echoes of Mrs Barbauld's second and fifth *Hymns in Prose*. In chapter 4, Mrs Nannicantipot argues with Mrs Sinagain about the virtues of regular church attendance, taking a liberal, anti-institutional line, and though we cannot with absolute certainty identify her with Mrs Barbauld, her type is at least clear. Quid, generally agreed to be Blake himself, responds to 'Nurse's Song' with 'The Little Boy Lost,' picking up the former's theme of protection, and providing an oblique comment on the earlier 'Holy Thursday' by stressing the importance of parental rather than institutional protectors. In short, beneath *Island*'s nonsensical surface, we can glimpse, among other themes and concerns, the outlines of an argument or discussion about children and their needs. The topic flows easily and naturally out of the dialogue, and is shown to be very much a part of the everyday interests of Quid/Blake and his friends.

Though Blake's 'unbending deportment'[9] eventually caused him to break with the Mathew set sometime after 1785, he soon became associated with a circle of intellectuals, artists, and social reformers who met at the home of his friend and sometime employer, the radical publisher Joseph Johnson.[10] Johnson's weekly dinners attracted well-known Jacobin celebrities, notably Priestley, Dr Price, Holcroft, Paine, and Joel Barlow. They also included a number of educational theorists and children's book authors, among them David Williams, perhaps the best known radical educationalist of his day, Mrs Barbauld, her brother Dr John Aiken, Mary Wollstonecraft, and William Godwin, all of whom, except Williams,[11] Blake seems to have met through Johnson.

Blake had professional as well as personal reasons for keeping in touch with Johnson and his set. By the end of the 1760s, demand for children's literature had grown to such an extent that publishers had at last begun to concern themselves with the physical appearance of their books, something only the miraculously successful John Newbery, about whom we shall be hearing shortly, had been willing to do earlier in the century. No longer content to rely upon a limited stock of old and often worn or crudely executed wood-block illustrations (many of them bearing little or no relation to the text), children's booksellers and publishers began instead to commission original designs both in wood and in the more expensive medium of copper. This trend coincided with, or was an expression of, a more general growth in late eighteenth-century engraving and illustration, one that included scientific, technical, antiquarian, and commercial as well as literary and artistic interests. Blake's career as a free-lance illustrator and engraver encompassed all these fields. It also involved several commissions for children's books, though unlike those of his contemporaries, Stothard and the Bewicks, they brought neither fame nor fortune. In 1780 Johnson commissioned Blake to engrave Stothard's designs for *The Speaker: or Miscellaneous Pieces Selected from the Best English Writers, and disposed under proper heads, with a view to facilitate the Improvement of Youth in Reading and Speaking.* In 1791 he asked him to engrave sixteen of fifty-one designs by Chodowiecki, the Berlin painter and illustrator, for Mary Wollstonecraft's translation of Ernst Salzmann's *Elements of Morality for the Use of Children,*[12] and six of ten of his own designs for Wollstonecraft's own *Original Stories from Real Life.* These, the last in particular, we shall return to in later chapters. As far as we know, they were Blake's only commissions as a freelance children's book illustrator.[13]

In 1793, though, a year before the combined *Songs* appeared, Blake ventured forth with a juvenile book of his own entitled *For Children: The Gates of Paradise.* This he printed and published himself, though he took care to issue it under Johnson's as well as his own name, perhaps in hopes of attracting some of the many juvenile readers who had made Johnson's children's books so lucrative a branch of his business. Though children's books tend to be worn out, that only five copies of the work survive (only one of which seems to have belonged to a child),[14] suggests that it cannot have been much of a success; and Blake's plans for a companion volume seem never to have got beyond a title-page sketch bearing the inscription *For Children: The Gates of Hell.*[15] In addition to these ill-fated projects, Blake may also have intended his *History of England* as a children's book, since it too, like *For Children: The Gates of Paradise*, is described in the 1793 *Prospectus* as 'A small book of Engravings. Price 3s.' (E670).[16] No copies, however, survive.

Blake's attempts to enter into the world of children's literature took place during the single most creative and controversial period in its history. His was an age in which artists, intellectuals, social reformers, teachers, and parents were passionately and sharply divided in their attitudes towards childhood and education. All the major figures of the early Romantic period – from Jane Austen in *Mansfield Park* and Scott in *Waverley* to Wordsworth in *The Prelude* and elsewhere, and Coleridge in his Lectures and the *Biographia* – took their stands. That the terms of this debate were dictated by wholly antagonistic views of human nature – views of great social and political moment – gave new seriousness and importance to discussion of the sorts of books children should read. In the past, authors of children's literature had been largely unconscious of the principles upon which their books were based. Now, in Darton's words, those principles were either 'seen openly,' or 'strongly suspected of being there.'[17] Until the last half of the century, Calvin, through his Puritan disciples, had been the spiritual father of respectable English juvenile literature.[18] In 1757, the year Blake was born, most books intended specifically for children of his age and class were still deeply influenced by the harsh severities of seventeenth-century Puritanism. By the 1780s, though, a change was at hand. Locke's *Some Thoughts Concerning Education* (1693) and the 1763 English translation of Rousseau's *Émile* (the former gradually and indirectly, the latter with a great dramatic burst) helped give definition to that change. They symbolized a growing dissatisfaction, among Dissenters as well as Conformists, with the harsh severities of the Puritan legacy, one which was to alter immensely – to soften and humanize – educational theory and juvenile literature. Calvin, though, in a multitude of subtle and indirect ways, remained a powerful and pervasive influence. It is with him, therefore, that any discussion of the underlying principles upon which late eighteenth-century children's books are based – principles with which *Songs* itself is intimately involved – must begin.

2

At the heart of the Puritan attitude towards childhood lies a rock-hard belief in original sin. Calvin voices it succinctly in Book Two of the *Institutes*:

> And therefore infants themselves, as they bring their condemnation into the world with them, are rendered obnoxious to punishment by their own sinfulness, not by the sinfulness of another. For though they have not yet produced the fruits of their iniquity, yet they have the seeds of it within them; even their whole nature is as it were a seed of sin, and therefore cannot but be odious and abominable to God. Whence it follows, that it is properly accounted sin in the eyes of God, because there could be no guilt without crime.[19]

'You must know Parents,' writes Cotton Mather, the influential early American Puritan, and author of several children's books (including the lugubriously titled *Ungodly Children*), in his *A Family Well-Ordered: or, an Essay to Render Parents and Children Happy in One Another* (1699), 'that your Children are by your Means born under the dreadful Wrath of God: and if they are not New-Born before they dy it has [sic] been very good for them, that they had never been born at all.'[20] Even among more tolerant or enlightened Puritan circles, Calvin's emphasis on original sin continued to figure prominently in attitudes towards childhood. Milton, for example, though hardly a strict Calvinist, begins *Of Education* (1644) by reminding his readers that 'The end then of learning is to repair the ruins of our first parents by regaining to know God aright, and out of that knowledge to love him, to imitate him, to be like him, as we may be the nearest by possessing our souls of true virtue, which being united to the heavenly grace of faith, makes up the highest perfection.'[21]

Of the 261 juvenile books (not counting school texts) published between 1557 and 1710, nearly all, according to

William Sloane, their cataloguer, not only shared Milton's aim, but lay great stress on the dread consequences of its neglect.[22] Time and again, seventeenth-century children's books communicate what Darton calls 'the plain dogmatic belief that a definitely revealed heaven and hell existed on every side of this mortal life, and that contact here on earth leads invariably (but for the mercy of God) to the one or the other.'[23] Hence Abraham Chear's ' 'Tis pity such a pretty maid/As I should go to Hell,'[24] or Thomas White's *A Little Book for Little Children*, 'Wherein are set down several directions for little children; and several remarkable stories both ancient and modern, of little children: divers whereof are of those who are lately deceased,'[25] or the prefatory poem to John Bunyan's *A Book for Boys and Girls* (1685) (later, around 1781, called *Divine Emblems*), with its warning to children that

> each fingle-fangle
> On which they doting are, their souls entangle,
> As with a web, a trap, a gin, or snare,
> And will destroy them, have they not a care.[26]

or the sub-title to James Janeway's equally well-known *A Token for Children: being an Exact Account of the Conversion, Holy and Exemplary Lives and Joyful Deaths of several young Children* (1671–2).

The reasons for this doleful severity are worth recalling, since they prevent any easy and unfair condescension to Puritan parents and educators. To begin with, the association of death with childhood was inevitable in the late seventeenth and eighteenth centuries; much more so than that of death with old age, something few people ever lived to attain. Life expectancy at birth in the 1640s was only thirty-two years.[27] In London, even by 1764, almost a decade and a half after the level of infant and child mortality had begun to fall, 49 per cent of all children were dead by the age of two, and 60 per cent by the age of five. Blake himself, one of a family of four, was born two years after the death of his infant brother, John. 'To preserve their mental stability,' writes Stone, seventeenth- and early eighteenth-century parents 'were obliged to limit the degree of their psychological involvement with their infant children.'[28] This was, of course, especially true of Puritan parents and educators, whose religion taught them, in Janeway's words, from *A Token*, that if 'children are not too little to die, they are not too little to go to hell.'[29] 'It is not surprising,' writes Ivy Pinchbeck of Puritan parents, 'that they devoted as much thought to the spiritual upbringing of their children as conscientious parents spend today on health and general personality development.'[30]

When Blake began work on *Innocence* in the 1780s the Calvinism of Janeway and Bunyan was far from dead. He himself may well have had direct access to it, having been born into that class of 'ordinary merchants and prosperous shopkeepers' among whom what J. H. Plumb calls 'the traditions of seventeenth century life' or 'the Puritan attitude' were still very much alive.[31] Though the first half of the eighteenth century was marked by reaction against Puritan excess, in the latter half of the century, with the rise of Methodism and the Anglican Evangelical movement, the Puritan spirit returned in force, accompanied by a species of juvenile literature much like that of the previous century. Methodism encouraged parents, in the words of Wesley's 1783 *Sermon on the Education of Children*, to 'break the will of your child, to bring his will into subjegation to yours, that it may be afterwards subject to the will of God.'[32] 'Thrift, abstinence, hard work, and concentration'[33] were the virtues it sought to inculcate. Play of any sort was discouraged (games were outlawed at Wesley's school at Kingswood); study of Scripture and Catechism was deemed sufficient education; idleness, the greatest of sins. Though Wesleyan hymns, particularly Charles's *Hymns for Children* (1763), betray a tenderness of feeling closer to Watts than to, say, Janeway or Bunyan, they too, like the works of their Puritan predecessors, were obsessed with death (Charles's funeral hymns, writes Martha England, 'sound like Christmas carols ... *Puer natus est* became for him a gospel of joy fraught with pain'),[34] and with the constant threat of sin; they too present to children a world of critical and deadly choices, one in which 'every event in real life takes its true reality from being subsumed in Myth.'[35] Nor, in their theoretical writings at least, do the Wesleys betray the slightest respect for the child-like qualities of children: 'There are two ways of writing or speaking to children,' writes John Wesley,

Dr. Watts has wrote in the former way, and has succeeded admirably well, speaking to children as children, and leaving them as he found them. [With my hymns, though,

8

when children] do understand them, they will be children no longer, only in years and stature.[36]

The upper or Anglican Evangelical branch of the mid-eighteenth-century Puritan revival shared similar attitudes towards childhood and education.[37] The passion and industry it brought to its campaigns for the abolition of slavery, and the reformation of upper-class manners, were no less marked in its attempts to provide suitable reading matter for the young, or to create day and Sunday schools for the children of the poor. To the Evangelicals, sin could be overcome by salvation in Christ, but salvation was only possible once a believer had attained knowledge or conviction of his essential sinfulness. Pressure for the recognition of human rights and dignities went hand in hand with an obsession with what Wilberforce, the spearhead of the movement, called 'the universal corruption and profligacy of the times.'[38]

The effect of obsessiveness of this sort upon the schools Wilberforce and his fellow reformers helped to set up, and the children's books they inspired, was to strengthen old-fashioned Calvinist attitudes. Hannah More, for example, the most prominent of Evangelical educators, thought it, as she wrote in 1799, 'a fundamental error to consider children as innocent beings, whose little weaknesses may perhaps want some correction, rather than as beings who bring into the world a corrupt nature and evil dispositions, which it should be the great end of education to rectify.'[39] Of what Darton calls the 'horde of minor moralists'[40] whose books for children were influenced by Evangelical fervor, Mrs Sherwood and Mrs Trimmer provide well-known and representative examples. Mrs Sherwood, the younger of the two, was the author of a number of juvenile books, among the best known of which were *The Infant's Progress* (1809–10), *The Indian Pilgrim* (1810), and the immensely popular *The Fairchild Family* (1812), with its famously un-Wordsworthian description of a family's instructive outing through dark woods to see the body of a man hanging in chains from a gibbet.[41] Like Hannah More, Mrs Sherwood was also a teacher as well as a preacher, and had even been to India as a missionary. A true daughter of Calvin, she believed that children

are by nature evil, and while they have none but the natural evil principle to guide them, pious and prudent parents must check their naughty passions in any way that they have in their power, and force them into decent and proper behaviour and into what are called good habits.[42]

Mrs Trimmer, whose works appeared several decades earlier, shared similar views, despite strict allegiance to the High Church faction.[43] Not only were her books immensely popular, especially *The Fabulous Histories* of 1786 and the 'Series of Prints' (1782–6) illustrating sacred and profane literature (with an accompanying volume of 'Lessons' loosely modelled after those of Mrs Barbauld), but her editorship of *The Family Magazine* (1778–9), a work 'designed to counteract the pernicious tendency of immoral books,'[44] and later, from 1802 to 1806, of the monthly *Guardian of Education*, gave her the broader powers of a censor. Any hint either of Jacobin sympathy or of the influence of Rousseau was roundly condemned. Newbery's publications, for example, were considered insufficiently pious. Perrault's *Cinderella* was said to depict 'some of the worst passions that can ever enter the human heart, and of which children should, if possible, be totally ignorant; such as envy, jealousy, a dislike of mothers-in-law and half-sisters, vanity, a love of dress etc. etc.'[45]

Blake's antipathy to foolishness of this sort derived not only from its underlying Calvinist vision of God and human nature, but from the political conservatism and anti-imaginative bias which accompanied it. Puritans had always frowned upon light reading, especially for children. But in the late eighteenth and early nineteenth centuries it was fear of revolution as much as fear of God which fueled the neo-Calvinist campaign of Methodists and Anglican Evangelicals against children's fantasy and fairy literature. Mrs Sherwood and Mrs Trimmer attacked fairy tales not just because 'fanciful productions ... can never be rendered generally useful,'[46] but because so many of them came from France. Opposition to Rousseau (who, however, also disapproved of fairy stories), the Encyclopaedists, and any other French or German theorists the new Puritans happened to come across, was a product as much of political as of religious or educational disapproval.

Nor was such disapproval confined to the upper or Anglican Evangelical branch of the Puritan revival. Wesley's politics were at least as conservative as Wilberforce's. 'The greater the share the people have in government,' he writes, 'the less liberty, civil or religious, does a nation enjoy.'[47] Wilberforce, out of similar convictions, called for a reformation of upper-class morals not only as a way of saving souls, but as the most effective means of blocking incipient revolt on the part of the lower orders. 'The rich,' writes W. H. Stevenson of Wilberforce's unspoken assumptions, 'were to return to God to save their skins. The poor were to learn resignation in the face of adversity – such adversities as famine, high prices, injustice, and oppression.'[48] Hence the approval of the dominant culture; a culture which was rationalist, empirical, and, of course, politically conservative. Since zealous devotion and social upheaval could no longer be equated (enthusiasm in its bourgeois acceptation now being at least partly reconciled to common sense and accommodation), Methodists and Anglican Evangelicals were spared much of the opprobrium heaped upon the Puritans of an earlier era, and in the last years of the century Calvinist attitudes towards children and their reading gained enormous strength and respectability.

3

John Locke, the second of the three figures, after Calvin and his heirs, whose educational views helped shape late-eighteenth-century debate about childhood and instruction, was the first figure of influence in England to challenge the severities of Puritan-inspired juvenile literature and educational theory. *Some Thoughts Concerning Education*, Locke's manual 'for the breeding of a young Gentleman,'[49] was, in its own sphere, as influential as the *Essay Concerning Human Understanding* (1690) or the two *Treatises of Government* (1690). It appeared in new editions once every five years throughout the eighteenth century, and all manner of children's book authors, from the commercially-minded Newbery (whose sales of children's books went up twelve fold from 1742 to 1800)[50] to pious Dr Watts, justified their work in the light of its teachings. Blake's own attitude towards it, given the Calvinist alternative, was, as we shall see, decidedly mixed.

Like others of Locke's writings, the *Education* both conformed to and helped to mould a growing latitudinarian spirit in Restoration and eighteenth-century society. Though the severity of a number of its passages (notably those calling for discipline and self-denial) hearkens back to Locke's own

Puritan upbringing, its overall effect on educators and children's book authors was essentially liberating. Locke's reputation lent seriousness and authority to the eighteenth century's growing distaste for harsh punishment, both psychological (children should be addressed in a 'grave, kind, and sober' manner, neither bullied nor frightened into learning)[51] and corporal ('a sort of slavish discipline [which] makes a slavish temper').[52] Reasoning with children, argues Locke, 'is the true way of dealing with them.' 'They understand it as early as they do language; and if I misobserve not, they love to be treated as rational creatures sooner than is imagined.'[53] Nor is it right to expect or force children to be perpetually serious or high-minded: 'All their innocent folly, playing and childish actions,' writes Locke, 'are to be left perfectly free and unrestrained, as far as they can consist with the respect due to those that are present.'[54] Though play is not in itself educative, it has its uses: by observing it, for example, we can discover a child's true nature (and Locke, paradoxically, laid great stress on the importance of tailoring the pace of a child's education to individual temperament and character) and, if properly structured, it can become a sort of disguise or camouflage to learning (wherein 'the chief art is to make all that they have to do Sport and play too').[55]

Blake no doubt approved the liberalizing effect of many of these tenets, both on pedagogy inside and outside class, and on the style and subject matter of children's books. What he would not have approved were the larger principles upon which the *Education* was based; principles whose ultimate influence was at least as abhorrent to him as that of Calvin. Locke's interest in childhood and education was the inevitable product of a larger philosophical concern with the mind's growth and development, its 'natural history.' That the *Education*, in James Axtell's words, was but 'the *explicit* application of the philosophy of knowledge latent in the *Essay*,' is what gave its theories their authority.

> The values of Locke's Restoration society were shared by many men, and there are a multitude of educational writings that contain recommendations similar to some of his. ... But there is none which bases these recommendations upon a philosophical analysis of the human understanding as Locke's does, nor upon such a

comprehensive view of the total human organism as Locke's.[56]

The broad outlines of Locke's philosophy reappear in the *Education*. The child's mind, we are told, is like 'white Paper or Wax to be moulded.'[57] Children enter the world unburdened, neither innately (or originally) sinful nor blessed, and 'of all the Men we meet with, Nine parts of Ten are what they are, Good or Evil, useful or not, by their Education.'[58] Character is built out of custom and habit, and the business of education is the forming, early in life, of right, which is to say rational and useful, habits. 'Full soon,' Wordsworth warns the child,

> thy Soul shall have her earthly freight,
> And custom lie upon thee with a weight,
> Heavy as frost, and deep almost as life![59]

Such customs, 'being once established, operate of themselves easily and naturally without the Assistance of the Memory.'[60] In Blake's words, in the straw-man 'Argument' to the first of his two tracts entitled *There is No Natural Religion* (1788), 'Man has no notion of moral fitness but from Education. Naturally he is only a natural organ subject to Sense' (E1).

Against this philosophy Blake strove all his life, and for reasons which the *Education*, as often as not inadvertently, makes amply clear. If, for example, right habits are to develop properly, strict authority must be maintained on the part of the parent or tutor. Locke lays great stress on this point, and in language which Blake would have found objectionable in several respects:

> Would you have your son obedient to you when past a child? Be sure then to establish the Authority of a Father, *as soon* as he is capable of submission and can understand in whose Power he is. If you would have him stand in Awe of you, imprint it *in his Infancy*; and, as he approaches more to a Man, admit him nearer to your familiarity: So shall you have him your obedient subject (as is fit) whilst he is a child, and your affectionate Friend, when he is a Man.[61]

The note of calculation in this passage (it reminds us of Chesterfield)[62] is characteristic. Though Locke's ultimate objective is to promote affectionate friendship between father and grown son, retaining a son's obedience 'when past a child' is the aim with which he begins. An 'obedient' son can, of course, be an 'affectionate' friend to his father, but in the context of this passage, with its references to 'Authority,' 'submission,' 'Power,' 'Awe,' and 'obedient subjects,' we begin to wonder. We know what Locke intends, just as we do when he tells us that 'The right way to teach children ... is to give them a Liking and Inclination to what you propose to them to be learn'd,' but we are troubled by the manner in which it is put.[63] Parents and educators must, to some extent, manipulate their children; no one would object to Locke's ends. It is just that his preoccupation in the *Education* with means and authority, his tendency to treat children as objects, to manipulate them, can breed unsettling habits of its own.

What is one to think, for example, when Locke proposes that corporal punishment (which, we remember, he largely opposes) be adminstered by a servant in the presence of a parent, so that the parent's authority shall be maintained, but 'the Child's Aversion to the Pain it suffers ... be turned on the Person that immediately inflicts.'[64] Locke's advice, though both 'rational' and 'practical,' can only be carried out at the expense of admirably human instincts. What makes the episode doubly disturbing, moreover, is the ease with which manipulation of children slides into a further manipulation of adult servants. Blake, as we shall see, was particularly sensitive to the corrupting influence of calculation of this sort, both on those who are used, and those who use others. Authors of juvenile books who, by way of Locke, saw amusement as a means of 'cheating/Children into learning' (Newbery, *The Child's Plaything*, 1744), or who sought to 'decoy children into Reading' ('J.G.,' *A Playbook for Children*, 1694) or to 'allure' the child and 'lead him on' into reading through the use of games and riddles (William Ronksley, *The Child's Week's Work*, 1712) represented a real and welcome advance over the severities of Puritan compulsion. Blake would not have approved Scott's objection, in *Waverley*, to 'an age in which children are taught the driest doctrines by the insinuating method of instructive games. ... The history of England is now reduced to a game at cards, the problems of mathematics to puzzles and riddles.'[65] Yet the philosophy upon which this approach relied is not, as phrases like 'insinuating,' 'decoys,' and 'allures' suggest, without its dangers.

The ultimate aim of the conditioning Locke advocates, the precise nature of the habits he values, is equally abhorrent to Blake. Again, reason stands triumphant over feeling and instinct:

> It seems to me, that the Principle of all Vertue and Excellency lies in a Power of denying ourselves the Satisfaction of our own Desires, where Reason does not authorize them. This Power is to be got and improved by Custom, made easy and familiar by *early* Practice ... I would advise, that, contrary to the ordinary way, Children should be used to submit their Desires and go without their Longings *even from their very Cradles.* The first thing they should learn to know should be that they were not to have anything because it pleased them, but because it was thought fit for them.[66]

Locke substitutes submission to an abstract 'Reason' for Puritan subservience to God and his Word. But as both species of denial are enforced by earthly protectors who seek to inspire 'Awe' in the 'obedient servants' who are their children, and who clothe themselves in 'the Authority of a Father,' mysteriously, to a child, refusing them their natural impulses and desires, the ultimate effect on the young is, in many respects, the same. This, at least, is how Blake seems to have seen the matter,[67] and though he is often unfair to Locke, choosing to ignore or overlook palpable benefits and liberties inspired by the *Education* and by Locke's other writings as well, that there *are* underlying similarities between the two systems is undeniable. Both, after all, value austerity, self-denial, and strict obedience to authority. Both breed passivity and hidden resentment in children.

How the seemingly incompatible Lockean and Calvinist visions of childhood and education could and did merge is amply documented in the life and works of Isaac Watts, the gentle hymnographer and polymath who, in Johnson's words, 'left neither corporeal nor spiritual nature unexamined.' Watts taught 'the art of reasoning and the science of the stars'[68] – hardly the syllabus to appeal to Blake. But he also wrote genuinely child-like hymns for children; hymns to which Blake's *Songs*, as has long been recognized, are deeply indebted. Before turning to Rousseau, therefore, I want to look briefly at Watts's immensely popular attempts to merge the traditions of Locke and Calvin. These attempts became models for a whole generation of children's writers. They represent a tradition still strong in the 1780s, one which Blake, as we shall see, knew well.

Watts's writing for children grows out of the 'Good Godly' tradition of Bunyan and Janeway.[69] What distinguishes him from that tradition, though, is the gentle kindliness of his voice, the product in part of temperament, in part of a conviction, by way of Locke, that 'the minds of Children' must be given 'a *relish* [my italics] of Virtue and Religion.'[70] How Watts sought to resolve the tension between 'Good Godly' severity and rationalist tolerance, is hinted at in his justification of children's verse in the Preface to *Divine and Moral Songs for Children* (1715):

> Verse was at first designed for the service of God, though it hath been wretchedly abused since. ... There is a great delight in the very learning of truths and duties this way. There is something so amusing and entertaining in rhymes and metre that will incline children to make this part of their business a diversion. ... What is learned in verse is longer retained in memory, and sooner recollected. ... This will be a constant furniture, that they may have something to think upon when alone, and sing over to themselves. This may sometimes give their thought a divine turn, and raise a young meditation. Thus they will not be forced to seek relief for an emptiness of mind in the loose and daring sonnets of the day.[71]

At first glance this seems a simple case of Locke triumphing over Calvin. Yet distrust of imaginative literature was as much a rationalist as a Puritan tendency, and so too was stress on use, on 'the very learning of truths and duties.' What Vivian de Sola Pinto calls Watts's lifelong compromise between 'the old Puritanism of the age of Cromwell and the new humanism of the age of Addison,'[72] was less of a problem for him than that of the compromise between artistic (or visionary, in Blake's terms) and doctrinal (whether Calvinist or Lockean) obligations. Though the *Education* lent support to Watts's initial decision to abandon the relentless severity of most Puritan juvenile books, what is most admirable and distinctive about his best poems — their gentle respect for and sensitivity to the young — is no more

Locke's gift, for all his empirical observation of children at play, than it is Calvin's.

The real tension in Watts's work is found in those moments when what he should feel, either as a humanist or as a Puritan, runs counter to what he does feel, as in the following lines from 'On the Hazard of Loving the Creatures,' the first poem in the second section of *Horae Lyricae*:

> Nature has soft but pow'rful bands,
> And reason she controuls;
> While Children with their little hands
> Hang closest to our souls.
>
> Thoughtless they act th'old serpent's part;
> What tempting things they be!
> Lord, how they twine about our heart,
> And draw it off from thee! ...
>
> Dear Sovereign, break these fetters off,
> And set our spirits free;
> GOD in himself is bliss enough,
> For we have all in thee.[73]

Here, reason and religion, Locke and Calvin, join forces in opposition to Watts's true feelings; while children, with their 'thoughtless' (that is, pre-rational and impulsive as well as innocent) acts, inspire in him an affection intense enough to over-ride both. What Watts fears in children and in himself is precisely that power which gives life to his lines: the 'little hands,' for example, whose vividness and particularity inspirit an otherwise abstract and perfunctory argument.

Blake's 'Holy Thursday,' to which I want now to turn, makes just this point, and in terms which provide a convenient opening to other as yet undiscussed aspects of Locke's influence over educators and children's book authors; aspects that lead us on to Rousseau.

> Twas on a Holy Thursday their innocent faces clean
> The children walking two & two in red & blue & green
> Grey headed beadles walkd before with wands as white as
> snow
> Till into the high dome of Pauls they like Thames waters
> flow.

O what a multitude they seemed these flowers of London
town
Seated in companies they sit with radiance all their own
The hum of multitudes was there but multitudes of lambs
Thousands of little boys and girls raising their innocent
hands.

Now like a mighty wind they raise to heaven the voice of
song
Or like harmonious thunderings the seats of heaven among
Beneath them sit the aged men wise guardians of the poor
Then cherish pity; lest you drive an angel from your door.

'Holy Thursday' describes a procession of orphan children into
St Paul's to celebrate the charity of God. In the opening stanza
an unnamed speaker, one whose character and identity have
aroused considerable debate,[74] remarks upon the 'innocent faces
clean' of the children. Cleanliness, an important virtue in both
'Good Godly' and 'humanist' or post-Lockean juvenile
literature, is mentioned nowhere else in *Innocence*, and its easy
association with the word 'innocent' in line 1 is but the first of a
series of troubling details which gradually distance us from the
speaker. 'The children's faces,' writes Bloom, 'have been
scrubbed clean, and are innocent, in a debased sense – because
they ought to appear brutalized, which they are, and yet do
not.'[75] This the speaker is either unwilling or unable to see,
despite the fact that charity school abuses were so common in
Blake's age that one social reformer, writing in 1786, could
describe as 'well-known' the fact 'that apprentices for labour of
either sex seldom turn out well, whether bound by the parish or
a charity school.'[76]

In the second line our attention is drawn to the orderliness of
the procession, its careful regimentation underlined by the
regularity of the meter. Though the speaker notes the colors of
the children's uniforms, he is attracted less to their brightness
than to the fact that each is neatly coupled with its own kind:
'two and two in red and blue and green.' The beadles who lead
the procession are wholly colorless, their grey hair and 'wands as
white as snow' suggesting a frozen, lifeless contrast to the
children who flow into St Paul's like the life-bearing waters (not
here 'charter'd') of the Thames. 'Wands' are probably
ceremonial staffs, but they also call to mind the switches used to

enforce discipline in charity schools. Their 'touch,' like that of a magician's, transforms the children, freezing life, movement, and energy into strict order and obedience. Though none of this the speaker consciously understands, his imagery hints at a deeper and more complex reaction than that of simple, sentimental approval. Throughout the poem, what he intends is consistently undermined by the language he uses, so that the reader begins to sense in him an internal conflict much like that of Watts in 'On the Hazard of Loving the Creatures.' The speaker would like to feel, along with Addison ('that most accurate reflector of contemporary moods'),[77] that processions of this sort are 'pleasing both to God and Man.'[78] His conscious or explicit reaction conforms startlingly to Mandeville's ironic description of a comparable scene in the famous 'Essay on Charity and Charity Schools' (1723):

> there is a natural Beauty in Uniformity which most People delight in. It is diverting to the Eye to see children well match'd, either Boys or Girls, march two and two in good order; and to have them all whole and tight in the same Clothes and Trimming must add to the comeliness of the sight; and what makes it still more generally entertaining is the imaginary share which even Servants and the meanest of the Parish have in it, to whom it costs nothing; Our Parish Church, Our Charity Children. In all this there is a shadow of Property that tickles every body that has a Right to make use of the Words, but more especially those who actually contribute and had a great Hand in advancing the pious work.[79]

R. F. Gleckner, in comparing this passage to 'Holy Thursday,' argues that 'Blake's *method* of attack upon charity is similar to Mandeville's: both men reveal that the schools were based not on kindness, altruism, and Christian charity, but upon the self-love and what Mandeville called the "private vices" of their sponsors.'[80] But 'Holy Thursday' is a more complex and sympathetic work than Mandeville's 'Essay.' Its speaker, like Watts, is genuinely moved by children, unconsciously attracted to those very qualities – energy, life, movement, and creativity – which set them apart from their adult supervisors. Nor is he unaware that the supposedly 'wise guardians' are in fact oppressors. Like Watts, though, he is frightened, for the virtues of the true innocent fly in the face of all that he has been taught to value. How he copes with his fears in the lines that follow again recalls Watts.

Stanza 2 opens with the speaker inside St Paul's. The sheer numbers of the children awe him. Though still regimented ('seated in companies') their 'multitudes' take on 'a radiance all their own,' one that sets them apart from the surrounding cathedral, the beadles who arrange their seating, and the speaker himself. Theirs is the radiance of things which live and grow. Hence the fifth line's reference to 'flowers of London town,' which picks up the colors of the uniforms mentioned in line 2. The noise the children make is 'a hum of multitudes ... but multitudes of lambs,' with the second clause delicately hinting at the speaker's unacknowledged fears. 'Multitudes' is a word rich in Biblical association, and though it appears in both positive and neutral Scriptural contexts (see, for example, Mark 6:34, 39), others which come to mind are of suffering and oppression grimly, often apocalyptically, redressed, as in Isaiah 13:4: 'The noise of a multitude in the mountains like that of a great people; a tumultuous noise of the kingdoms of nations gathered together: The Lord of hosts mustereth the host of the battle.'[81] Benjamin Malkin, a friend and supporter of Blake, and an educational theorist to whom we shall be returning, associated the word with Revelation 19:6: 'And I heard as it were the voice of a great multitude, and as the voice of many waters, and as the voice of mighty thunderings, saying, Alleluia: for the Lord God omnipotent reigneth.'[82]

When the speaker of 'Holy Thursday' reminds us that the multitudes before him are 'multitudes of lambs,' he may well be trying to force out of his mind a vague but troubling sense that danger cannot but attend so great a gathering of grievances. That he fears the children is also suggested in line 8, where 'hum of multitudes' is replaced by a vision of thousands of children raising their hands all at the same time. The power of the gesture alarms the speaker, which accounts for his reassuring reminder that these are 'little' boys and girls, and that the hands they raise are 'innocent.' The effect of the line, even to a reader who finds little irony in the poem, 'is simultaneously one of simple, rather helpless gracefulness, and of grandeur.'[83] Without realizing it, the speaker, in his fear, diminishes the power of the children's gesture. Their helplessness is, of course, a fact, but recalling it in this context is a form of self-protection, one which allies the speaker to the beadles whose function is that of order and control.

As the poem progresses the speaker's attitude to the children shades delicately, almost imperceptibly, from simple, unthreatened admiration in the opening lines, to awe in the second stanza, and then, in stanza three, when they begin to sing, to fear. In the end, frightened as much by his own powerful feelings as by the vital energy of the children themselves, the speaker unconsciously retreats to the last line's comfortable but limiting platitude. He can follow the children, and the imaginative energies they release in him, only so far : from the ominously disquieting 'hum of multitudes,' to a vision of thousands 'raising' their hands, to voices surging 'like a mighty wind,' to the very 'thunderings' of heaven itself. Finally, though, as if dizzied by imaginative flight, he forces himself back down into the company of 'aged men.' In real life, 'wise guardians' bring high-flying children 'down to earth.' So too, in this poem, the wise guardian or 'aged man' within the speaker – that part of him which needs and values order and control – reasserts itself in line 11, quickly returning us to the beadles seated 'Beneath' the children. The speaker is neither hypocritical nor 'usurous' as Mandeville or the experienced 'Holy Thursday' would have us believe. Nor is he really 'obtuse,' as Erdman argues,[84] since the imagery he uses suggests that he sees through to the true meaning of the procession and to the support his approval lends to it. Somewhere inside him he knows and is troubled by what his fears have done to his own vital energies and to those of the children, and this is why we cannot treat him harshly. He is a kind of Theotormon (from *Visions of the Daughters of Albion*) in embryo, too weak to embrace true innocence – to join Oothoon in rejecting a limited, reason-bound vision – yet aware that that vision, for all its safe and reassuring coherence, is both inadequate and harmful.

The ease with which Lockean and Calvinist attitudes towards children – attitudes such as those hidden in the innocent 'Holy Thursday' – dovetail, not only in late-eighteenth-century educational theory and practice, but in the juvenile literature of Watts and others like him,[85] derives, in large part, from the growing respectability and political conservatism of eighteenth-century Puritanism. Watts's background, the source of what Sloane calls that 'unpleasant air of bourgeois self-satisfaction'[86] he sometimes shares with the speaker of the innocent 'Holy

Thursday,' is worth recalling at this point. Doctrinally, Watts was an orthodox Calvinist, little different from Bunyan, his predecessor and model in children's verse. Socially and politically, though, the two were poles apart, Bunyan being 'a sectarian mechanick preacher with considerable class antipathy and hatred of wealth,' Watts 'a typical rich man's minister.'[87] Dissent, for Watts, was compatible with political conformity. His views on education and class order, like those of the Methodists and Anglican Evangelicals who succeeded him, belonged essentially to the establishment; an establishment whose vision of society and how it should be run owed much to Locke. Watts's support of the charity school movement provides a case in point. Like Locke, he was for educating the poor, but not at the expense (literally, for Locke, who saw charity schools as a means of abolishing Tudor poor law provisions) of the existing social hierarchy. Charity school children were not to be allowed 'an education which might permit them to compete in the labour market with the children of their betters,'[88] an attitude later taken up not only by Anglican Evangelicals like Mrs Trimmer's friend Robert Raikes, who in the 1780s sought, by reviving and expanding the facilities of the church Sunday schools, to continue, on an attenuated scale, the original charity school movement of the 1690s, but by Methodists as well.

4

Radical opposition to the alliance of Lockean and new Puritan conservatives was itself deeply indebted to eighteenth-century rationalism, as the example of Rousseau, the third of the three figures whose educational views I want here to examine, and the single most important and controversial educational theorist of Blake's age, makes clear. Rousseau galvanized debate, in England as well as on the Continent, over the sorts of books children should read.[89] He also helped sharpen the political dimensions of that debate, not only because *Émile*, like Locke's *Education*, was in many respects the practical application of its author's earlier and politically and philosophically broader works, notably the *Discours sur l'origine de l'inégalité* (1754) and the *Contrat social* (1762), but because so many of its ideas and followers were intimately connected to the revolutions in America and France. David Williams, for example, the earliest and most influential English educator to experiment with

Rousseau's theories, and author of the *Émile*-inspired *Treatise on Education* (1781), was a founding member of the radical Club of Thirteen, a London version of the Birmingham Lunar Society, the members of which included Benjamin Franklin as well as Edgeworth, Day, and Robert Owen. In 1776, Williams, aided by the Club, produced the deistical *Liturgy on the Universal Principles of Religion and Morality*, a work which subsequently contributed to the cult of the worship of Reason and the Supreme Being in France in 1793–4, and for which the Revolution awarded him French citizenship.[90] That Blake took full note of connections of this sort – between, that is, educational innovation, political radicalism, and reason worship – *Experience*, as I shall argue, makes clear.

Émile itself is based on the premise that man can be returned to freedom (or 'Nature') through education.[91] Its influence, Rousseau hopes, will breed a whole new generation of men and women, one which will build a truly just and natural society. First, though, contemporary education, which systematically strips us of our natural rights, must be radically reformed. Its lessons of perpetual restraint, physical as well as mental, must no longer be tolerated, for they breed dangerous and ignoble resentments in children – resentments which later blossom into the evils of adult society. 'With each item of precocious instruction which we would cause to enter their heads,' writes Rousseau, 'we plant a vice in the depth of their hearts.'[92] Though conventional schooling makes a child 'supple,' 'docile,' and 'passionless' ('For the passions are never aroused so long as they are of no effect'),[93] 'the more children are held in constraint under your eyes, the more turbulent they become the moment they regain their liberty.'[94]

Blake too warned his readers of the dangerous consequences of educational repression, and nowhere more emphatically than in the concluding lines of 'Tiriel,' written some time between 1789 and 1793, years in which he was working on *Songs*. Tiriel's final speech rings out in passionate denunciation of the Lockean-Calvinist educational alliance, and in terms which call *Émile* immediately to mind:

> The child springs from the womb. the father stands ready to form
> The infant head while the mother idle plays with her dog on her couch

The young bosom is cold for lack of mother's nourishment
and milk
Is cut off from the weeping mouth with difficulty and pain
The little lids are lifted and the little nostrils opend
The father forms a whip to rouze the sluggish senses to act
And scourges off all youthful fancies from the new-born
man
Then walks the weak infant in sorrow compelld to number
footsteps
Upon the sand. &c
And when the drone has reachd his crawling length
Black berries appear that poison all around him. Such was
Tiriel
Compelld to pray repugnant & to humble the immortal
spirit
Till I am subtil as a serpent in a paradise
Consuming all both flowers & fruit insects & warbling birds
And now my paradise is falln & a drear sandy plain
Returns my thirsty hissings in a curse on thee O Har
Mistaken father of a lawless race. ...

(12–28: E281–2)

Rousseau's insistence that 'constraint' breeds dangerous
reaction lies at the heart of this passage, and of 'Tiriel' as a
whole. In addition, several more specific echoes are sounded.
Lines 13 and 14, for example, remind us of Rousseau's attack
upon frivolous and indifferent mothers:

since mothers, despising their first duty, have been no
longer willing to nourish their own children, they must be
intrusted to hire-ling nurses, who ... have felt no anxiety
but to rid themselves of their burdens.

Where there is no mother, there can be no child. ... The
child should love his mother before he knows that this is his
duty. If the voice of kin is not strengthened by habit and
duty, it dies out in early life, and the heart is dead, so to
speak, before it is born. Thus, at the very start, the path of
nature is forsaken.[95]

while the father of line twelve who 'stands ready to form/The
infant head,' calls to mind Locke's advice to 'Be sure ... to

establish the authority of a father, as soon as [the child] is capable of submission and can understand in whose power he is.' The 'whip' of line 17, used to 'rouze the sluggish senses to act,' allows Rousseau's violent opposition to the deforming physical constraints of parents and nurses (not just swaddling and tight-laced stays, both of which Locke also opposed, but giving 'the heads of infants a more proper form by a sort of moulding'),[96] to slide neatly into an attack on the brutalities of empirical education: 'The little lids are lifted and the little nostrils opend.' It also 'scourges off all youthful fancies,' so that the child, losing its child-likeness, becomes a 'new born man,' one without imagination. Erdman reads 'compelld to number footsteps' in line 19 as a sign that the infant, having reached school age, must now walk, as do the children in 'Holy Thursday,' 'two by two.'[97] But numbering can also refer to the imaginative limitations imposed by a Lockean-Calvinist education.

In the end, the child who has been 'compelled to pray repugnant & to humble the immortal spirit' (note the linking of religious orthodoxy with anti-imaginative rationalism) becomes 'subtil as a serpent,' and the very thing his education has been structured to prevent – lawlessness – lies at the heart of his being. Tiriel's education 'in the crucifying cruelties of Demonstration' (*J* 24.55: E168), has led him, like all true sons of Albion, to assume 'the Providence of God' (*J* 24.56: E168) and attempt to slay his father. The violated child grows into a violating adult, as in *For Children: The Gates of Paradise*, where the son who slays his father in plate 8 becomes 'Aged Ignorance' in plate 11, clipping his own son's wings. 'My Son! My Son!' reads the corresponding 'Key' to plate 11 in Blakes 1818 re-working of the series, entitled *For the Sexes: The Gates of Paradise*, 'thou treatest me/ But as I have instructed thee' (31–2: E266).

Formally, *Émile* is an educational romance somewhat along the lines of Rabelais's *Gargantua*, a welcome change – in Blake's eyes at least, if not in those of radicals of a more rationalist temperament (like Williams)[98] – from the dryness of earlier theory. Its ideas and advice are set out with great rhetorical energy, and in a fashion consciously distinct from the orderly and systematic procedures of Locke's *Education*. Its use of a single named fictional protagonist may also, in part, be a protest against the generalizing tendencies of previous educational theorists, like its habitual exaggeration and repetition. The theories themselves cluster around certain key words: 'natural,' 'simple,' 'progressive.' Teaching, writes Rousseau, should be stripped of all 'artificial' methods, books included;[99] a view implicitly endorsed, as we shall see, in both volumes of *Songs*. Locke's elaborate strategies for the forming of virtuous habits are not only useless but counter-productive;[100] so too are the endless admonitory precepts of 'Good Godly' and eighteenth-century neo-Calvinist children's books. Children must find things out for themselves, even when freedom entails suffering. 'The blessings of liberty,' Rousseau tells us, 'are worth many wounds. My pupil will often have bruises; but in return he will always have good spirits. If yours have fewer, they are always perverse, always restrained, always sad.'[101]

Rousseau's distrust of authority, his insistence that personal discovery is the one true path to learning, was the most radical, and from Blake's point of view, most welcome, of his teachings. Unfortunately it went hand in hand with a wholly traditional distrust of the imagination. The child's thoughts and interests, argues Rousseau, should be confined to the world about him; his 'most important lesson ... to desire nothing in the way of knowledge save what is useful.'[102] Since words are valueless unless connected with the ideas or objects they represent, mere verbal lessons, as in geography, are not only useless but pernicious; and the same applies to moral lessons as well.[103] The limitations and dangers of an approach of this sort are hinted at in the following passage:

> if, instead of transporting the mind of your pupil to a distance; if, instead of incessantly leading him astray in other places, in other climates, in other centuries, to the extremities of the earth, and even into the heavens, you make it your study to make him always self-contained and attentive to whatever immediately affects him – then you will always find him capable of perception, of memory, and even of reasoning: this is the order of Nature.[104]

What, though, of the imagination, of the child's creative capacities? Does education serve only sense perception, memory, and reason? Is training a child to be 'self-contained and attentive to whatever immediately affects him' a way to set him free? Blake did not think so; and with ample justification, judging from *Émile*'s English offspring.

The great irony of *Émile*'s enormous influence on 'advanced' or radical English educational theory and practice in the late eighteenth century is that the application of its theories led to less rather than more freedom for children. At the heart of *Émile* lies Rousseau's belief that childhood should be respected; that instead of 'always looking for the man in the child, without thinking of what he was before he became a man,' we should 'take the reverse of the current practice.'[105] 'Be reasonable,' Rousseau implores us, 'and do not reason at all with your pupil, especially to make him approve of what is displeasing to him.'[106] This is precisely the lesson, though, that Rousseau's English followers tended to forget, despite its centrality to *Émile*.[107] Instead they allowed Rousseau's championing of useful or practical information to take precedence over more important aspects of his teachings. Rousseau's disapproval of fantasy became, for men like Day, Williams, and Edgeworth, an excuse for providing children with what was good for them rather than with what they wanted. As long as tutor or author managed to convince a child that good behaviour paid off and bad did not, the spirit of *Émile* was thought to be upheld.

One final aspect of this radical revision of *Émile*'s precepts ought here to be mentioned, since it clearly bears on Blake's early interests. (Others, more closely linked to *Experience*, will be examined in later chapters.) Chief among the educational innovators who differed from Rousseau on the matter of infant instruction were Johann Oberlin, Samuel Wilderspin, and James Buchanan, founding fathers of the first infant schools in Europe. All three were Swedenborgians, prompting one authority to claim that 'If the early infant schools can be said to have any theoretical basis at all it was Swedenborgian.'[108] By 1788–9, of course, Blake was deeply interested in Swedenborg and the New Church, and in April of 1789 he and his wife attended its first meeting and signed its manifesto: though almost immediately their enthusiasm seems to have waned. If Blake was familiar with Swedenborg's educational principles his feelings about them must have been mixed. Though he cannot but have approved the New Church's teaching that children were spiritual beings in earthly bodies, what he thought of its insistence that they should begin their education in infancy, and that its prime object should be 'the cultivation of the memory of things that come within the range of the physical senses,'[109] is another matter. Whatever he thought, though, it is clear that here too, in

Blake's spiritual as well as his professional life, educational issues figured prominently.

5

That Blake was no stranger to contemporary children's literature, or to the larger implications of the debate about childhood and education that lay behind it, ought by now to be accepted. *Songs*, I hope to show, was a comment on, and contribution to, current debate. It was also the most comprehensive and successful of Blake's early attempts to give artistic expression to his theory of 'Vision,' the key to his own larger religious, social, aesthetic, and philosophical views. The extent to which that theory grew out of, or was merely tailored to, current debate, is impossible to tell. That it fits it so well, though, attests to the prominence of children and childhood, both as metaphors and models, in Blake's thought. Before turning to *Songs* itself, therefore, I want to say a word or two about Vision. Since we are concerned with the period just before and after the publication of *Innocence*, most references will be drawn from the Tracts of 1788 and the annotations to Swedenborg and Lavater.[110]

Blake believed, at all periods of his adult life, in the divinity of man. Since Jesus or God was for him man's 'Poetic Genius which is the Lord' (Annotations to Swedenborg's *Divine Love*: E592), those who fail to exercise their imaginative powers, who give themselves over to a false and unnecessarily limiting empiricism, are, in effect, denying their own divinity. Because all religions and deities 'are derived from each Nation's different reception of the Poetic Genius,' and the source of all religions is 'The true Man ... he being the Poetic Genius' (*All Religions Are One*: E2, 3), then, in Lavater's words – altered, underlined, and praised ('True Worship') by Blake – 'He, who [hates] <loves> the wisest and best of men, [hates] <loves> the Father of men; for where is *the Father of men to be seen but in the most perfect of his children*' (Annotations to Lavater's *Aphorisms on Man*: E586). Or, as Blake himself puts it in *Jerusalem*,

> the Worship of God, is honouring his gifts
> In other men: and loving the greatest men best, each according

To his Genius, which is the Holy Ghost in Man; there is no
other
God, than that God who is the intellectual fountain of
Humanity.

(97.7–10: E248)

Vision, or the exercise of the Divine Imagination or Poetic
Genius, is, therefore, both means and end for Blake. To see
God, one must be Him, which is why Heaven, in Blake's later
work, is conceived as a place of intellectual battle rather than an
achieved or settled state. The man who realizes his divinity
through the free exercise of his creative perception is Christ, for
Christ's divinity, in Lavater's words, lies in his power to 'see
objects through one grand immutable medium, always at hand,
and proof against illusion and time, reflected by every object,
and invariably traced through all the fluctuation of things'
(E573). To Christ, as to the man of vision, '*all life is holy*'
(Annotations to Lavater's *Aphorisms on Man*: E579).

Children, to the extent that they are untouched by adult or
'experienced' habits of mind, express or realize their divine
humanity instinctively, and those who find their innocent
behavior offensive do so, as Blake wrote in 1788, 'because it
reproaches them with the errors of acquired folly' (Lav.: E589).
Blake sees the child's life as god-like, lived within what he calls
an 'Eternal Now' (Lav.: E581), unhampered by time or
consequence. We, on the other hand, are mired in 'a dull round
of probabilities and possibilities' (*DC*: E534), prisoners of
memory and foresight. Children people their world with
imaginary friends and foes, half-create what they see, animate
inanimate objects, and take a spontaneous and unselfconscious
delight in creation. Their God is human, figured in the loving
sympathy and omniscience of earthly parents. Ours, abstract and
alienating, like the 'reality' we inhabit, lives in an 'allegorical
abode' (*E* 6.7: E61). Happiness, to children, is found 'in
pleasure which unsought falls round [their] path'; ours is sought
for 'in spaces remote' (*FZ* 9.121.9–10: E375). 'Has he not,'
writes Fuseli in his *Remarks on Rousseau* (1767), 'to the
abhorrence of every good schoolmaster, affirmed, that the idea of
God can have no meaning for a boy of ten years; that to him
Heaven is a basket of sweet-meats, and Hell – a school?'[111]

Finally, and most important, whereas adults divide their world
into self and other, subject and object, to the child all creation is

of a piece, as in the following lines from 'Spring,' perhaps the simplest and most transparent of all innocent Songs:

> Sound the flute!
> Now its mute.
> Birds delight
> Day and Night
> Nightingale
> In the dale
> Lark in the sky,
> Merrily
> Merrily Merrily to welcome in the year.

The first thing we note here is how authentically child-like these lines are. This child-speaker[112] is wholly at one with what he describes. The vivid clarity and directness of his simple exclamations suggest an immediacy of response to creation so intense that subject and object become almost indistinguishable. The child's world, like Christ's, or like that of the man of vision, is one of joyous unity, and to enter rather than to alter it should be our goal. 'That,' Samuel Palmer recalls Blake's proclaiming to a friend as they overlooked children playing in Fountain Court, 'is heaven.'[113] If anyone is to be educated, therefore, it is the adult. And the child should be his teacher:

> He who would see the Divinity must see him in his
>   Children
> One first, in friendship and love; then a Divine Family, and
>   in the midst
> Jesus will appear; so he who wishes to see a Vision; a
>   perfect Whole
> Must see it in its Minute Particulars.
>
> (*J* 91.18–21: E249)

'His' in the first line of this passage can refer either to our own or God's children (that is, ourselves), a characteristic Blakean ambiguity. In the latter sense, Los–Blake seems to be telling us that if we wish to see God, we must turn first, with unfeigned friendship and love, rather than with the theorist's abstract admiration for 'childhood' – his frequently callous disregard for individual 'Minute Particulars' – to a single, flesh-and-blood child. If approached in such a spirit, the individual child, whose god-like attributes we have already discussed, affords us a glimpse of the true Jesus, the Christ within us, by transforming adult modes of perception and understanding of the sort most children's books (whether influenced by Calvin, Locke, or Rousseau) seek to inspire, into the child's capacity to see the world as 'a Vision; a perfect Whole.' At the same time, contact with children also evokes in us those divinely human attributes – pity, love, protectiveness, forgiveness, tenderness – conventionally associated with parents. When Jesus appears 'in the midst,' he does so both as child-lamb and as parent-shepherd. Vision produces 'a Vision.'

In view of beliefs of this sort, Blake, as I have suggested, was hardly more likely to have championed the views of Rousseau and his followers than those of the followers of Calvin and Locke. Rousseau, after all, writes of the glories of childhood, and of our need to protect and cherish them, as if their demise were inevitable:

Why would you take from those little innocents the enjoyment of a time so short which is slipping from them, and of a good so precious which they can not abuse? Why would you fill with bitterness and sorrow those early years so rapidly passing which will no more return to them than to you? Fathers, do you know the moment when death awaits your children? Do not prepare for yourselves regrets by taking from them the few moments which Nature has given them. As soon as they can feel the pleasures of existence, allow them to enjoy it, and at whatever hour God may summon them, see to it that they do not die before they have tasted life.[114]

For Rousseau, childhood's glories and pleasures are different from its virtues. Émile's nobility as an adult is somehow related to his naturalness, a childhood inheritance preserved by scrupulously 'enlightened' education. Yet his virtues as a man exclude those qualities of imaginative exuberance, spontaneity, creative perception, and open and unembarrassed trust and affection, which make childhood 'a time so short ... a good so precious.' For the Blake of *Songs*, though, the virtues and glories of childhood are identical. Moreover, as we shall see in chapter 4, they can be preserved. 'Childhood and Age,' writes Blake in his Annotations to Reynolds' *Discourses*, 'are Equally belonging to Every Class' (E637). 'Neither Youth nor Childhood,' he writes in a letter to Dr J. Trusler, author, we remember, of several children's books, 'is Folly or Incapacity. Some Children are Fools and so are some Old Men.'[115] 'Innocence,' sings the old shepherd in an early 'Song' of 1784, obviously echoing *Lear*,

> is a Winter's gown;
> So clad, we'll abide life's pelting storm
> That makes our limbs quake, if our hearts be warm.
>
> (E457)

Keeping our hearts warm, rekindling within us the visionary flame of childhood – these are Blake's aims, not only in *Innocence* and *Songs*, but in all his works. *Innocence* focuses on child-like modes of perception and understanding in order

> To open the Eternal Worlds, to open the immortal Eyes
> Of Man inwards into the Worlds of Thought; into Eternity
> Ever expanding in the Bosom of God, the Human
>   Imagination
>
> (*J* 5. 18–20: E146)

and *Experience*, for all its darkness and disillusion, seeks, as we shall see, a similar end.

Though its poems are of a sort that 'Every child may joy to hear,' and though many of its themes and conventions are drawn from seventeenth- and eighteenth-century juvenile literature and educational theory, *Innocence* was intended primarily for adult or sophisticated readers. No attempt was made to advertise it as a juvenile book in the manner of *For Children: The Gates of Paradise*, nor, so far as we can tell, was it treated as such by its original purchasers. It was, in effect, a children's book for adults. What attracted Blake to so novel and paradoxical a creation has already, in part, been explained: he knew, through personal acquaintance and professional experience, a great deal about juvenile literature; lived in a world which took children's books seriously; disagreed with the theories and assumptions upon which most of them were based; and saw all too clearly that their ultimate effect, if not aim, was to deny children what he felt were their most valuable qualities. Furthermore, since most juvenile literature was illustrated, a children's book for adults would provide Blake with a perfect opportunity to extend his recent experiments (the three Tracts of 1788, themselves reminiscent of children's books [116]) in illuminated printing. The deceptively simple and reassuring rhythms of nursery rhyme, folk-song, jingle, lullaby, ballad, and hymn, when combined with an equally child-like pictorial style (the primitiveness of which may have appealed to Blake for other reasons as well), would lull the reader into expecting conventional themes – laziness, for instance, or disobedience – to be conventionally treated. When expectations were then subtly undermined, the larger implications of the themes and conventions of traditional children's books would be thrown into relief.

Which is not to say that *Innocence* is a satire. Though it may indeed, as Frye suggests, have been born out of the 'glint in the eye of the poet who wrote *An Island in the Moon*,'[117] true rather than false innocence is its primary concern. Nor do I mean to suggest that its borrowings from children's literature were wholly ironic or satirical. Blake heard a genuinely child-like voice not only in the Biblical-pastoral idiom of what Hirsch calls 'the dissenting tradition of children's literature from Bunyan through Watts to Mrs Barbauld,'[118] but in the short, emphatic, declamatory mode of such reading exercises as Mrs Barbauld's *Lessons for Children* or Mrs Trimmer's commentaries on her 'Series of Prints.' Though the content of the following passage reminds us of the experienced 'Nurses Song,' what it sounds like is 'Spring,' or the child-like peremptoriness of the infant voice in 'Introduction':

Come hither, Charles, come to Mamma.
Make haste.
Sit in Mamma's lap.
Now read your book.
Where is the pin to point with?
Here is a pin.
Do not tear the book.
Only bad boys tear books.
Charles shall have a pretty new lesson.
Spell that word. Good boy.
Come and give Mamma three kisses.
One, two, three.
Little boys must come when Mamma calls them.
Blow your nose.
Here is a handkerchief.

Come and let me comb your hair.
Stand still.
Here is a comb for you to hold.[119]

Another of Blake's debts to juvenile literature, similarly un-ironic, is the air of child-like mystery and wonder in several of the Songs. The puzzling, gnomic quality of 'The Blossom,' for example, or 'The Lilly' of *Experience*, owes much to the evocative riddles and aphorisms of juvenile reading books like Ronksley's *The Child's Week's Work*;[120] while the haunting simplicity of 'The Little Boy Lost/Found' poems in *Innocence* reminds us of chapbook ballads and folk-rhymes. Even the frequent ambiguity of many of the designs may owe something to the 'strange and distorted pictures,'[121] often haphazardly arranged, found in many cheaply produced children's books.

Blake's most important debt to juvenile literature, though, is one of structure and function. A. P. Davis's description, in his biography of Watts, of Bunyan's *A Book for Boys and Girls*, one of the half dozen most influential of late seventeenth- and eighteenth-century children's books, as 'at once an alphabet, a reader, and a guide to doctrine,'[122] applies equally well not only to Watts's *Divine Songs* but to a great many other juvenile books. Witness the difficulties historians and scholars of children's books encounter when trying to classify or categorize their material. Though Joyce Whalley, for example, divides her study of illustrated juvenile literature into separate chapters on alphabet books, reading books, history, geography, and natural history books, books of street cries and occupations, of religious instruction, and of moral improvement, we soon discover that 'Before the middle of the nineteenth century almost all books had either a religious or a moral content – and frequently both;'[123] that history, geography, and natural history books were frequently religious in intent, with the Divine Will as protagonist; that many reading books contained alphabets; and that even alphabet books contained short reading lessons, usually of a moral or religious character.

The multi-purposed structure of these books points to a characteristic convergence of means and ends, precepts and practice in juvenile literature. The infant reader lives out the virtues about which he reads through the very act of reading. To the Puritan, for example, reading not only encourages in children the traditional virtues of obedience to parents, application, and self-discipline. It is also the one true path to salvation through God's Word. So closely was salvation intertwined with the act of reading that even the simplest hornbook alphabets and primers included, at the very least, a Lord's Prayer or Catechism. The relation between reading and what the child read was thought of as complementary. Being saved and reading about being saved were one and the same, as in Janeway's advice to his 'dear lambs' to

> hear what other good children have done, and remember how they wept and prayed by themselves, how earnestly they cried out for the Lord Jesus Christ: you may read how dutiful they were to their parents: how diligent at their books: how ready to learn Scriptures and their catechisms ... if you love me, if you love your parents, if you love your Souls, if you would escape hell-fire, and if you would go to Heaven when you die, do you go and do as these good children.[124]

Nor was it only the Puritans who pressed home a connection between precept and practice, ideal child and infant reader. When Dr Johnson protested that 'Babies do not want to hear about babies,'[125] Richard Edgeworth rightly took his words as a challenge as much to the followers of Rousseau, with their endless procession of good and bad little boys and girls, as to those of Calvin. The child reading *Sandford and Merton*, for example, is doing precisely what Day's all-knowing fictional tutor, Mr Barlow, would have him do: using his time to advantage, pleasing his elders, focusing on the 'real' rather than the imaginary world. No doubt he is even feeling a rush of self-satisfied virtue of the sort we detect in the voices of Mr Barlow's prize pupils.

Innocence too, like a children's book, merges means with ends, though instead of cultivating adult powers of mind (the most important of which Watts lists as 'the understanding, the memory, the judgement, the faculty of reason, and the conscience'),[126] it teaches us to approach the world as a child would. Those qualities it invites us to admire in the innocents who sing and people its Songs are the very ones we need when reading: unselfconsciousness, for example, emotional and imaginative daring, a refusal to abstract and generalize. How Blake gradually 'tricks,' 'allures,' and 'delights' us into adopting these qualities will be discussed in chapter 3. For the moment I want only to note the source and nature of the special relation *Innocence* establishes between practice and precept, reader and text (or design); the fact that we too, like a child at his book, are made, while reading, to embody the virtues (or rather 'powers of mind,' since *Innocence* is a book of visionary as opposed to 'moral' instruction) about which we read.

Experience, which Blake added to *Innocence* in 1794, puts our newly acquired child-like percipience to the test. Though many readers have mistaken it for a repudiation of innocent truths, or as an inevitable product of Blake's own disillusioning growth into maturity, its ultimate purpose is to strengthen rather than weaken visionary habits. If we think of *Innocence* as an 'alphabet' or 'guide' to vision, one which teaches us *how* to read, *Experience* functions as a kind of exercise book or 'reader.' The two are bound together in a single volume much as they would be in a children's book, so that *Songs*, like its models, is 'at once an alphabet, a reader, and a guide to doctrine.' Chapter 5, the first to look closely at *Experience*, argues this point in detail, and as with so many others of the points I have been making in these last few pages, its proof will depend ultimately on the readings in the chapters that follow. Since those readings give equally close attention to text and design, we must turn next, in chapter 2, to the special problems posed by illuminated printing.

CHAPTER 2
THE DESIGNS

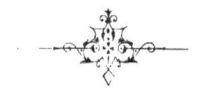

This chapter begins with a familiar refrain, since critical studies of Blake's verse continue to appear which ignore his visual art, or pay it only lip service: Blake meant the poems and designs of his Illuminated Books to remain together. When picture and poem are separated the result is 'Loss of some of the best things.' The designs, he writes, turning the equation around, 'perfect accompany Poetical Personifications and Acts, without which poems they never could have been Executed.'[1] Nor would he have approved of readers who treat the designs as so much attractive but irrelevant decoration. Painting, he believed, ought to be 'as poetry and music are, elevated to its own proper sphere of invention and visionary conception' (*DC*: E532). Pictures ought to be studied as closely as poems:

> I intreat that the Spectator will attend to the Hands and Feet the Lineaments of the Countenances they are all descriptive of Character and not a line is drawn without intention and that most discriminate and particular <as Poetry admits not a Letter that is insignificant so Painting admits not a Grain of Sand or a Blade of Grass <insignificant> much less an Insignificant Blur or Mark>.
>
> (*VLJ*: E550)[2]

Explicit statements of this sort are backed by great personal sacrifice. Critics who fail to read the poems in light of the designs forget how high a price Blake paid to create his illuminated pages '– in time, money, patronage, friendship and spiritual energy.'[3] 'I know myself both Poet and Painter,' Blake insists, defying those (often, as in this case, important patrons) who would prevent his 'more assiduous pursuit of both arts.'[4] Only a few sympathetic contemporaries understood the nature of the designs: Coleridge spoke of 'Blake's poesies, metrical and graphic'; Robinson mentions 'poetic pictures of the highest beauty and sublimity'; the anonymous author of 'The Inventions of W.B., Painter and Poet' (Keynes thinks it C. A. Tulk), finds 'The figures surrounding and enclosing the poems ... are equally tinged by a poetical idea'; to Allan Cunningham, writing in the same year, 1830, text and design are 'intertwined ... so closely in his compositions, that they cannot well be separated.'[5]

This book takes as one of its starting points a somewhat more timid version of David Erdman's 'working assumption' that 'every graphic image has its seed or root in the poetry':[6] almost every graphic image bears some relation to – colors if it does not, in fact, grow out of – the poetry. It argues that we cannot properly appreciate the larger meaning or 'vision' of *Songs* without a knowledge of the designs, and in a few cases it even questions the extent to which certain poems can stand alone. 'Spring,' from *Innocence*, provides a case in point. Robert Gleckner complains that in the poem's last stanza 'the "I" is not identified, except possibly as Blake himself, [and] the lamb's appearance is unprepared for.'[7] But in the scene at the bottom of the second plate we are shown a child petting (or 'pulling') the 'soft wool' of a 'little lamb.' We notice lamb and child as soon as we turn the page (before we read the last stanza) and we identify them with similar figures on the first plate. When we turn then to the last stanza we realize at once that the child (not Blake) must be the poem's speaker and that the lamb he refers to is pictured in the designs. Text and design 'cannot well be separated.' Gleckner's complaint disappears when 'Spring' is returned to its original format.

'The Little Girl Lost' and 'The Little Girl Found' provide an example of a subtler and more frequently recurring interdependence of text and design. They also bring us closer to understanding the difference between Blake's illuminations and conventional illustration. 'Lost' tells the story of little Lyca's separation from her parents and her wanderings in 'desart wild.' Exhausted, she lies down beneath a tree, falls asleep, and is soon approached by magical 'beasts of prey' who undress her (while she sleeps) and carry her off to their caves. 'Found' tells of the wanderings of Lyca's distraught parents. They too encounter a magical beast (a lion who becomes 'a spirit arm'd in gold') who leads them to where Lyca sleeps 'among tygers wild.' In the final stanza the parents are said to 'dwell/in a lonely dell,' no longer fearing wolves and tigers.

A story of this sort, rich in folk and fairy-tale motifs, and 'obviously nonsensical on the level of natural fact,'[8] is bound to give rise to elaborate symbolic readings. One of the more plausible of these readings takes 'Lost' as an allegory of sexual awakening in which Lyca's separation from her family is to be seen as a fall; her wanderings in 'desart wild' as the stirrings of desire; the tree under which she sleeps as a type of the Tree of the Knowledge of Good and Evil; and her eventual abduction by 'beasts of prey' as a symbolic sexual initiation.[9] 'Found' is then read as Blake's account of the necessary adjustments parents must make when their children grow into experience. A number of suggestive details lend support to the reading: the southern setting (traditionally associated with the passions);[10] our twice being told of Lyca's loveliness; the seductive influence of 'wild birds song'; Lyca's calling out to 'sweet sleep' in the manner of a lover; the lion's licking her neck and bosom; the loosing of Lyca's 'slender dress.'

Those who object to a sexual interpretation of this sort[11] begin with line 13, in which Lyca is said to be 'Seven summers old' – hardly an age of sexual awakening. Details such as the story's setting or the removal of Lyca's 'slender dress' are interpreted along Neoplatonic lines, their sexual overtones ignored or minimized. If the poems are taken in isolation, this approach has some merit. But the designs lend strong support to a sexual reading. On the first plate a couple embraces. We notice them before we turn to the text, and our first impulse is to identify the female in the design with the 'Little Girl' of the title. Once we begin reading, though, we are forced to retract the identification (Lyca being alone in 'desart wild' and too young to have a lover). When we turn to the second plate, still in search of some connection between the lover's embrace and Lyca's story, our uncertainty deepens. A young woman lies alone in a forest beneath a tree. Again, our immediate impulse is to identify her with Lyca, interpreting the design as an illustration of stanzas 5 through 8. But what of her age? Like the female on the first plate, she wears a gown whose folds reveal a woman's body. We begin to wonder about line 13. Perhaps we were not meant to take Lyca's age literally? Perhaps Blake chose the number seven for its symbolic associations?[12] This is what the design on the third plate seems to imply. Below the text, a naked female lies asleep next to a lioness. A male lion sits off to the right. Three children, two male and one female, caress and play with the lions. To the right of the text two trees entwine, their smooth curves like those of human limbs in embrace. There can be little doubt about the identity of the maiden on this plate. She is Lyca, naked and asleep among beasts of prey. The identification confirms our suspicions about the young women on the previous plates. Once we have overcome our doubts about Lyca's age, we return to the maiden on the first plate and notice that her hair and dress are similar in color[13] to those of the maiden on the second plate, now more confidently identified as Lyca. We return to the problems of the first design: how are we to connect Lyca's story with a lover's embrace?

Questions of this sort – no matter what their answers – affect the way we read the 'Lyca' poems. They direct our attention along specific lines, adding emphasis and point to subtle sexual suggestions in the text. Though we are not confined by the designs to any single level of meaning, they make it impossible for us to ignore the story's sexual dimension. Like most of Blake's 'illuminations,' the pictures occupy a middle ground between illustration and interpretation. They provide no missing information, as do the designs to 'Spring,' but they prevent partial or misdirected readings. They also have a larger and more general effect: by taking certain liberties with the text (why lions and not tigers on the third plate?) they encourage a similar freedom in our own interpretations. We find ourselves looking for what Blake calls 'mythological and recondite meaning, where more is meant than meets the eye' (*DC*: E522).

Designs of a more abstract nature can affect our readings in equally complex and subtle ways. On the first plate of 'A Cradle Song,' for example, the text (a mother's lullaby to her sleeping child, sung in response to the child's smiles, moans and sighs) is set against a night sky and surrounded by a tangle of flame-like vegetative forms and tiny human figures. Our initial reaction to the design is uncomplicated. The decoration, we feel, neatly captures the poem's dominant note of security and protection. Delicate intimations of identity between mother, child, and all creation are echoed in the swirling continuity of text, vegetation and human form. To Keynes, 'the dreamy tangles of falling vegetation ... suggest the feeling of the first line: "Sweet dreams form a shade." ' He also points to the 'soft female form with arms stretched out in benison' above and to the right of the second stanza who 'seems suggested by ... "Sweet sleep Angel mild,/Hover o'er my happy child." '[14] Erdman writes of 'Suggestive, indeterminate vegetable and human forms of dreams, smiles, sweet moans, and sighs which fill the verdure backed by night sky.' When comparing this plate with other examples of flame-plant decoration, continues Erdman, 'we see that the lullaby form of energy and desire thins into "pleasant streams" and "happy silent moony beams." '[15]

But the poem is not all gentle sweetness and content. Its delicate beauty, like that of Coleridge's 'Frost at Midnight,' is faintly disturbing and enigmatic. We wonder, for example, at the ease with which the mother overcomes her sense of Christ's sorrows. 'The tears of the Christ child,' writes Bloom, 'were not an image of infant helplessness, but a lament for all mortality, for the transience of Innocence. Yet the mother singing "A Cradle Song" will not see this, but converts the infant god of Innocence very rapidly into a father god of the same state, with a supposedly inevitable movement from "Wept for thee, for me, for all" to "Smiles on thee, on me, on all." '[16] The mother's steady, unvarying tone fails to dispel the darker implications of moans, sighs and tears. A gap opens between what we feel and what the mother's tone would make us feel – a gap anticipated in the design on the first plate. What Erdman sees as 'pleasant streams' and 'happy silent moony beams,' others see quite differently. Wagenknecht, for example, writes of the 'terribly twisted and dark vegetation which winds against a dark background like seaweed ... in one place tinged with red which suggests flesh as well as vegetation.'[17] Vague premonitions of threat and danger soon complicate any initial impression of exuberant organic life. This vegetation, we realize, is thicker, darker and heavier than the light curlicues and intertwinings found elsewhere in *Innocence*. The more we look at its swirling strands, the less likely we are to associate them with the dream-formed 'shade' of line 1. 'The hedging of each stanza,' writes Eben Bass, 'implies protection for the cradled child, but the stanzas are also, in fact, nearly oppressed by the design.' The decoration begins to affect the way we read. Bass wonders if ' "Sweet dreams form a shade" could imply the mother's clouding, as well as protective, influence.'[18] Words like 'hovers' and 'beguiles' take on new and more ambiguous meanings. As the thinning strands of vegetation work their way into the text, tiny ripples of doubt disrupt the reassuring flow of the mother's words. We turn to the second plate secure in our sense of a world bounded and fused by the loving identity of mother and child, but we are also vaguely troubled. The design catches out and alerts us to subtle intimations of threat and danger in the text – even as it sounds the poem's dominant note of protection and contentment. It is like Bellini's *The Madonna of the Meadow* in the National Gallery (figure 1), in which the Virgin looks down, in prayer, on a naked infant whose pose reminds us of those of the dead Christs of countless Renaissance Pietàs.[19] Here and elsewhere in *Songs* the marginal decoration repays close attention. We must learn to take seriously Blake's claim that 'not a Grain of Sand or a Blade of Grass [is] <insignificant> much less an insignificant Blur or Mark.'

Even when a design seems awkward, crude, or perfunctory we ought not to dismiss the impressions it makes upon us. The second plate of 'A Cradle Song' provides a convenient example. Our first impulse is to seek some extra-literary excuse for its unpleasant appearance. Damon speaks of 'a sort of Raphaelesque hardness, which in these days is not pleasant'[20] (but refers to it nowhere else in *Innocence*); Keynes calls the second plate 'uncomprising in the hard outlines of the mother's clumsy chair and the child's wicker cot,'[21] leaving us with the impression (since he gives no reasons for its oddly 'uncompromising' character) that Blake himself has been clumsy or careless in execution. Erdman's off-hand reference to 'the thickly wrapped, perhaps even threateningly swaddled, infant,'[22] is equally puzzling. Though he is hardly likely to charge Blake with clumsy or careless execution ('A failure to find the textual referent is a failure to find something that is there'),[23] he records no other discrepancies between the poem's designs and its textual lullaby. Why, then, does the child's appearance disturb us?

There is no mistaking the design's unpleasantness. The stark backdrop of dark, draped cloth is like nothing else in *Innocence*. Its strong, straight lines are of a piece with the 'hard outlines' of the chair, the large, hooded cradle, and the folds of the mother's dress. The ground's dark mottled colors suggest a patterned carpet, but the patterns lack definition or outline. Like much else in the design, it reminds us of a similarly enclosed scene in 'Infant Sorrow,' a poem about the stifling, oppressive weight of parental influence.[24] The hooded wicker cradle looks coffin-like, in part because of its length. Is this an accident, the wholly fortuitous result of Blake's habitual 'clumsiness' with perspective?[25] And what of the mother? Why does she look so much less attractive and appealing than the mother on the first plate of 'Spring'? 'Amply, almost redundantly gowned,'[26] with a head-dress like a wimple, she is stiff and awkward as she bends over her child. 'It is surely not by chance,' writes Keynes, 'that the child's pillow is so arranged as to form a conspicuous halo around its head.'[27] But what of more disturbing details? Is it chance that wraps the child's bedclothes around him as tightly as a cocoon? Why not attribute their unpleasant, 'threatening' appearance to the mother, a woman whose own clothing wholly conceals the curves of her body?

'The cradle's hood,' writes Bass, 'and the draped cloth behind are the mother's way of sheltering her child from cold and drafts, but both testify as much to danger and mortality as they do to protection.'[28] Our doubts about the poem's concluding stanzas increase as we look at the second plate. The world, it seems, is not as benevolent as the mother's words would have us believe; protection takes on the appearance of something more threatening. We worry again about 'hovers' and 'beguiles.' Maternal affection is frequently ambiguous in *Innocence*: nurture slides easily into dependency, protection tightens into possessiveness. On 'The Blossom' plate, for example, a tiny child is almost totally obscured by the embrace of a winged female dressed in green, presumably its mother. She faces *against* the cycle of generation traced by the other figures in the design.[29]

The designs to 'A Cradle Song' hint at the dangers implicit in the mother's easy passage from tears to smiles. Innocence must be protected, enclosed against an outside world whose threatening harshness is figured in the acanthus-shaped leaves at the top of the second plate or the nightmarish tangles of plate 1. But the domestic scene offers its own dangers. The disturbingly 'uncompromising' nature of the design on the second plate is no accident. Blake was a careful and conscious craftsman with a professional engraver's eye for detail. He thought seriously about technique, and knew how to adapt his style to different moods. No artist who supported himself by illustrating or engraving other men's works could have 'missed' or 'overlooked' the design's want of delicacy. Had he been displeased with the harsh outlines on the original copperplate, Blake could have softened them with color, as he did in earlier copies.[30] When a design seems crude or perfunctory, the impressions it makes upon us ought not to be dismissed too quickly. Blake has flaws, both as poet and as painter — the pictorial language of his designs is, at times, as in the case of *Tiriel*, inappropriate — but his visual art deserves the same respectful scrutiny as his poetry. 'In the art of the late eighteenth century,' writes Robert Rosenblum, 'a one-to-one correlation of style and subject was as frequently the exception as the rule';[31] in Blake's art, it was more often the rule than the exception. 'Not a line is drawn without intention,' he insists, 'and that most discriminate and particular.' We ought to try to take him at his word.

In some plates, though, Blake seems subject to purely technical or formal limitations. The text of 'The Chimney Sweeper' in *Innocence*, for example, fills almost the whole plate. Blake, we feel, has no choice but to squeeze his design into a half-inch strip along the bottom of the plate. As a result, sweep-heaven seems neither airy, light, nor particularly pleasant. But Blake need not have confined himself to a single plate. Had he spread the text over two pages, as he does in 'Spring,' a poem only three lines longer than 'The Chimney Sweeper,' he would have had ample room to depict a heaven every bit as joyous as lines 15 to 18 describe. Plate 1 could have been bleak and dreary, a picture of the sweeps' grinding poverty and oppression, plate 2 bright and energetic. At this point a host of insupportable conjectures suggest themselves. Perhaps Blake was short of copperplate (we know he sometimes used both sides)?[32] Perhaps he had not realized how much room the text would take up? Was he in a hurry that day? Or distracted? (In that case, he must also have had an off day thirty-seven years later when coloring Crabb Robinson's copy.) But no critic can take this sort of speculation seriously. Doubtless Blake fell victim to all sorts of technical difficulties (both as poet and as painter), but these are of no more value to a reading of the designs than they are to a reading of the poems. We must look first to the work itself, and when we do, we shall discover subtle but important reasons for the design's depressing appearance.

As 'The Chimney Sweeper' opens, an older and more

experienced sweep, the speaker, comforts a younger sweep ('little' Tom Dacre) against the pain of a newly encountered experience. Little Tom has just had his head shaven, a ritual initiation and subjugation 'like those given in prison or the army.'[33] (Its ostensible purpose was to reduce the risk of hair catching fire from pockets of smoldering soot.)[34] Tom has but newly entered his apprenticeship and cries for the loss of his curly white hair (an echo of 'softest clothing wooly bright' in 'The Lamb').

The speaker's instinctive sympathy and fellow-feeling has a profound effect on young Tom. So, too, his thoughts on 'duty.' Tom's dream ends with an admonition from the liberating angel identical in spirit to that of the poem's last line, and equally disturbing:

> And the Angel told Tom if He'd be a good boy,
> He'd have God for his father and never want joy.

In this case, being a good boy entails doing what one's told, and doing it without complaint.[35] Tom may have picked up such 'advice' from any of several sources: the father who sold him; the master who exploits him; perhaps a priest of the sort we encounter in 'A Little Boy Lost,' or one of the 'Wise guardians of the poor' in the innocent 'Holy Thursday.' But he is also likely to have picked it up from the older sweep, whose experience has no doubt taught him the painful consequences of disobedience. That Tom dreams of the eventual salvation not just of himself but of 'thousands of sweepers Dick, Joe, Ned and Jack,' suggests that he has also caught something of the speaker's spirit of compassion.

The very existence of the dream seems to owe something to the older sweep's influence. 'It is not for nothing,' writes Wicksteed, 'that the child's vision follows immediately after his being given the idea that his "white hair" is potentially "there" just as much when it is shaved off as before.'[36] Like his friend the speaker, Tom builds an imaginary ideal out of the bleakest and most depressing of realities. The 'coffin of black' is an obvious example. 'To wash in a river and shine in the sun,' sporting 'naked and white' in the landscape of innocence, is another. As Martin Nurmi writes:

Nakedness is not here merely a symbol of innocence. In dreaming of it Tom is making a connection between his dream imagery and his ordinary life. For sweeps often went up chimneys naked. ... Naked immersion in soot, therefore, is Tom's normal state now, and white naked cleanliness is its natural opposite.[37]

The sweeps' trust in the justice and benevolence of the very world that has injured them is terribly pathetic. We see all too clearly the price they must pay for their few moments of warmth and happiness. Though they still retain some sparks of imaginative life, much has already been lost. Tom learns to submit to the loss of his hair with all the docility of a sheep; the cheerless anapests of the older sweep's matter-of-fact tone, especially in the first stanza, sound only the faintest echoes of the more energetic speech of children in other Songs. The off-hand manner in which he recounts the cruelties of his life ('His mother's death he puts in a dependent clause ... his being sold by his father ... he emphasizes less than the fact that he was very young'),[38] suggests a spirit numbed by suffering. Only when recounting the imaginary joys of Tom's dream does the speaker recapture the animated rhythms of childhood. The cold, dark mornings must soon, we sense, take their inevitable toll.

The poem concludes with what Bloom calls 'a new fierceness for Blake.'[39] The sweep lacks sufficient strength or security to question what he has been taught, and his call to duty is without conscious irony. The last line is a brutal indictment of the sorts of traditional pieties we encounter again and again in 'Good Godly' books, or in Watts's *Divine Songs* or Mrs Barbauld's *Hymns in Prose*. Yet the poem belongs in *Innocence* because, unlike its experienced counterpart, it inspires neither outrage nor indignation. Our attention is almost wholly absorbed in the sweeps' last few glimmers of imagination and fellow-feeling.

The scene at the bottom of the plate depicts Tom's heaven. To the far right a robed and haloed figure (presumably the angel with a bright key)[40] reaches down to lift a small boy out of a black coffin.[41] The flowing curves of his gown suggest a figure out of a dream. To the left, eleven sweeps rejoice at their liberation.[42] Those furthest from the coffin run towards a river (tinted blue in copy Z). The sweeps are barely more than stick-figures. Their 'heaven' is compressed into a space too small to provide any visual equivalent for the wide expanse suggested by the line, 'down a green plain leaping laughing they run.' The dark blue-green of the mottled landscape, and the pale yellow wash[43] behind the poem's last stanzas, sound but the faintest echo of 'wash in a river and shine in the sun.' No attempt has been made to capture the airy lightness of 'rise upon clouds and sport in the wind.' The scene lacks the very qualities the sweeps most long for: open spaces, sun, warmth, clear, bright colors. The great block of text presses down upon Tom's dream like a weight,[44] stunting and crushing it much as Innocence itself is ground down by a life of poverty and oppression. That the poem is 'illuminated' by the design's cramped and unpleasant appearance encourages us (here and elsewhere) to take our initial reactions seriously – even when we might plausibly relate them to circumstances beyond Blake's control.

Failed or flawed designs in *Songs* are the product less of carelessness or incompetence than of ambition. Some simply ask too much of us. The oddly inoffensive creature on 'The Tyger' plate provides a notorious case in point. Blake might easily have drawn a fearful or ferocious tiger. 'He had no trouble drawing a fearful were-wolf,' Erdman reminds us, 'or for that matter a fearful flea.'[45] And on the sixth page of the Notebook (or 'Rossetti Manuscript'), another page of which contains a draft of the poem, we find two genuinely ferocious beasts, one unmistakably a tiger (figure 2). Yet in none of the extant copies of *Songs* is there a creature remotely comparable to the picture created by the poem's awestruck speaker. 'Comical,' 'inquisitive,' 'simpering,' 'quaint,' 'gentle,' 'tame,' 'patient,' 'worried,' 'fatuous,' 'supercilious' – these are the adjectives critics use to describe the visual equivalent of the poem's bright burning beast. Even at its most ferocious, in copy U, the tiger is only 'formidable,' not yet the 'heroic Tyger' Grant and others seek (figure 3).[46] Keynes speaks of an unspecified 'ferocious carnivore,' but neither Erdman nor anyone else has seen it.[47]

Once we accept the obvious discrepancy between poem and design, a whole range of possibilities opens: the design is Blake's attempt 'to portray the smile of the Deity on its [the tiger's] lips, and to show the ultimate "humanity divine" of Nature's most terrific beast'; or it is 'a mask, deriding those who expect upon a mortal page the picture of the Deity at work';[48] or a depiction of 'the final tiger, who has attained the state of organized Innocence as have the adjacent lions and tigers of "The Little Girl Lost"

and "The Little Girl Found" ';[49] or a joke, not so much on us as
on 'the awestruck questioner, or the Tyger, and perhaps on the
Creator himself.'[50]

I tend towards the last of these possibilities. Blake and the
poetic voice ought not to be confused, especially in a Song of
Experience. Much of what the awestruck questioner says implies
a world (and a way of looking at it) that Blake would have found
unnecessarily limited and limiting. He might well have sought to
undermine the speaker by domesticating or defanging his tiger,
just as he cuts Behemoth and Leviathan down to size (Paley calls
them 'houshold pets') in plate 15 of the *Illustrations to the Book
of Job* (figure 4).[51]

But an 'explanation' of this sort makes the design no less
jarring or unsatisfactory. Hagstrum is still right, the tiger *is*
'unworthily illustrated,'[52] even if Blake thinks the speaker's
celebration of its fierce majesty wrong or misguided. The poem
is simply too powerful to be undercut so brutally. We have
neither time nor inclination to make the necessary adjustments
of perspective the design demands of us.

This is also a common problem for readers of the later
prophetic books. Blake's poems and designs suffered
increasingly from an absence of public recognition. Lacking
informed and sympathetic criticism, he grew less and less
inclined to anticipate (or even consider) the needs and
expectations of his almost nonexistent audience. At times, in his
eagerness to attain the widest and most comprehensive vision,
Blake would alter his works substantially, often at the expense of
their coherence and our comprehension. The revisions that
turned *Vala* into *The Four Zoas*, for example, introduce so
many new themes and connections that the original narrative
sequence and allegorical pattern become hopelessly confused;
those to what was, in effect, its visual counterpart, a huge Last
Judgment design, turned one version, according to
Cumberland's son, 'black as your hat'[53] – so feverishly was it
worked over and elaborated. We can reconstruct Blake's
intentions in these cases, and find subtle and complicated
justifications for the thematic coherence of much of the
additional material, but each new idea makes the poem or the
design less accessible and attractive, even to the most learned
and partisan of Blake's readers.

The design to 'The Tyger' is marred by a comparable lack of
restraint. Blake is so eager for us to see the whole, so delighted

with the ease with which he can expose his speaker, that he momentarily loses his sense of tact. The reader is much too abruptly wrenched out of the mood of the poem. On occasion, abruptness of this sort can produce astonishing effects, as in plate 9 of *Europe*, where all of human history is condensed into three lines:

> Eighteen hundred years, a female dream!
> Shadows of men in fleeting bands upon the wind;
> Divide the heavens of Europe
>
> (9.6–8: E61)

but here we feel betrayed and bewildered. 'The Tyger,' though, is an extreme case. More often than not, when a design undercuts a poem's speaker, or adds an unexpected twist, the poem is enriched.

A subtler and more problematic example is provided by 'The Little Boy Found.' Our difficulties begin with the figure Keynes calls 'a person in the image of God.' If, as the poem tells us, the child's rescuer is 'God ever nigh,' who appears to him 'like his father in white,' why is its form in the design 'ostensibly female, so appearing to be in disagreement with the poem'?[54] Keynes is not alone in thinking this an oddly feminine Savior. Others have made much of the figure's long flowing hair, lack of beard and high-waisted gown, which, in the shading of some copies (Z among them), suggests a female bosom.[55] Erdman, Grant, and Bindman take a dim view of such speculation. Erdman disdains comment, simply assuming the figure's masculinity;[56] Grant points to nine other unmistakably male figures wearing high-waisted gowns in *Songs*, as well as to numerous depictions of Christ outside the *Songs*, many of which bear a striking resemblance to the figure on this plate;[57] Bindman relegates the controversy to a footnote.[58] We ought not to be bullied. No matter what its appearance in other copies, or how much it resembles Blake's Christs elsewhere, in copy Z the little boy's rescuer looks more like a masculine female than a feminine male. Our first impulse is to identify it as the little boy's mother. But the text clearly tells us that 'God ever nigh' (or the 'father') 'by the hand led' the little boy. Besides, what of the smaller female figure in the bottom half of the plate whose arms reach out just below the word 'Found' in the title? Is she not a more plausible mother, as Grant argues?[59] We are soon forced to

conclude, with Keynes, that the design's 'God ever nigh' is
'Probably ... one of Blake's not infrequent androgynous figures,
having both mother and father attributes.'[60] Blake may be
suggesting that the little boy sees the watchful benevolence of
both parents in the divinity of the father. He almost never spoke
approvingly of God the Father, and the sexual ambiguity of the
little boy's rescuer may well be an attempt to forestall criticism
of the child for believing in the wrong kind of Savior.[61]

Yet we remain troubled. Though we can find plausible
explanations for the figure's androgyny, our initial confusion is
distracting. We are made to move too quickly from problem to
problem. The design is another of Blake's attempts to do too
much – to make too many points, answer too many questions. As
in 'The Tyger' neither carelessness nor incompetence need have
anything to do with the design's failings. When 'God the father'
looks feminine, as in copy Z, Blake's ambition has simply got the
better of his tact. Though the design may be flawed, we still
sense a complex and subtle intelligence at work.

Let us return to 'The Tyger' for a moment, since it provides a
convenient opening to larger and more general questions of
pictorial style in *Songs*. 'The Tyger' is disappointing, argues
Ann Mellor, because 'Blake was forced to re-use Stothard's
illustrative style in the companion volume to *Songs of Innocence*.
Stothard's sentimental decorative mode is by 1794 clearly
inadequate to Blake's poetic vision.'[62] Stothard, a friend of
Blake's from bachelor student days, had already begun to make
a name for himself by 1780 as 'a prolific inventor of charming
vignettes for the booksellers.'[63] What William Gaunt calls his
'modest faculty for design,'[64] Stothard put to the service of
fashionable allegory and *conversazioni*. 'At their worst,' writes
Hagstrum, Stothard's illustrations 'place preposterous medieval
cavaliers and white-clad society ladies in the wooded parks of
English country estates or fill the sky with allegorical heads
derived academically from Raphael, Guido Reni, Correggio, or
the antique.' Only 'now and then' do they capture 'authentic
echoes of the greater tradition from which he and his fellows
sprung.'[65]

Until the abrupt and bitter termination of their friendship in
1806, Blake engraved a number of illustrations after Stothard.
Bindman thinks he may even have worked in partnership with
Stothard, producing, by 1785, as many as thirty-three
engravings of the latter's illustrations.[66] While openly admitting

the similarity between Stothard's style and that of his own early work, Blake vigorously denies any influence on Stothard's part. 'Heath and Stothard were the awkward imitators at that time,' writes Blake of his early artistic career. Praise for Stothard's draftsmanship, he claims, is almost wholly derived from 'those little prints which I engraved after him five and twenty years ago' (*PA* : E561). Though Blake's remark about 'awkward imitators' is that of an embittered rival, a friend who thought himself cruelly wronged ('Resentment for Personal Injuries has,' Blake admits, 'had some share in this Public Address' (*PA* : E563)), it points to real, if subtle, differences between his own style in *Songs* and that of more fashionable contemporaries.

Anthony Blunt was among the first of Blake's modern critics to detect Stothard's 'sentimental decorative mode' in the designs for *Innocence*, but even when he thinks Blake most artificial or mannered, as in 'Laughing Song' or 'The Shepherd,' Blunt also notes details 'typical of Blake's best illumination.'[67] Though the idiom may be conventional, 'the movement is equally personal.'[68] Mellor notes that, on the whole, Blake's figures are less artificial than Stothard's, their sturdier and more muscular bodies frequently set off by clinging or transparent drapery.[69] (Compare, for example, the child on the cloud in the frontispiece to *Innocence* with what Hagstrum calls the 'simpering cupids' of more fashionable society allegories.)[70]

Blake rings subtle changes on the conventional mode. His pictorial style in *Innocence* is as deceptively familiar as the nursery and lullaby rhythms of the poems. Though at first it reminds us (as it means to) of Stothard and others like him,[71] we soon discover delicate discordances, subtle and unexpected touches (the sharp-pointed fingers of the winged figure in 'Infant Joy,' the 'naive rigidity' of the children's procession in 'Holy Thursday,'[72] the claw-like roots of the tree on the second plate of 'The Little Black Boy') which hint at a deeper and more complex vision. This is even more true in *Experience*, where the poems invariably undercut and overturn the expectations we bring to them from the designs. The text of 'The Angel,' for example, is clearly meant to indict all that the mannered gestures of the figures in its design imply. When Mellor suggests that by 1794 Blake had somehow outgrown the sentimental style of an earlier and more optimistic poetic vision,[73] we should bear in mind Frye's witty reference to the artist of *Experience* as 'no longer a child of thirty-two but a grown man of thirty-seven.'[74]

Of all the designs in *Innocence*, that of 'Laughing Song' owes most to Stothard.[75] The faintly Neoclassical arrangement of figures, the 'rather Roman or Hellenistic chairs,'[76] the highly stylized gestures and attitudes of the seated revellers, even the 'fine hat' (with its feather or plume)[77] which the standing youth holds aloft in his left hand – all point to the attenuated pastoralism of Stothard's designs (engraved by Blake in 1783) for Joseph Ritson's *A Select Collection of English Songs* (figure 5). Nor is this an accident. Blake subtly adapts his pictorial style to the mood and spirit of a text, and if the design to 'Laughing Song' strikes us as more derivative than others in *Innocence* – more in tune with the fashionable pastoralism of eighteenth-century illustration – so too does the poem. Not only is its world one of 'green woods,' 'dimpling streams,' 'painted birds,' and 'merry wit,' but its speaker closes with the traditional pastoral 'invitation':

> When the painted birds laugh in the shade
> Where our table with cherries and nuts is spread
> Come live and be merry and join with me,
> To sing the sweet chorus of Ha, Ha, He.

The poem's daringly unselfconscious refrain prevents a well-worn pastoral convention from sounding calculated or disingenuous. Though 'Laughing Song' owes more to the traditions of late eighteenth-century pastoral than any other poem in *Innocence*, its celebration of simple rustic pleasures is natural and unaffected. Blake largely avoids what Hallett Smith calls the 'transparent pretence'[78] of most post-Elizabethan pastoral by making his poem as simple or 'native' as possible. The latinized names of the early manuscript version, for example, become common English names in *Innocence*; 'Mary and Susan and Emily' are substituted for 'Edessa and Lyca and Emilie.' Blake knows and uses the tradition, but carefully adapts it to his needs. So too in the design: the flat outline style, with its minimum of interior modelling, though hardly 'native,' mutes 'transparent pretence' – in this case, that of Stothardian rococo. Spartan Neoclassicism, like that of Flaxman, subtly undercuts what Rosenblum calls the 'Neoclassic Erotic.'[79] Similarly, though the youth in the center holds a plumed hat of a sort that suggests the stylized jauntiness of traditional pastoral illustration (and is unlike any other hat in *Innocence*), neither his unfashionably simple costume nor his sturdy, muscular body are in the least like anything Stothard might have produced. Though Blake may have inherited what Roger Fry calls 'the worn-out rags of an effete classical tradition,'[80] he used them in *Songs* – or at least those of Stothard (there being nothing 'effete' about the monumental Neoclassicism of David, for instance, or of Blake's own early 'Joseph' watercolors (1785) or of the 'Job' and 'Ezekial' prints of the following years) – to piece together the visible garments of a deceptively complex and shifting set of attitudes and themes.

Blake's relation to the several varieties of late eighteenth-century Neoclassical theory and practice is an extremely complex business – almost as complex as late eighteenth-century Neoclassicism itself. One of its smaller mysteries – that of the depiction of facial expression – is worth noting at this point, since it affects the readings that follow. Despite his early approval of Lavater, author of *Physiognomical Fragments* (1775–8), as well as of the previously mentioned *Aphorisms on Man* (1788), the Blake of *Songs* belongs, in the matter of physiognomy at least, to the school of Winckelmann (and Lessing and Mengs), which is also that of Fuseli and Reynolds, despite their disapproval of the subtleties of German interpretation.[81]

Though other aspects of Blake's art suggest a belief, with Lavater, that 'Each part of an organized body is an image of the whole, has the character of the whole,'[82] the physiognomy of his figures all too frequently (and sometimes incongruously) suggests 'noble simplicity and sedate grandeur in Gesture and Expression'[83] – Winckelmann's oft-quoted terms of praise for the sculpture of the Greeks. The oddly remote, generalized placidity of the faces of Blake's figures (their bodies are another matter, as capable of violent or passionate distortion, especially in the later Lambeth books, as the figures of Mortimer or Fuseli), when combined with the frequently minute scale in *Songs*, makes interpreting physiognomy (always a tricky business) especially difficult. On the whole, therefore, I try to avoid readings based on facial expression.

Other aspects of Blake's visual art require similar caution. Very little has been written about the formal or compositional aspects – the general geometry – of Blake's pictures; or at least about those of his illuminated books. Aside from sections of W. J. T. Mitchell's *Blake's Composite Art*, and Mellor's book, which makes use of Heinrich Wölfflin's distinction between closed (or 'tectonic') and open (or 'atectonic') composition, we have only Wicksteed's theories of right and left (together with subsequent controversy),[84] several brief but interesting essays in *Blake's Visionary Forms Dramatic*, and a dazzling (if somewhat bizarre) essay on *The Marriage of Heaven and Hell* by Morris Eaves.[85]

My book adds little to the little already written about formal or compositional meanings in the designs. Aside from brief remarks in passing, and a short section in a discussion of the introductory plates to *Experience* (where Blake's careful distinction between Gothic and Graeco-Roman motifs is especially pronounced), I avoid, on the whole, the study of what Arnheim calls 'elementary form patterns.'[86] My reasons are two-fold. First, I lack the training. Second, the meanings yielded by previously published formal analyses of the designs, or at least those with which I am familiar, tend to be large and relatively abstract generalizations, on a level apart from (and of little use in delineating) the subtle variations of tone and point of view so important to a proper understanding of *Songs*. Take, for example, Eben Bass's reading of 'The Divine Image' in *Blake's Visionary Forms Dramatic*.

'Innocence,' writes Bass, 'is the line of the Piper's instrument in the frontispiece (pl. 2), lower left to upper right. Experience is the line of the flames in the general titlepage (pl. 1) or of the falling snow in "The Chimney Sweeper" (pl. 37), upper left to lower right.' The reversed 'S' curve of the flame-plant in 'The Divine Image' ('which *is* the Divine Image') 'resolves thrust into counterthrust [and] is part of Blake's dramatization of the "Two Contrary States." ' As for the design's tiny human figures, Christ raises up the reclining male and female in the lower right corner, and the four figures at the top of the page represent 'Mercy Pity Peace and Love,' since 'in the sense of composition, four figures are expressive of four virtues.'[87] Though Bass can be a close and perceptive reader of Blake's designs, his preoccupation with formal elements in a passage like this obscures or distracts us from important (if more obvious or specific) connections between poem and picture. The text to 'The Divine Image' teaches us that God is both immanent and transcendent and that, in Hirsch's words, 'the relationship of the transcendent God (Father-Christ) to the immanent God (Man-Christ) is the feeling of sameness in difference which is the essence and meaning of love.'[88] The repetition in the second stanza,

> For Mercy Pity Peace and Love,
> Is God our father dear:
> And Mercy Pity Peace and Love,
> Is Man his child and care.

is but one of several ways in which 'sameness in difference' is suggested. The arrangement of the design's human figures is another.

The haloed Christ who stands upon the green earth at the foot of the flame-plant stretches his left arm over two naked human figures[89] in a gesture of blessing or release. He is Hirsch's 'transcendent God (Father-Christ)' come to earth to free us from the 'distress' (line 14) of what in *Europe* Blake calls 'The Night of Nature' (9.3: E61). At the same time, in the top left corner of the design, directly above the poem's title, a haloless female,[90] carrying a 'pitcher or cruet' in her left hand, and 'something round under her right arm, possibly a loaf of bread,'[91] moves towards two figures at prayer, the 'All' of line 2 who 'pray in their distress.' A second gowned figure, also without a halo, points the way.

Though 'in the sense of composition, four figures are expressive of four virtues,' something subtler and more important is going on at the top of the design. An earthly Savior, Hirsch's 'immanent God (Man-Christ),' brings worldly relief, in the form of food and water (or, perhaps, bread and wine) to those who, with backs turned to human goodness, seek help from above.[92] The scene at the bottom of the plate is balanced by the scene at the top, just as the first two lines of the second stanza are balanced by the second two. Christ walks on the green earth; heaven above is but a world of earthly virtues, of distinctly human figures whose actions realize the divinity of the human image. In this case, at least, Bass's concern with formal or compositional meanings causes him to overlook what is most artful and illuminating about the design.[93]

Much has been written about Blake's use of tradition, both poetic and pictorial. His iconography, drawn from an astonishingly wide range of sources,[94] mixes Christian, Classical and esoteric meanings, sometimes within a single design.[95] In *Songs*, of course, it also draws frequently upon the specific motifs of instructional literature: from the fruit-picking children of Lily's famous Latin Grammar, or the anonymous late eighteenth-century children's book, *Mirth Without Mischief*, so like the youths on plate 2 of 'The Ecchoing Green' (figure 6), to the countless scenes of maternal instruction on the frontispieces of seventeenth- and eighteenth-century readers and alphabets (figures 7 and 8), obvious analogues to the title-page to *Innocence*. But as even the most dedicated iconologist is quick to admit, Blake's borrowings are peculiarly selective (or 'creative' or 'eccentric'). Tradition, whether 'heterodox' (Yeats's phrase) or established, was for him double-edged. Take, for example, the following confession in his description of *The Last Judgement*, painted in 1810:[96]

> <The Greeks represent Chronos or Time as a very Aged Man this is Fable but the Real Vision of Time is in Eternal Youth I have <however> somewhat accomodated my Figure of Time to <the> common opinion as I myself am also infected with it and my Visions also infected and I see Time Aged alas too much so.>
>
> (*VLJ*: E553)

Though students of Blake's iconography are unlikely to find an annotation of this sort reassuring, tradition is at least upheld. Elsewhere Blake abandons it completely:

> The Ladies will be pleased to see that I have represented the Furies by Three Men and not by three Women It is not because I think the Ancients wrong but they will be pleased to remember that mine is Vision and not Fable The Spectator may suppose them Clergymen in the Pulpit Scourging Sin instead of Forgiving it.
>
> (*VLJ*: E547)

The tone of these passages is as revealing as their iconoclastic content. I belong to that school of readers for whom Blake at his wildest is often Blake at his most ironic or purposefully extravagant. Phrases like the second passage's 'The Ladies will be pleased to note ...,' or the 'alas' of the first, suggest gentle mockery rather than other-worldliness; a parody or joke at the expense of the sorts of iconographical explanations or 'programmes' upon which both esoteric and traditional

Renaissance (and post-Renaissance) art works were frequently based. Given irreverence of this nature, the source-hunter ought to take care. Of what use is it to the reader of 'The Lilly,' for example, a Song of Experience the meaning of which is much debated, to know that Jacob Boehme associated lilies with 'the Birth of the Life and Love and Joy of God in the lives of men'?[97] Even if one could determine Blake's feelings about Boehme in 1794 and/or 1825 (the coloring of the design is of importance) what would that prove? Similarly, do we really need Swedenborg to tell us that the circle represents harmony, or the stone truth? Would the latter correspondence apply, for instance, to 'The Clod and the Pebble,' or to the dreaded 'Stone of Night' in *Jerusalem*?

The critical commonplace, in other words, is worth repeating: tradition plays its part in a study of Blake's iconography, but context and careful attention to detail are infinitely more important. Many of the plants, flowers, birds and beasts in *Songs* are iconographic in nature, but their meanings, whether traditional or not, change and develop from plate to plate. Even the most famous of Blake's symbols – the giant compasses we associate with Urizen, Newton, and the Ancient of Days – can be utterly transformed, as in *Christ in the Carpenter's Shop* (*c.* 1800) (figure 9) where they find their way into the hands of an heroic, unironized Christ.

This view of the unfixed nature of Blake's symbols, and of their relative freedom from (or rather 'with') tradition, lies at the heart of my interpretation both of *Songs* and of Blake's whole life and career. Its only 'proof' is the readings that follow; readings from which, for reasons that will soon be apparent, I am loath to have it abstracted. Nevertheless, several traditional misconceptions (or misconceptions about tradition) ought here to be mentioned. It is often assumed that Blake's is a Neoplatonic and/or Kabbalistic philosophy of symbolism.[98] This is true, though, only in a restricted and frequently misunderstood sense. Blake was an inveterate foe of mystery and priesthood: he could not have adhered to – except, as we shall see, when less than himself – a philosophy of symbolism the central feature of which was 'The augur interpreting a portent, the mystagogue explaining the divinely ordained ritual, the priest expounding the image in the temple, the Jewish or Christian teacher pondering the meaning of the word of God.'[99] For Blake, fixed systems were enemies, the creations of a priesthood that 'took advantage of and enslav'd the vulgar by attempting to realize or abstract the mental deities from their objects ... [c]hoosing forms of worship from poetic tales' (*MHH* 11: E37).

Blake's symbol system in *Songs*, like Fuseli's,[100] has much close affinities to the rival Aristotelian or analogical tradition exemplified by the emblem books of Ripa, Quarles, and Wither; a tradition in which the icon defines as well as represents the given concept. This is as one would expect, given Blake's training as an engraver (engraving being one of the last fields in which Renaissance iconology survived),[101] and his poetic apprenticeship to the school of Thomson, the Wartons, Collins, Gray, and other admirers of the personified abstraction.[102]

Blake's connection to the Neoplatonic philosophy of symbols lies less in the nature of the images he uses (only rarely of a mysterious or apophatic sort, in which like represents unlike), than in the seriousness with which he takes them; his refusal to treat visual symbols as sophisticated games, clever analogues upon which the full meanings of motifs or whole designs so frequently depend. For Blake, as for the Neoplatonist, the visual symbol was more than a mere sign or metaphor: the Neoplatonist saw his symbols as theophanies, the forms in which God Himself chose to appear to the limited human mind;[103] Blake saw them as no less divine, but only because they were human, an expression of man's god-like creative or poetic faculty, the only true divinity.

The other point of similarity between Blake's use of visual symbols and that of the Neoplatonists is the value he places on their power to communicate on a pre-rational level. For the Blake of *Songs* this power need entail no repudiation of analogy or rational analysis; it is simply another, though at the moment repressed (and *therefore* more important), way of arriving at meaning. Blake's attitude to pre-conscious ways of knowing, and the ease with which it can be misunderstood, is paralleled in the following definition, from E. H. Gombrich, of the Renaissance emblem or *impresa*: 'an image [that] reveals an aspect of the world which would seem to elude the ordered progress of dialectic argument.'[104] We ought to note and emulate Gombrich's care here: 'would seem' not 'does.' With Blake too, it is easy to mistake what seems (a hatred of reason *per se*, and of the analytic habits of the Aristotelian) for what is (hatred of the mis-use of reason, and fear for the dangerous consequences of its abuse). That Blake himself, as we shall see, was prone to such mistaking, has much to do with its continued occurrence.

Finally, a brief word about recurring gestures in Blake's designs. Figures who crouch, stride, raise or stretch their arms, cross their legs or clutch their heads, appear so frequently in Blake's art that Laurence Binyon can barely bring himself to forgive what he calls 'the endless repetitions of attitude and gesture.'[105] Many, as Bo Lindberg and others have suggested, are derived from, or subtly allude to, past traditions,[106] others take on uniquely personal meanings. Again, the key to understanding lies in context and careful attention to detail.

In the following chapters, the next two in particular, I shall try to put these and other such stern admonitions into practice by looking as closely as possible at the designs, beginning with and testing this chapter's central assumption that they are as carefully and thoughtfully executed as the poems. I shall also try to prove what I have so far only suggested: that the meanings of the work's verbal and visual symbols not only cannot but should not be imposed upon them from outside; that recourse to Blake's 'symbolical philosophy,' in the case of *Songs* at least, violates its very purpose.

CHAPTER 3
ENTERING *INNOCENCE*

John Beer, writing of Blake's penchant for aphorism and apothegm, rightly warns us that

> single statements which seem truly central are rare. Blake's philosophy consists rather of interlocking statements, each modifying the others. In consequence, a whole nexus of ideas must be grasped before the exact significance of single statements can be weighed.[1]

These remarks are equally true with respect to the individual plates of *Songs*. Each poem or design is but a 'single statement,' the exact significance of which depends upon a number of other statements. Even when a Song seems clear and explicit, its full meaning almost always depends upon other plates.

The themes in *Songs* develop gradually, and as their meanings subtly evolve, so too do our reading habits. Suggestive details constantly tempt us into interpretations and identifications which, at the time, we can neither verify nor dismiss, but which subsequent plates almost always confirm. As a consequence, we begin to take more chances when we read. Slowly, imperceptibly, from one plate to another, we discard our old, conventional ways of looking at the world, and replace them with the habits of vision. This, as I have suggested, need entail no repudiation of selfconscious critical procedures; Blake's heaven, after all, has room for Bacon, Newton, and Locke, as well as Shakespeare, Milton, and Chaucer (see *J* 4.98.9: E254). It is merely a way of offering encouragement, like so much else in Blake's life and work, to pre- or un-conscious intelligence. For Blake, as for Carlyle, selfconsciousness *per se* is not the disease, but 'the symptom merely; nay it is also the attempt towards cure.'[2]

This chapter traces the early stages of the reader's visionary awakening, examining the first seven plates of *Innocence* in sequence. Because we are concerned with matters of development and continuity, little reference will be made to *Experience*, or even to later plates of *Innocence*. On occasion we will leave open questions of interpretation which cannot be answered until we move on to subsequent plates. Our goal is twofold: to trace the process through which the reader begins to learn how, as well as why, he should adopt child-like ways of seeing; and to note the numerous echoes and overturnings of the themes and strategies of instructional literature – Blake's way of reminding us of the irony of our position as adult readers at school to children and innocents. Each discussion of what we learn will be woven into a discussion of the way in which we learn it.

The frontispiece

The frontispiece to *Innocence* introduces the plates that are to follow in several ways. It illustrates the poem 'Introduction'; it provides our first encounter with important visual motifs; and, because it is unaccompanied by quotations or explanatory epigraphs, it encourages us to approach subsequent designs as this one must initially be approached: as a source of meaning independent of any text.

The frontispiece not only depicts the events described in the poem 'Introduction,' but it also anticipates the physical structure of the plate on which the poem is etched. Just as the characters and relationships depicted on the frontispiece are framed on either side by healthy tree-trunks whose branches form an arch at the top of the plate, so the words of 'Introduction' (words which describe similar characters and relationships) are framed by sturdy, healthy entwining vines which give off vegetative sprigs and tendrils at the top, and which come together over the poem's title.

Though similar in type, the trees in the background of the

frontispiece are smaller and less distinct than those in the foreground. They form a protective enclosure for the sheep, the shepherd-piper, and the child (who appears against a cloud-shaped patch of sky outlined by the tops of the trees),[3] and we attribute the calm of the sheep, in part, to the protection afforded by the setting. In the next plate, the title-page to *Innocence*, no such protective enclosure is provided for the design's characters, and some part of our sense that the seated mother, or nurse, and her two children are vulnerable, is derived from their exposure to the empty landscape. When we turn then to the fourth plate, which contains 'Introduction,' and we see that the entwined vines and their vegetative outgrowths form an enclosure or frame for the poem's words, we recall not only the similarly framed composition of the frontispiece (and something of the protective security it provided), but the very different title-page whose absence of frame and enclosure made innocence seem vulnerable.

Blake is quick to establish his key visual motifs: enclosed settings – whether composed of naturalistic trees, shrubs or vines, as on the frontispiece; or of more abstract, decorative vegetation, as on the 'Introduction' plate – invariably frame words or visual scenes which express a secure, unthreatened innocence. He suggests throughout that innocence is a state in which one feels protected, cut off from experience (even when in its midst), guarded as sheep are guarded by the shepherd. The designs reinforce this suggestion not only when they serve as illustrations – when they present us with a piper who is a shepherd or with a flock of sheep protected or enclosed by healthy trees – but when they are more abstract and seem to perform only a decorative function.

'Trees of different kinds,' writes Keynes, 'signified for Blake varying aspects of life on earth; their leaves are in the sky, but their roots are firmly buried in the ground. The twisting trunks of the tree on the poet's left symbolize earthly love.'[4] No one could possibly argue with the first half of this statement, but when Keynes tells us that the trees on the left of the poet (notice how quickly the shepherd-piper becomes 'the poet') symbolize earthly love, we want to ask certain questions of him: In what ways do they symbolize earthly love? Which of the various kinds of earthly love do they symbolize? And if they do symbolize earthly love, why should such a symbol be depicted on this plate? As with other poetic or pictorial details, a proposed symbolic identity of this sort ought first to be tested against the actual impressions a plate makes upon us. For example, the twining trees on the right of the plate possess certain qualities. They are healthy trees, as we have said, but it is also worth mentioning that they are relatively young (certainly younger than the trees on the title-plate to *Innocence*) and that their trunks seem smooth, soft, and pliable. The smoothness and softness of the trunks, together with the gentle flow of the curves that allow them to entwine, suggest limbs or human bodies in embrace. But do all twisting trees (or entwining vines, or vines twining around trees) give rise to the same impression, as Keynes's remarks seem to imply? The curves of the vine-entwined trees on the title-page or on the first plate of 'The Little Black Boy,' for example, are neither flowing nor sensual. If every embrace of tree and vine symbolizes earthly love, we must either ignore the particular qualities of these trees and vines, or content ourselves with a symbolic significance ('earthly love') too broad to mean much of anything.

Other aspects of Keynes's reading disturb us, in particular his reference to the Piper as poet. The sheep associate the Piper with the shepherd. The Piper who becomes a poet in 'Introduction' is not referred to there as a shepherd, but in light of the earlier plate, we think of him as one. And when we look back to the frontispiece after having read 'Introduction,' we associate the shepherd-piper with the poet whose songs compose the *Songs of Innocence*. Though Keynes was right to call the shepherd-piper a poet, his immediate disclosure of the figure's full identity works against Blake's purpose, because it encourages the wrong kinds of reading habits. Blake is concerned that we should approach *Songs* as active not passive readers; he would not be content with those who merely 'understood' its themes. Keynes's reading, in this case at least, tends to inhibit in us the very imaginative and visionary powers Blake is most anxious to rouse.

The child, like the shepherd, is a protector. His position above the scene, and his outstretched arms, suggest blessing as well as watchful guardianship. And since he seems to float in the air, resembling traditional depictions of angels or cherubim, we think of him, at first, as divine. But he lacks wings or a halo, which qualifies our impression. If he is not an angel, though, how are we to account for his weightlessness? Kathleen Raine proposes one possible explanation:

> The apparent weightlessness of Blake's figures, the ease with which they fly without the use of those cumbersome wings Baroque, and still more, Victorian angels require, arises from the realization that life, as Blake understood it, is not subject to the forces of nature. Life – consciousness – moves freely where it wills. To leap in thought along the line of a hill, or on a cloud, is to be there in imagination ... in *Songs of Innocence* Blake's figures have attained freedom from the gravitational forces which constrain material objects.[5]

Though few readers are likely to arrive at an interpretation of this sort upon a first viewing, most will come away from the frontispiece with a sense that the wingless child's world lies outside the laws of our everyday experience.

Irene Chayes, in a discussion of similar, though winged, figures on 'The Blossom' plate, suggests another way of accounting for our reactions to the floating child. She believes that creatures of this sort are 'Blake's version of the *putti* or *amorini* of Classical and Renaissance painting, which survived in the eighteenth century mainly in rococo decoration. In other words, they are figures of Cupid ... and the erotic meaning of their playful flights was thoroughly conventional when Blake turned it to his own use, in this design and elsewhere.'[6] The child's presence, together with the entwining trees at the right of the plate, and the form-fitting, flesh-colored costume worn by the Piper ('Is it a garment,' asks Coleridge of the ambiguous drapery of *Songs*, ' – or the body incised or scored out':[7] here the matter is resolved by what should be a point of connection between trousers and hose just below the Piper's knees),[8] contributes a subtle sexuality to the design, one which at first we only vaguely sense.

While none of these accounts of the possible meanings of the figure 'explains' it, the impressions they suggest – of divinity, of a realm freed from the conventional laws of nature, and of healthy and unembarrassed sexuality – all play a part in the reader's reaction. Why this should be so, and in what ways these impressions fit together or relate to one another, are questions which we cannot yet answer. Blake is merely laying the groundwork here, planting suggestions or intimations of themes and relationships which he will set out more explicitly on later plates.

The title-page

The tree which dominates the title-page to *Innocence* is not at all
like the trees on the previous plate. It is old (there is a knot-hole
in its trunk and the central branch is broken), and has little
foliage, and yet it still bears fruit, in the form of two pairs of
apples just to the left of center between the words 'SONGS' and
'Innocence.' The curve of the right branch, which swoops up
and over to the left, is much less smooth and flowing than the
curves of the branches on the frontispiece trees, and reinforces
our sense of the tree's age. The smaller branchings, especially
those just above the two children absorbed in their reading, are
also gnarled, and reinforce the dominant impression. The tree
contrasts sharply with the soft, supple curves outlined by the
branches of the trees on the frontispiece.

The single vine, loosely but snakishly twining around the
tree's trunk, is usually interpreted as a symbol of 'Christ
embracing what we consider the Tree of Sin.'[9] But an
interpretation of this sort raises problems similar to Keynes's
'earthly love.' Though supported by symbolic and iconographic
tradition,[10] it ignores the actual appearance of tree and vine, both
of which are singularly unpleasant. A truer and more Blakean
interpretation would begin by taking the design's appearance
seriously.

While the trees on the frontispiece formed a protective
enclosure around the central scene, the apple tree seems to
threaten rather than protect the objects it encircles. The smaller
branchings which arch over the children's heads are too sparse
and jagged to provide much shade or shelter. They seem to reach
out at the children as the legs of a spider reach out to trap a fly.
The branchings that surround the word 'Innocence' also appear
threatening. They do not so much protect the word as encroach
upon it. The vine encircling the trunk of the tree adds another
ominous note. Because it too suggests encroachment,
constriction, and danger, and because the tree round which it
circles bears forbidden fruit (apples which dangle directly over
'Innocence' and over the two children who embody it)[11] it is
much more likely to suggest the serpent in the Garden of Eden
than Christ.[12] This is not to deny Blake's knowledge of the
traditional connection between Edenic Serpent and crucified
Christ – or J. B. Trapp's insistence that 'in any work of art made
by or for a Christian which portrays the Fall, there must always

be a more or less explicit proleptic reference to Redemption and/or Judgement'[13] – it merely allows the impressions created by tree and vine to change and develop from plate to plate. Some vines remind us of serpents, others do not; the identification depends upon context and careful attention to detail. If we allow so singularly unattractive a vine to symbolize Christ, then all vines can be Christ symbols and all the trees round which they twine symbols of sinful life. We need only look ahead to the delicate beauty of the vine-entwined sapling on 'The Lamb' plate to see how wholly wilful and inappropriate an approach of this sort can become.

Other aspects of the title-page disturb us. The background landscape, which contrasts sharply with the rich and luxuriant vegetation of the enclosure on the frontispiece, is menacing in its own way. A single tiny tree on the distant horizon provides the only suggestion of shelter aside from the central apple tree (an effect similar to Tennyson's 'no other tree did mark/The level waste, the rounding gray');[14] a river or stream (with an island in it) stretches across empty plains and looks, at first glance, as if it might have been drawn with a straight edge; the sky, bursting with turbulent energy, contrasts sharply with the stillness of the landscape, but it too is vaguely disturbing. We feel as if a great wind, presaging a storm, had blown all the vegetation of the apple tree, the fantastic lettering of the word 'SONGS,' the decorative sprigs and volutes which grow out from it, and the tiny birds and human figures which are scattered round and within it, up into the air.

Nor is it only in late colorings that this plate disturbs. From its earliest incarnations, the title-page announced a complex and unsettling Innocence, though in copies issued separately from *Experience* its menace was rarely turbulent. The pale blue-green and peach washes of pre-1794 (even pre-1800) colorings reinforce the bleak bareness of tree and prospect. In some copies (*In*.B and *In*.I, for example), inky black shadows surround and further isolate the figures. In Malkin's copy (*In*.P) the sky is a uniformly pale blue-green; which paleness, while it lends delicacy to later plates, here sharpens the jagged outlines of tree-trunk and branchings (though it also discloses lighter notes, as in the literal notes floating above the piper's head in *In*.E and *In*.F, but obscured in Z and other late colorings).

The children are oblivious to their surroundings. They are totally absorbed in the book on their mother's (or nurse's) lap, their backs turned to the threatening apple tree, the empty landscape, and the turbulent sky. The mother is presumably reading to them or teaching them how to read, as common a motif not only in Blake's early works but in all types of illustrated children's books, as lost infants or talking robins, sparrows, and emmets.[15] Though they are still innocents, they are gathering the knowledge that will transport them into a world of experience. Perhaps once they look up from their book, they will catch sight of the forbidden fruit which dangles above them on the Tree of the Knowledge of Good and Evil, and their newly whetted thirst for 'knowledge' will cause them to reach up and hence out of their childhood. We think back to the general title-page, and the sufferings of Adam and Eve, and wonder if the children on this plate are a pre-lapsarian version of those same figures.

If we do begin to feel that the children are being 'fould in Knowledge's dark Prison house,' as Blake wrote in *Then She Bore Pale Desire* (E438), our attitude toward the mother will begin to change. At first glance we include her in the innocent grouping, assuming along with Damon, 'that maternal instruction was not the education to which Blake objected.'[16] But as we look more closely, we sense something a bit too rigid and proper about her. Despite her youth and pleasant face, she sits straight-backed, stiffly 'composed' in the manner of a queen or some other figure of authority. 'Her dress,' as Eben Bass points out, 'has the fullness and authority of a robe, and its color of purple is authoritative.'[17] The propriety of her ample gown (it also reminds us of Puritan or Methodist costume) and of the clothing she has presumably provided for her children, contrasts sharply with the form-fitting garment worn by the Piper on the frontispiece and the nakedness of the child who floats above him.

The Piper's oddly stylized costume is worth returning to for a moment, since it reappears throughout the plates that follow, often in telling contrast to costumes similar to those on this plate. Despite Coleridge's previously-quoted confusion (Is it a garment ...?'), the form-fitting clothing of so many of Blake's innocents was no mere rococo fantasy or convention. Nor was it only an expression of his more general preference for revealing drapery; his belief, with Winckelmann, that the noblest costumes, like those of Greek statuary, 'clasped the body and discovered the shape.'[18] It also had a contemporary social reference: that of recent (and radical) innovations in child fashion, notably the so-called 'skeleton suits' of the 1780s, the objects of which were to facilitate free and easy movement in the young, and to distinguish them, clearly, from their parents. (Previous to the mid-eighteenth century, children's clothes were little different in style from those of adults.)[19] Both these aims, with their implied approval of the natural in children, were inspired and encouraged, of course, by Rousseau and his followers.

'As the person so is his life proportiond' (*FZ* 9.120.31: E375). We begin, then, to suspect that the mother's influence is not wholly protective or benevolent. Despite their obvious interest and absorption – suggested in part by the unselfconscious trust with which they lean against her – the children may actually be threatened by the mother's care. 'Reading is the scourge of infancy,'[20] writes Rousseau, and though these children bear few signs of the 'sighing and dismay' with which other children are said to face instruction in 'The Schoolboy,' they are equally in danger of losing or forgetting the 'youthful spring' of innocence. The maternal figure on this plate is somehow implicated in that loss. Her presence undoubtedly helps make possible the calm, unselfconscious absorption of the children (she does, in part, represent comfort and security), but it also hints at forces which will stifle and repress a free expression of the child's instinctive innocence.[21]

The cursive script used for the word 'Innocence,' in contrast to the fantastical, green, flame-like block capitals of 'SONGS' or the smaller, non-italic script used for the barely visible 'of,' softens the word (as does the reddish-gold glow which backs it) and gives to it an appearance of quiet delicacy like that of the children below. A piper leans against the first letter, wearing a wide-brimmed, 'merrily'[22] curved hat such as we know Blake himself wore,[23] and which his mythic *alter ego*, Los, wears on the frontispiece to *Jerusalem*. The first stroke of the 'N' of 'SONGS' swirls down in acanthus-like volutes to a place just above the piper's head, so that once we have taken note of him, it is possible to imagine his music rising up from the pipe and gradually, as it moves along the volute, taking on the form of the actual word 'SONGS.' At the same time, it is equally possible to see the word as part of the tree below it. For at first glance it is difficult to determine where the tree's leaves and branches end, and where the letters of the word begin. This is just the first of many plates on which we shall discover tree-like texts, plant-like flames, and music which rises into human, bird-like, or vegetative form. Only after we realize that Blake intends the words of his titles and texts to melt into and play a part in the designs, do we return to the title-page and note that 'SONGS' seems to be both a creation of the Piper (a work of art or imagination) and a part of the 'natural' world of the tree. For the moment, we are much more likely simply to register its strangely mixed appearance. The energetic beauty and exuberance of the lettering seems to go hand-in-hand with the disturbing harshness or jaggedness of its acanthus-like or flame-like flourishes.

The tiny human figures who stand or rest within the letters of the word 'SONGS' also provoke a mixed reaction. The outstretched arms of the figure who kneels within the 'O' could suggest either distress or exultation, and a similar ambiguity attends the female figure who stands within the 'G.' Between them, leaning against the diagonal stroke of the 'N,' we can barely make out a haloed, winged figure who, according to Erdman,[24] is meant to signify the author, writing with a pen. Tiny figures like these tease us into thought. They tempt us to make conjectural identifications like Erdman's, and they encourage us to look both more closely and more imaginatively at the design's 'Minute Particulars.' Once we have identified them as human beings, we are tempted to transform the even tinier and more obscure shapes within the two 'S's' and above the 'N' into human forms as well. They are impossible to identify, of course, but we are meant to try. For Blake is seeking to foster in us the same imaginative, visionary capacity that he himself possesses. He wants us to learn that we play a part in the creation of what previously we had thought of as an independent or 'objective' reality, and that it is within our power to transform our world and to interpret it according to our own vision.

'Introduction'

The text of 'Introduction' tells us a good deal about the poems and designs that are to follow. Its narrative accounts for the inspiration or inception of *Innocence* (the vision of the child on the cloud), the format the artist is to give it (he is to write songs in a book with a rural pen and colored inks), and what its purpose is to be ('Every child may joy to hear'). It also suggests to the reader both how the poems and their accompanying designs are to be read, and, through its depiction of the Piper's reaction to the child upon the cloud, how innocence itself is to be confronted. At the same time it reveals that the scene on the frontispiece was no less one of instruction than that on the title-page.

The child issues a set of orders to the Piper, and he does so with a marvelously well-rendered child-like peremptoriness: 'Pipe a song,' 'Piper pipe that song,' 'Drop thy pipe,' 'Sing thy songs.' At each command the Piper obeys. His obedience is easy and immediate. Like any sympathetic adult (we cannot help but see the Piper as the mature figure of the frontispiece) who plays with a child, the Piper must give in to the rules of the child's game and put aside his adult's perception of the senselessness of the child's way of doing things or of seeing the world. 'Piper pipe that song again,' says the laughing child, as have countless children who ask for the umpteenth repetition of a favorite story, or who push spoons off tables with what begins to seem, alarmingly, like an inexhaustible supply of energy and interest.

'So I piped ...,' responds the Piper. He is neither bored nor irritated. Instead he is prepared to join the child's game, the word 'So' hinting at the gently tolerant nature of his compliance. Gillham offers an illuminating contrast between the Piper's response in 'Introduction,' and the response Wordsworth's speaker makes to another child in 'To H. C. Six Years Old.' Unlike the speaker in 'To H. C.,' 'The piper does not have to contend with a clumsy, grasping self, has no impulse to pull the child from its cloud and put it on earth where it should be, and has so much enjoyment in the child because he takes it exactly as it comes.'[25] Because the Piper allows himself to play, to enter into the child's world, instead of patronizing him (which is a way of not looking at him) or forcing him to become a 'defective adult' (Evelyn Waugh's term for children), he is granted the power to create the very 'Songs' (the designs and poems) that are to follow. 'Introduction' implies that adults have something to learn from children and that it will be worth their while to listen attentively and sympathetically to the things children have to say.

Once the amused, tolerant adult of the first four stanzas takes on the child's way of seeing and speaking, the floating, wingless boy disappears. 'The characteristic of genius and of all its creations,' writes Lavater, in a work for which, as we remember, Blake engraved several prints sometime around 1788–9, 'is, in my opinion, *apparition* ... like the apparition of an angel, it comes not, but is suddenly present, leaves not, but is gone. Like the apparition of an angel, it moves us to the marrow; its immortality rouses the immortality in us; it vanishes, but continues to act after it is gone, leaving us in sweet trembling, in tears of fright, and the pallor of joy.'[26] This, of course, is what happens here: 'The child,' writes Wicksteed, 'is now something within. It is himself, and the only outside inspiration is the fact of actual living children on this earth.'[27]

When the Piper is asked to drop his pipe and 'Sing thy songs of happy chear,' the song he chooses to sing is 'the same again.' Like a child, he takes delight in repeating the song a third time. We also note his manner of speaking once the child vanishes:

> So he vanish'd from my sight,
> And I pluck'd a hollow reed.
>
> And I made a rural pen,
> And I stain'd the water clear,
> And I wrote my happy songs,
> Every child may joy to hear.

The simplicity and directness of these lines reminds us of the way children tell stories. The Piper connects each new bit of information with the words 'And I,' much as a child punctuates a story. This child-likeness, interestingly, was a quality noted in the most famous educator of infants in Blake's day, the previously mentioned James Buchanan, Swedenborgian founder, along with Brougham and James Mill, of the Westminster Infant School. 'The first I remember of him,' recalls an ex-pupil,

> is seeing him with a hundred or more little children in the great room in Vincent Square. ... I should have hardly distinguished him from some of the children, for he was very small, and had an infantile expression, one might have called it angelic, when he was leading his troop of little ones marching to the sound of his flute.[28]

Buchanan used no books or slates in his school. His lessons were conveyed through songs, recitations, and games; their texts, the Bible, *The Arabian Nights*, and Swedenborg. Like the Piper, he thought of infants as angels.

As we watch the Piper enter into innocence, we too 'find ourselves, almost without realizing how, in a new world.'[29] But in order to enter this new world, we must approach it properly, with the Piper's sympathy, gentle tolerance and respect, rather than with the adult's instinctive desire to anatomize or abstract or categorize. We must be wary of interpretations, often based on a misguided notion of the way Blake uses symbols in *Innocence*, which prevent us from taking the poem 'exactly as it comes.' For example, critics often draw attention to the symbolic significance of the child's insistence that the Piper pipe his song about a lamb. The lamb, we are told, is, of course, a symbol of Christ, and since Christ's life entails tragedy as well as joyful and miraculous deliverance, the child reacts to the Piper's song in line 8 with tears of sorrow. Several highly elaborate and ingenious interpretations have developed out of a symbolic approach of this sort. Some, implying that the poem can be properly understood only by a reader familiar with the whole of Blake's work, ignore or obscure the literal meaning of the words, as well as the poem's dramatic context. Gleckner, for instance, whose interpretation relies heavily on the sorrowfulness of the tears in line 8 (rather than on a 'Joy even to tears' (*M* 31.51: E130)), becomes so involved with Blake's symbolic system that he fails to explain why the child thinks of the pipe that has produced the song as 'happy' or why, in the line that follows, he calls it a song of 'happy chear.'[30] Gleckner also patronizes the poem's speaker, looking for a series of abstract correspondences instead of listening sympathetically, as the Piper listened to the child on the cloud.

A proper reading of the poem ought to begin on a literal level. The child asks the Piper to sing and to write a song about a lamb because he is a child, and because children's songs and jingles – from 'Mary had a little lamb' to 'Ba Ba Black Sheep' to 'Bo-Peep' to 'Little Boy Blue'[31] – are frequently concerned with sheep and lambs. The request is one more carefully crafted detail in a poem which emphasizes the human qualities of the child on the cloud. If we instantly identify the lamb as a symbol of Christ it is almost impossible not to suspect some measure of 'intent' or selfconsciousness in the child's request. And if we feel this, we may well lose sight of the fact that this child, despite its cloudy perch, acts and sounds (though in a stylized fashion) like a human child. If he is a divine representative or spiritual guide, it is only *because* he is a child. The critic who instantly identifies the lamb as Christ and the child as some sort of heavenly messenger is guilty of the very process of abstracting the divine from the human which Blake consistently opposed throughout his life.

The Piper has had a vision of the divinity of innocence. The child is placed on a cloud because he is divine, but he is made to speak and act like a human child for the same reason that Blake's depiction of him on the frontispiece omits the expected angelic wings and halo. The divinity of the child is the divinity of children or innocents in this world. 'He who would see the Divinity must see him in his children,' writes Blake in *Jerusalem*. Only after we realize this, can we go on to speculate not only about the symbolic associations of 'lamb' and Christ, but about the fact that children in this world traditionally have been attracted to nursery rhymes and jingles which deal with lambs.

When we look closely at the design on the 'Introduction' plate we begin to see (as with the lettering of the word 'SONGS' on the title-page) an apparently organic connection between the text and the surrounding decorative vegetation. The words appear against the background of a light blue wash of sky. Their realm is sky, as sky is the realm of the vision of the child (both in the words of this plate and in the frontispiece design). But the lettering is also related to the entwining vines or branches on either side of the plate in that the vines give off vegetative sprigs and smaller, curling vines which reach into the text and resemble the letters in both size and color. The parent vines are clearly darker than the sprigs they produce, and their dark greenish-brown color is identical with the ground or earth out of which they grow. The entwining parent vines are connected with the earth; the vegetative sprigs and smaller, curling vines are connected with the actual words of the poem (most clearly in the final line, where the 'y' of 'May' grows out of a sprig from bottom left). The poem is both of this world and apart from it, like the child upon the cloud, or the word 'SONGS' on the title-page.

The figures drawn within the loops of the parent vines are too small or too indistinctly printed and colored to be identified with much certainty. While in some copies the top left-hand loop seems to be inhabited by a seated woman and a standing child,[32] in copy Z only a single seated figure of indeterminate sex can be identified. Even less can be said about the bluish-purple blotch of color in the loop at the bottom left. As for the yellow-gold bird in the top right-hand loop, it is almost impossible to make out in copy Z unless one has seen it in other copies.

While figures who seem to sit or crouch or huddle suggest to us that they are trapped or constricted by the looped vines which surround them, other figures stand upright and give quite different impressions. The naked female figure in the second loop from the top on the left margin, for instance, is either flying or, as Damon suggests,[33] dancing – neither activity indicating anything at all like constriction or entrapment. Erdman says that her outstretched arms are meant to remind us of the child on the cloud in the frontispiece, just as the position of her legs echoes the piper's stride.[34] But he offers us no clue to the significance of so artful a conflation of gestures. Anthony Blunt suggests that the decoration on either side of the text resembles a Tree of Jesse, of the sort found in illuminated manuscripts and church windows,[35] and Erdman believes that 'as a symbol of God and his Mercy [the Tree] makes a suitable emblem of Innocence.'[36] But once again, while this interpretation is attractive, it does not help us to interpret the actual scenes within the loops or to relate those scenes to the text itself, which is what the connection between text and surrounding decorative vegetation encourages us to do. Though Erdman provides descriptions for the scenes within each loop, he does not tell us what these scenes mean or whether they tell a story. Yet this is precisely the sort of information the reader seeks.

Even if one accepts Erdman's descriptions, the most one can say about the tiny vine-framed scenes which decorate the margins of this plate is that they suggest a range of moods and human activities. Perhaps we are to think of them as part of the 'earth' out of which the vision of the poem grows? Perhaps Blake wants us to realize that a vision of innocence is born out of the moods and activities of everyday earthly experience?[37] In the end, though, the specific identities and meanings of the vine-framed scenes on this plate remain teasingly elusive. Like so many of the designs' details they tempt the reader to take chances as he reads, to half create what he sees. Those who *are* prepared to accept the fact that the vision of 'Introduction' grows out of the earthly experiences depicted in the marginal decorations and the earth-colored vines or branches which enclose them, can go on to liken the relation of text to surrounding vegetation to the relation of a child to a parent. The decorative vegetation can be seen, then, not only to give birth to but to shelter (because of the protective enclosure it provides) the innocent vision of the poem. While at first such an interpretation may strike the reader as far-fetched, it will seem less so when he gains similar impressions from later plates.[38] For the moment, though, we are likely to move on to the next plate with only the vaguest understanding of the design's implications. Our barely conscious sense that there is some organic connection between a vision of innocence and the 'realities' of earthly experience, between guarded and guardian – a connection implied in the parent-child relation of margin to text – prepares us, however, for what we will encounter on the next plate. For just as certain aspects of the title-page hint at the central themes of 'Introduction,' so themes which are only vaguely suggested here lie at the very core of 'The Shepherd.'

Such a process of interweaving and anticipating themes makes it hard for a critic to group the songs thematically, but this is all to Blake's purpose. Unlike earlier 'instructional' literature, *Innocence* is not meant to be broken down into a series of detachable moral lessons.[39] Instead Blake wants each plate to hint at the existence of a larger, unified vision. He wants us to 'see the world in a grain of sand,' to realize that each part of the vision implies the whole. The fiction of the Piper is introduced on this plate for the same reason. It unifies *Innocence* by encouraging us to think of each plate that follows as one of the Piper's songs 'about a lamb.' Even when the Piper is not a poem's actual speaker, we think of that poem as one of his creations, because our response to it is made up of the attitudes he displays in 'Introduction.' When we react to 'The Chimney Sweeper,' for example, we echo the sympathy and gentle tolerance of the Piper's words to the air-borne child. And if we find we cannot accept the poem's tone, we will also have difficulties with the Piper's voice. What these difficulties are we shall discover in the opening lines of 'The Shepherd.'

'The Shepherd'

The Piper's voice not only provides continuity from plate to plate, it also plays a crucial role in the reader's growth into vision. The child-like quality of the opening line of 'The Shepherd,' 'How sweet is the Shepherd's sweet lot,' instantly identifies the speaker as the Piper. The 'bold repetition'[40] of the word 'sweet' not only reminds us of the concluding lines of 'Introduction,' but puts us in a position similar to the Piper's.

We too are being asked to show sympathy and tolerance, to take the imaginative and emotional risk of abandoning our adult selfconsciousness. Though Wicksteed claims, with some justice, that the 'twice repeated "sweet" of the first line does not cloy the ear because the accent is far weaker on the second than the first,'[41] not all readers will agree. Blake is taking a chance with the line; it is one of those 'daring simplicities,'[42] to use Hirsch's phrase, which either alienate or disarm us. A critic like Lord Jeffrey, probably the most influential reviewer of the period, and one whose key terms of rejection were 'silly,' 'babyish,' and 'puerile,' would have been much discomfited.[43]

As the shepherd tends his flock, he praises the 'lamb's innocent call' and the watchful and tender protectiveness of the ewe's response. He himself embodies the qualities he praises in lamb and ewe, providing the larger 'peace' which allows the ewe to be a protector (this is what the word 'for' implies in the poem's last line),[44] and sharing in the lamb's innocence by straying through his day 'from the morn to the evening' with the carefree instinctiveness of a child.[45] The shepherd's straying recalls the Piper's carefree piping in the opening line of 'Introduction.' It provides another delicate link between the two figures, one which their resemblance in the design reinforces.[46] At the same time, of course, it also provides a marked contrast to the traditionally purposeful activity of positive figures in most children's books.[47]

Though the poem's religious implications are impossible to miss ('The Shepherd' is almost a paraphrase of Psalm 23), Blake carefully avoids explicit reference to Christ or the Lord. 'We are free,' writes Gillham, 'to see a relationship between the shepherd and Christ the Shepherd if we wish, but we are expected, first, to see the operation of watchfulness and protection on which the relationship is based.'[48] Out attention is focused on a single, literal shepherd and the literal lamb and ewe under his charge. The symbolic identity of the shepherd, like that of the child on the cloud, is made to shine through or emerge out of a divinity which is recognizably human. The same is true of the symbolic identity of the lamb. Though the shepherd's praise can be understood as praise for Christ the Lamb, Blake wants us to begin on a literal level. Hirsch cites John 17: 21–23, almost as important a source for this poem as Psalm 23: 'Thou, Father, art in me, and I in thee, that they also may be one in us. ... And the glory which thou gavest me I have given them; that they may be one, even as we are one: I in them and thou in me, that they may be made perfect in one.'[49] We must look for Christ in men on earth, in guarded as well as guardian. Man, the earthly shepherd, protects Christ on earth by protecting the lamb, just as Christ protects the human shepherd who is part of his earthly 'flock.' Though it is dangerous to argue from Blake's use of capital letters, Ann Mellor is probably right when she points to the final line's 'spiritual fusion of Man and God ... implied both in the inclusive pronoun ("they" can include lambs, ewes and mortal shepherd) and in the capitalization of Shepherd (which thus includes both the mortal and the divine shepherd).'[50]

The design manages to sound not only the poem's dominant note of protection and security, but also the delicate intimations of threat and danger implicit in its stress on guardianship. What Erdman calls the 'luxuriant density of the flock, emblem of close content and comfort,'[51] is watched over by the shepherd, and both shepherd and flock are nestled within an enclosure of trees, rich and healthy with vegetation, which block out most of the distant landscape. Though the tree to the right of the shepherd provides a further note of protection, the creeper or flowering vine which twists around the trunk reminds us of the vine-entwined tree on the title-page. That there are little flowers growing from this vine, however, mutes the sinister intimations of the previous plate. We sense only the faintest echo of a knowledge inimical to innocence. If the vine-entwined tree is meant to suggest experience, then it is of a protective not a threatening variety – hence the resemblance of vine to shepherd's curving body, and tree to upright crook. The turbulent and energetic sky also recalls the title-page. A large bird of paradise (we expect a dove in this 'valley of the shadow'), similar in appearance and position on the plate to the bird found below and slightly to the left of the initial 's' of the word 'SONGS' on the title-page, soars over and is irradiated by a fiery sun. The sun's shafts of light, bright with gold-leaf in the original, stretch from the distant hillside almost to the light wash of sky in which the words of the poem are set. Even the branches of the protective tree look as if they are being stirred by a breeze from the right side of the plate. We are left with the impression of a world of energy and motion, one from which the peaceful shepherd and his flock are cut off.

In earlier and less opaquely colored copies, including copies of *Innocence* issued separately from *Experience*,[52] though the tree still seems blown by a breeze from the right of the plate, the sky is awash with pastel blues and pinks, and the sun is neither bright nor fiery (in *In*.I, the sun and its rays are banished completely). The earlier colorings mute and soften the background (in Malkin's copy, *In*.P, the twining vine is even replaced by a blameless, free-standing St Bernard's lily), emphasizing the tranquil calm of shepherd and flock. In copy Z the contrast between backdrop and enclosure creates a wholly different impression. The world outside, with its dark blue sky, white-hot sun, and orange-red rays of light, strikes us as a potential threat to the quiet security of the innocent scene. If we believe, with Erdman,[53] that the fiery sun is about to rise, then the soaring bird heralds the dawn, and, presumably, our entry into a new world. But our feelings about this world are mixed. Are we to greet it with joy and hope? Is the bird's presence a sign of innocence, as it seems to be on the general title-page? Or does the day's dawning signal the end of quiet and security? At present the sheep are calm and content — their tranquility neatly captured in the flat, unruffled surface formed by their backs — but once they move out of the enclosure they will begin to separate, and little lambs such as the one who raises his head towards the shepherd, may find that their calls go unanswered. Time is passing, the background seems to suggest; the security of the innocent scene is but a thing of the moment. Even if we disagree with Erdman, and believe that the sun is setting, the design still leaves us vaguely troubled. Does the coming of night signal the onset of experience? Or does it merely contribute to our sense of 'close content and comfort?' In the next two plates such questions come to the fore. The rising or setting sun in the design to 'The Shepherd' merely introduces them.

The shepherd, like the piper, is a healthy young man, the outline of whose supple body is clearly visible through his clothing. He resembles the youths on the two plates of 'The Ecchoing Green,' the little boy on 'The Lamb' plate (because of position in the design, upright posture, and relaxed, healthy body) and the central figure on the 'Laughing Song' plate. The designs underline the superimposed identities of child, shepherd, piper-artist, Christ, and energetic youth that develop in the poems. They also encourage us to see Christ in those qualities that are good and beautiful in men. But if it is Christ we are seeing in the figure on this plate, then some part of his

divinity (or divinely human beauty) is sexual. For Blake, as for
D. H. Lawrence, the notion that a human being can be healthy,
young, beautiful, and sexless is a blasphemous impossibility. 'If
you love *living* beauty,' writes Lawrence, 'you have a reverence
for sex.' 'Sex and beauty are inseparable, like life and
consciousness.'[54] The shepherd's sensually curving body is part
of his attractiveness. It reminds us of the equally sensual
appearance of divinely human figures on other plates – the
healthy sexuality of the well-muscled piper, for instance, or the
erotic associations raised by the child who floats above him, and
by the naked little boy on 'The Lamb' plate. In later years Blake
was to put his vision of Christ as man to a radical test by
suggesting, in plate 61 of *Jerusalem*, that Christ was conceived in
adultery, and by allowing the rhetorical questions of *The
Everlasting Gospel* to ask whether Christ had

> A Body subject to be tempted
> From neither pain nor grief exempted
> Or such a body as might not feel
> The passions that with sinners deal
>
> (i.11–14 : E794)

The reader faces nothing quite so shocking in *Innocence*, but he
does sense that, for Blake, 'active love,' in Mark Schorer's
words, 'includes both "charity" or "good to the neighbor," and
sex love.'[55]

The subtle sexuality of the shepherd's appearance, like the
disturbing implications of the sun's rising or setting, occupies no
more than the briefest moment of our attention. Nor is it in the
least likely to undermine the larger sense of innocent security
both text and design convey. It does, however, work against any
complacent or limited conception of innocence. On the next two
plates the problems raised by time's passage and the relation of
sexual love to innocence take center stage. Gradually,
imperceptibly, Blake is calling our assumptions into question;
though the 'Ecchoing Green' helps us to understand troubling
details in the design to 'The Shepherd,' it also deepens and
complicates the meaning of innocence.

'The Ecchoing Green'

'The Ecchoing Green' is a triumph of Blake's illuminated verse.

No plates in *Innocence* are more carefully constructed, or more likely to reveal the conscious craftsman at work. Every detail of text and design plays a part in Blake's larger artistic purpose, and attests to his conviction that 'Execution is the Chariot of Genius' (Annotations to Reynolds's *Works*: E632). Because the poem shows Blake at his most controlled (and because the plates play so important a role in drawing the suggestions and intimations of previous poems and designs into a subtle and delicate unity) I shall pay especially close attention to the technical properties of the verse. Similarly, when discussing the designs, no seemingly 'Insignificant Blur or Mark' will go unexamined.

In the poem's first stanza the 'ecchoing' of the title increases in intensity. As the first seven lines of the poem touch upon the sun, the sky, the bells, the spring, the sky-lark and the thrush, they gather each image up until the last three lines of the stanza (composed of two full anapests each, contrasted with the previous five lines, each of which is composed of an iamb and an anapest) echo with a merriment that includes the cheer of previous lines and of the children at their sports. The bells of the third line are referred to in the eighth line (another echo), and the birds of the bush are said to sing louder, which contributes to our sense of increasing intensity. Skies, birds, and bells are made joyous one by the other, in a sort of chain-reaction of delight. The skies are made happy by the newly risen sun, the bells ring out (are 'merry') because the day has dawned making happy the skies, and the birds are set to singing by the sound of bells. We are reminded of *Resolution and Independence*:

> All things that love the sun are out of doors;
> The sky rejoices in the morning's birth;
> The grass is bright with rain-drops − on the moors
> The hare is running races in her mirth;
> And with her feet she from the plashy earth
> Raises a mist; that, glittering in the sun,
> Runs with her all the day, wherever she doth run.[56]

The second stanza presents echoes of a different sort. The memories of the old folk are 'echoes' of the echoing joy and jolly 'sports' of the young folk on the green. The old folk remember themselves, in Michael Tolley's words, *'as echoed*, as having been seen ("In our youth time were seen"), so that we have a pleasant receding image of old folk when they too were young, and so on.'[57] Their laughter, and Old John's, is an echo, if fainter, of the joy of the youths in the top half of the plate. The unselfconscious repetition of the word 'such' in line 17 is also an echo, one which serves to maintain the sense of wholeness and community experienced in the previous lines. Banishing objectivity and distance, it binds the old folk to the young, so that when the refrain is sounded at the end of the stanza (another echo), we feel as if the old folk have joined in with the sports of the youths. All phases of life – not just rising but darkening as well, not just the young but the aged, not just present sports but past sports remembered ('Such such were the joys') – contribute to the beauty of the poem's echoing rhythms. Though the darker aspects of natural process hint at inevitable loss, without them our sense of unity, participation and belonging – the heart of the innocent vision in 'The Ecchoing Green' – would be lost.

Hirsch accounts for the poem's complex tone – somehow both vaguely troubled *and* calm and accepting – by suggesting that 'The old folk who recollect their natural past in the joy of children see both their source and their rebirth in eternity,' and that 'in the full cycle of life the setting of this sun is a new and greater sunrise.'[58] But there is little reason to believe that either the old folk or the speaker (no longer the Piper, but one of the youths on the green) is conscious of any 'greater sunrise.' On the contrary, their very unselfishness is important to the poem's success, as a number of critics who compare this poem to 'I Love the jocund dance' (in *Poetical Sketches*) have pointed out.[59] The tone of 'The Ecchoing Green' recalls Keats's 'Ode to Autumn.' Natural process is simply described in both poems, and just as in 'The Ecchoing Green' aging and darkening, though a threat to the innocent vision, are essential to its beauty, so in Keats's poem, were there no winter to follow autumn, we would find its mellow glories less compelling. Neither poem's tone can be understood in terms of an implicit faith in eternity. Once we posit a greater sunrise in 'The Ecchoing Green,' we lose touch with that delicate state of the soul its speaker expresses. The poem, like the design on 'The Shepherd' plate, and like, in fact, *Innocence* itself, is poised between a vision of process in which all elements contribute to joy, beauty and security, and one in which process will itself soon end the possibility of such a vision.

The meter of the third stanza suggests the coming of twilight

and the weariness of the little ones who return to their mothers'
laps:

> Till the little ones weary
> No more can be merry
> The sun does descend
> And our Sports have an end;
> Round the laps of their mothers,
> Many sisters and brothers,
> Like birds in their nest,
> Are ready for rest:
> And sport no more seen,
> On the darkening Green.

The anapestic run is modified by an extra unstressed syllable at
the end of the two opening lines and of lines 25 and 26. This
makes the lines fall, and contributes to our sense that the echoes
are now fading. The double anapests of the two previous refrains
are also subtly altered. 'And sport no more seen' can be read as
an iamb followed by an anapest, or stresses can be placed over
both 'no' and 'more.'[60] In either case the effect is gained. Line
29 echoes what has gone before even as it breaks up the expected
rhythm. The result is a metrical equivalent of the effect
produced by the word 'darkening' in the last line.

Though the designs to 'The Ecchoing Green' make the
poem's subtle suggestions more explicit, their vision of
innocence is equally delicate and balanced. The top half of the
first plate depicts a securely enclosed green, the traditional figure
of the *hortus conclusus*. A tall, circular hedge blocks off the
background landscape, and a sturdy oak provides shade and
shelter. The curve of the foreground which gives the green an
oblong shape, creates a further sense of enclosure. Between the
hedges and the oak tree we notice what look like young trees,
with thin, spindly branches. Blake, as I have suggested, paid an
engraver's careful attention to the smallest details not only of his
own but of others' designs. Samuel Palmer remembers him
remarking of Claude's trees, for example, that 'when minutely
examined, there were upon the focal lights of the foliage, small
specks of pure white which made them appear to be glittering
with dew which the morning sun had not yet dried up.'[61] A
similar attention to minute detail lies behind his depiction of the
thin young trees on this plate; they suggest a world outside the

green, one which contrasts with the soft yet solid calm of the protective vegetation of hedge and oak. In the original printing, the trees' branchings are somewhat wilder and more threatening, but even in Z where the original outlines have been colored over and the trees are arranged symmetrically, the contrast between enclosed and unenclosed worlds is subtly disturbing.[62]

On the far left of the oak tree a boy bats a ball (obscured in copy Z) to a youth with outstretched arms. Beneath the tree, five small children, already weary, gather round the laps of their mothers and of one of the two seated males. To the right, three older youths stand around in relaxed or restless attitudes, as if bored with the green's sports. That all generations are present in the innocent scene contributes to our sense of inclusiveness and harmony, but it also suggests that time is passing, leaving us with the impression that the joys of the present moment are fading.

The bottom half of the plate creates a similar impression. The decorative vegetation, composed of three healthy young grapevines, squiggles and curls energetically, providing a visual equivalent to the exuberant rhythms of the verse. In the upper right-hand corner, one vine, bearing green leaves and what look like buds and blossoms, seems to grow out of the last word of the title. Erdman rightly notes its 'very active sexual parts,'[63] for Blake has clearly gone to some trouble to outline stamens and stigmas (a wholly plausible precision, given his familiarity with Darwin's *Loves of the Plants*, part 2 of *The Botanic Garden*, with its detailed verse descriptions of the sexual organs of flowers).[64] The longest of the vine's tendrils stretches down the right side of the text coming close to a larger tendril from a second vine at bottom right. This lower vine, while not quite as 'sexually active' as the one above, is every bit as energetic. One of its tendrils loops across the page between the first and second stanzas, reminding us of the smaller branching vines of the 'Introduction' plate, while another puts forth a bunch of grapes. A bird (Erdman identifies it as a swallow)[65] flies 'swift as arrow' towards the fruit.

Between the two vines to the right of the text a young boy (he is more like the youths to the left of the oak than those to the right) rolls a hoop. His carefree, unselfconscious play recalls the trustful innocence of the two children on the title-page. The vines which surround him, though much less menacing than the apple tree on the earlier plate, none the less signal the onset of experience. The upper vine's potency, and the swift swallow's flight towards the ripe grapes on the lower vine, suggest that innocence – the child's unselfconscious play – is but a passing thing, the product of a particular moment in process. Like any child absorbed in a game, the boy to the right of the text focuses all his attention on the hoop itself, and does not seem to see, as we do, that his play is leading him out of the world of this plate and into the dark blue skies of another place and time. We remember the deep blue background of 'The Shepherd' and title-page plates, and the disturbing contrasts they suggested between enclosed and unenclosed worlds. A similar impression is conveyed on the left side of the text, where a third vine, also bearing buds, curves up the length of the lower half of the plate and puts forth a single green leaf next to the title.[66] Another young boy, with a cricket bat in his right hand, appears to be standing on the vine. Though not actively engaged in play (his more passive stance reminds us of the boys at the upper right) he too seems oblivious to his surroundings.

On the second plate, below a text which speaks of 'darkening,' weariness, and the end of sports, several figures from the previous plate (and some who appear here for the first time) begin their journey home. The green is behind them now, and they move through a landscape without hedges or trees.[67] Only one mother appears on the plate. She holds an infant in her arms, and a weary child clings to her skirts. A youth with a brimmed hat offers the child a bunch of grapes. Hirsch calls the tall male figure in the center of the party 'an image of the father who gently guides his weary children home.'[68] He is also, as Erdman points out, 'Old John with white hair.'[69] The three youths in front turn to him for directions, and as he points the way with his right arm, his left gently guides, or urges along, the boy in green. Old John's central position is analogous to that of the protective oak on the previous plate.[70] His knowledge of the way home protects the group, and just as the oak's vegetation shades and encloses the green, so John's arms spread like branches, guiding, sheltering and keeping the party together. He too is a shepherd, embodying what Hirsch calls 'the sacramental implications of the poem.'[71]

Though the youth in red to the left of Old John carries a kite, he and the green-gowned girl next to him are clearly adolescents. The similarly clad girl on the far right of the plate is also an adolescent. The older the youths, the further they are from John and the mother, just as in the first plate the youngest children stay close to the protection of the oak tree, old folk and mothers, while the older boys move off to the green's periphery. In both plates, the youths on the left of the central, vertical axis seem to be slightly younger than those on the right. Though the young girl at the far left of the second plate is still attentive to John, the girl at the far right focuses all her attention on the bunch of grapes she is about to receive from an adolescent boy resting with sensual nonchalance on one of the grape-vine branches above her head. As she reaches up with her left arm, she lifts back her head and the wide-brimmed hat she wears haloes her head. In Hogarth's 'Evening' (plate 3 of the 1738 series, *The Four Times of the Day*), a similar illusion is put to satiric effect (figure 10). Instead of placing symbolic horns on a cuckolded London dyer, Hogarth positions a bull directly behind him, its horns seeming to protrude from the dyer himself. In *Innocence*, though, 'accidents' of this sort are much more than merely accidental. They represent a central truth or theme of the volume: that of the sacramental quality of everyday life.

Damon calls the grapes the haloed girl will soon be tasting 'grapes of ecstasy,'[72] and Keynes says that she and the two boys above her are 'on the road to Experience, passing from the Age of Innocence to that of sexual awareness.'[73] We are reminded of plate 15 of *America*, where another bunch of grapes appears in the design, and where the text tells of Orc's liberation of 'female spirits of the dead.' Once Orc appears these spirits

> Run from their fetters reddening, and in the long drawn
> arches sitting:
> They feel the nerves of youth renew, and desires of ancient
> times,
> Over their pale limbs as a vine when the tender grape
> appears.[74]
>
> (*A* 15:24–26: E26)

The sun is setting, the green is darkening, and the girl at the right of the second plate is growing into a new world. Yet she remains a part of the innocent scene, despite her symbolic sexual awakening. 'Infancy,' Oothoon tells us in *Visions of the Daughters of Albion*, is 'fearless, lustful, happy! nestling for delight/In laps of pleasure' (6.5–6 : E48). The girl's hat, which is made to look like a halo, as well as her delicately graceful body, are Blake's way of reminding us that sexuality and innocence are not mutually exclusive, that innocent sexuality is divine and beautiful.

Similar points are made in the top half of the plate. The three small vines of the first plate have now grown together, and two of them combine to form a sort of tree. Though still young, these vines need 'no elm for support.'[75] Their sensuous entwinings, which recall the tree-vines on the frontispiece and 'Introduction' plates, confirm our suspicions about the sexual character of earlier and equally suggestive vegetative embraces. Half way up the plate the vines separate to frame the text and support the same two boys, now more mature, who appeared in the lower part of the first plate. Cricket bats and hoops have given way to more 'adult' pursuits. The boy on the right, slightly older than the boy on the left, has already reached the grapes, but like the vine which is just barely strong enough to support him, he has not yet attained full maturity.

At this point our original interpretation of the Old John figure begins to change. What, we wonder, would Old John say were he to look behind him? Would he be pleased to see the girl in green reach up to receive the grapes? Instead of embodying what Hirsch calls the poem's 'sacramental implications' might he not represent a world opposed to innocent sexuality, one which seeks to thwart what it calls 'sinful delights/Of age and youth and boy and girl'? (*J* 18.16–17: E160) Grant believes that Old John is 'not really in charge because the gift of the grapes of pleasure behind his back unmistakably reveals him to be Mister Parental Spoilsport, rather than a good guide.'[76] He is right, of course, but so too is Hirsch. Old John, who has participated for a charmed moment in the joyous echoes of the poem, *is* a good guide, a human analogue to the central, sheltering oak. But he is also the sort of figure who might, in another context, seek to bind and repress youthful sexuality. To Hazard Adams, 'this picture of Old John with white hair sitting under the oak tree has just enough suggestion of white Urizen' to help produce 'an ominous note in the imagery.'[77] John is still the benevolent guide of the innocent party, but we are allowed a glimpse of what he might be in a world of experience, when the sun has finally gone down or the new day has dawned.

Almost every detail of text and design in 'The Ecchoing Green' suggests that the innocent vision is intimately bound up with a sense of time's passage. The world of these plates is no mere pastoral fiction or timeless Eden; it is neither untouched by nor prior to experience. Rather, as the innocent speaker's complex tone suggests, it is a world woven out of those moments in our lives (Blake refers to them collectively as a 'state of the human soul') in which we feel that all elements of process, even mutability and death, are part of a larger, unified picture. Blake's attempt to teach the reader to see 'a vision, a perfect whole' by adapting a child's way of seeing is neither escapist nor regressive; there is nothing of Tennyson's 'All things have rest, and ripen towards the grave' about 'The Ecchoing Green.'[78] Peter Coveney's distinction between 'those authors [of the late eighteenth century] who went to the child to express their involvement with life, and those who retreated towards the symbol from "life's decay," '[79] is worth bearing in mind. No one who has looked closely at 'The Ecchoing Green' can be in any doubt as to the camp to which Blake belongs.

'The Lamb'

Though the poem 'The Lamb' is all innocent harmony and inter-relation, the design's delicate suggestions of loss and threat echo the ambiguities and qualifications of previous plates. As in the design to 'The Shepherd,' the innocent foreground is tranquil and secure. The child and the flock are enclosed by a river, an oak tree, a hedge, and a thatched cottage or barn. If the latter is, in fact, a cottage, it suggests that parents are nearby, which adds a further protective note, and the two reclining sheep at the front of the flock 'looking relaxed and off to the left, framing with their complacence the lamb who is advancing towards the child' remind us, in Wagenknecht's words, of 'the apparent parents of the lamb in "Spring".'[80]

The enclosure, like the poem, is wholly reassuring. Outside it, though, the character of the design begins to change. Though the text is backed by a pale wash, the surrounding sky is darkest blue, with a deep purple patch of cloud louring behind the cottage. The air, we realize, is 'burdened,' as in 'The Argument' to *The Marriage of Heaven and Hell*. But lamb, child, and flock, like the innocents on the title-page and 'The Shepherd' plates, are oblivious to the threat it poses. While the stormy sky (almost as vividly purple in the earliest copies of *Innocence*, *In*.A–C) suggests the onset of experience, it also accentuates the very innocence it endangers. By literally 'defining' or outlining the two white doves perched on the cottage roof, for example, it not only draws them to our attention, but reminds us that 'peace' (the doves) is vulnerable, a thing of the moment.[81] It also emphasizes the fragility of the vine-entwined saplings that arch so beautifully over text and enclosure. Though Wagenknecht believes these vines and saplings contribute to what he calls the plate's 'erotic tensions,'[82] and though Erdman describes them as 'sinuous' and 'embracing,'[83] their predominating qualities, like those of lamb and child, are health, youth, and delicacy.

In order to appreciate the text's less disturbing subtleties we must pay especially close attention to the stylized child-likeness of the speaker's tone. Though Hazard Adams believes the speaker 'so universalized as to be anyone,'[84] both text and design suggest otherwise. The multiple repetitions of word and phrase, the sing-songy, jingle-like quality of three- and four-beat trochaic lines, diction and syntax of the utmost simplicity, all point to the child's way of seeing and speaking. A line like 'Softest clothing wooly bright,' for example, though perilously close to a cloying sentimentality, vividly captures the child's immediacy of response to and total absorption in what delights him. It also, like earlier 'daring simplicities,' challenges the reader to respond in a similarly unselfconscious manner.

Once we identify the speaker with the child in the design, we give the poem a dramatic context, one which subtly enriches its meaning. The lines 'Little Lamb I'll tell thee/Little Lamb I'll tell thee,' for example, no longer strike us as mindless repetition. We see them, instead, as an expression of the child's eager delight and pride in being able to teach what he has been taught. The child, we realize, like so many other characters in *Innocence*, is playing a game, 'pretending' (though he believes what he says) to be a teacher. 'When I was but a child of nine or ten years old,' writes Bunyan, 'in the midst of my merry sports and childish vanities, amidst my vain companions, I was often much cast down and afflicted in my mind therewith; yet could I not let go my sins.'[85] *Innocence* takes a wholly different view of sports and childish vanities. Here, for example, we are made to sense behind the child's lessons to the lamb the teachings of his parents, and what must have been, judging from his own gentle patience, an equally affecting sincerity and simplicity; and if we take the poem 'exactly as it comes,' keeping a literal child before our eyes, a family (the occupants of the cottage) appears, one whose authority is as gentle and benevolent as the God they have taught their child to praise. 'One first in friendship and love,'

Los tells his Spectre, 'then a divine family, and in the Midst/ Jesus will appear.'

Though 'The Lamb' is among the simplest and most transparent of Blake's lyrics, its delicately inter-related cluster of ideas not only reiterates but weaves together and clarifies a number of themes and suggestions from previous plates. Christ, line 3 tells us, creates and protects the lamb ('Gave thee life and bid thee feed'); the lamb is also protected by the child's teachings (because they encourage us to care for and reverence lambs); and the child is taught by the lamb's innocent beauty to recognize and reverence Christ on earth. We as readers see the truth of the child's teachings in his careful and loving sympathy. He becomes Christ-like in the very act of recognizing and reverencing Christ in others. The delicate suggestions of 'The Shepherd' becomes the child's explicit assertions in 'The Lamb.' As the identities of guardian and guarded fuse, we find ourselves in a world much like that of 'The Ecchoing Green.' Christ's gift to the lamb of 'such a tender voice' makes 'all the vales rejoice,' just as in 'The Ecchoing Green' the rising sun sets in motion a joyful song of skies, birds, and bells. We feel the benevolent unity not just of lamb, child, and Christ, but of all creation. The poem's structure, we realize, is one 'of identity, of the merging and interfusion which is the ultimate condition of harmonious oneness.'[86] The last two lines neatly epitomize the effect produced by the poem as a whole. The literal lamb of the design is being blessed in both lines; or the second line's echo is, as Wicksteed suggests, 'perhaps from the Poet, blessing the child, "himself a lamb" ';[87] or the child speaks the first line to the literal lamb and the second to Christ the Lamb. Though we wonder which lamb is being referred to, we also realize that the question is no longer important. The child's way of seeing and speaking, his love of repetition, is an example of, as well as a means of apprehending, 'the Eternal Vision: the Divine Similitude' (*J* 34.11 : E178).

The visual echoes set off by the child's appearance in the design extend the complex of identities established in the poem. The naked little boy reminds us not only of the child on the cloud in the frontispiece, but of the Piper as well. Like the Piper and the shepherd, he stands in front of a peacefully grazing flock and his body is healthy and muscular. He also reminds us of Old John on the second plate of 'The Ecchoing Green' in that he stands taller than his peaceful charges and gently reaches out towards the little lamb as John reaches out to the child in front of him. The text of 'The Lamb' teaches us to identify lamb and child with Christ; the design reminds us that the child who is Christ who is a lamb, is also the protective shepherd, the benevolent guide (Old John), the artist of imagination and vision (the Piper), and the source of the artist's inspiration (the child on the cloud). When we look at the little boy on this plate we see in him the divine attributes of previous human figures. Both text and design teach us to seek out Christ in the goodness and beauty of men on earth.

They also, of course, further the work's re-invention or re-vivification of traditional Christian symbols, so that when we turn from 'The Lamb' to the design on the first plate of 'Spring,' for example, we sense its delicate intimations of threat or danger, as well as those of protection, identity, and the divinity of innocence, without recourse to tradition – even to the traditional associations of its central motif. Knowledge of analogues or possible influences only reinforces (I am not, I want to emphasize, calling appeals to tradition pernicious or purposeless) what the work itself discloses. Leonardo's *St Anne* (figure 11), for instance, the subject of what Gombrich calls 'the best documented application of exegetics to a painting in the Renaissance,'[88] is a plausible analogue to the design on plate 1 of 'Spring.' According to Fra Pietro da Novellara's famous description of the painting,

> It represents the Christ Child, about a year old, as if about to slip out of his mother's arms, grasping a lamb and seeming to hug it. The mother, as if about to rise from the lap of St. Anne, grasps the Child to take him from the lamb, that sacrificial animal which signifies the passion. St. Anne, rising a little from her seat, seems to want to keep her daughter from taking the child away from the lamb: this would perhaps stand for the Church that does not want to have the passion of Christ prevented.[89]

A comment on the same picture, by Guolamo Casio, offers a somewhat different interpretation:

> St. Anne, as the one who knew
> That Jesus assumed the human shape
> To atone for the Sin of Adam and Eve

Tells her daughter with pious zeal:
Beware if you wish to draw Him back
For the heavens have ordained that sacrifice.

Though much of this (including what is contradictory in the two accounts) may be relevant to the design on the first plate of 'Spring,' *Songs* itself provides comparable associations and echoes. The identity of protector and protected, of lamb, mother, and child, the imminence of sacrificial danger, all these notes are sounded for the reader who brings to 'Spring' a knowledge of the plates that precede it. Even Novellara's identification of St Anne with the Church will be suggested, and so can be read back into this and other designs, by a complex of associations developed in later plates, especially those of *Experience*. Blake's symbols in *Songs*, I am suggesting – given that larger tradition Leavis seems to mistake for immutable truth, and Blake implies in appeals to 'the Public' – are self-revelatory and self-generating, despite their inevitable links to tradition.

To return, then, to 'The Lamb': by confirming our suspicions about the meanings of suggestive or mysterious details in previous plates, and tying those meanings together, both text and design play an important part in our growth into vision. Though the themes of 'The Lamb' are simple and straightforwardly stated, they provide a justification for the interpretative risks more complicated or problematic plates tease us into taking. Those risks, a product of the gradual unfolding of Blake's thought in *Songs*, subtly undermine our adult or experienced habits of mind. Every time we are tempted to half create what we see, to take seriously lines which sound sentimental or 'childish,' to trust in our feelings and intuitions, to see the whole in the minutest of minute particulars in text and design – we move closer to vision, to the child's way of seeing in 'The Lamb.' Blake, as this chapter has tried to suggest, wants us to realize, in both senses of the word, our own divine humanity. Like children at their books, we are to live out the themes of *Innocence* through the very act of reading.

CHAPTER 4
INNOCENCE IN MATURITY

Blake is fully aware of how difficult it is to maintain vision. Contact with innocents can afford us flashes of insight in which the distinctions between subject and object, self and other fall away, and in which man's creative powers are revealed as divine. But moments of this sort are hard to retain or prolong. They quickly dissolve with the return of adult or experienced habits of mind that obscure any sense of unity of inter-relation, and restrict our imaginative capacities.

The plates we shall examine in this chapter show us what happens once an adult attains a moment of vision. They invite us to enter into the minds of characters who are dragged away from genuine insight by conventional modes of perception and understanding as strong, deceptive, and dangerous as a swift undertow. In most cases, the powers that stifle vision remind us of the restrictions needlessly or arbitrarily imposed upon us by custom and law. In a few plates, they seem inevitable, like the passage of time and the seasons. Our task — to determine the extent to which these powers are beyond human control — is complicated by Blake's refusal or inability to provide unambiguous answers. When in some plates it seems as though 'reality' has displaced a moment of divine insight, closer scrutiny reveals that our return to a supposed objective world is an illusion, a sign of imaginative poverty. At other times, a clear line is drawn between what is real and what is imaginary; vision, we are made to feel, can do nothing to prevent the sun from setting.

In later works, Blake tries to simplify matters (even as he complicates them) by distinguishing between two states of vision: Beulah, the properties of which are much like those of Innocence; and Eternity, a higher and more active state, glimpses of which Beulah affords. Beulah is 'a soft Moony universe feminine lovely/Pure mild and Gentle' (*FZ* 1.5.30–1: E299), a respite from the rigors of Eternity; Eternity, as we know, is 'intellectual War,' for which one needs 'the golden armour of science' (*FZ* 9.139.8–9: E392). Beulah is a way through to Eternity.

Precisely when Blake conceived this distinction is impossible to tell, but in its first appearance, in *The Four Zoas* (*c.*1796–1803), it was inconsistently applied. Eternity there is remembered not only as a place of energizing conflict, but one in which 'the lamb replies to the infant voice and the lion to the man of years/Giving them sweet instructions Where the Cloud the River and the Field/Talk with the husbandman and Shepherd' (6.71.6–8: E341); and, even more pointedly, 'Where joy sang in the trees and pleasure sported on the rivers/And laughter sat beneath the Oaks and innocence sported round/Upon the green plains' (6.72.39–73.2: E343). In other words, Blake, through the recollections of his fallen eternals, continued to describe a life of vision, or Eternity, in innocent terms – as though the state of Innocence could and should be prolonged – well after the creation of *Experience*. In Heaven, 'To know sweet Science and to do with simple companions/Sitting beneath a tent and viewing Sheepfolds and soft pastures' (*FZ* 4.51.30–1: E328), seem to go together.

In *Jerusalem* (*c.* 1804–7), the distinction between Beulah and Eternity is more consistently applied, accompanied by explicit warnings against the danger of mistaking one for the other:

> O Vala! Humanity is far above
> Sexual organization; & the Visions of the Night of Beulah
> Where Sexes wander in dreams of bliss among the
> Emanations
> Where the Masculine & Feminine are nurs'd into Youth &
> Maiden
> By the tears & smiles of Beulahs Daughters till the time of
> Sleep is past.
> Wherefore then do you realize these nets of beauty &
> delusion
> In open day to draw the souls of the Dead into the light
> Till Albion is shut out from every Nation under Heaven.
> (4.79.73–80: E233–4)

But even in *Jerusalem* there are prominent exceptions, notably the introductory lyric to chapter 2, in which Jerusalem's 'Little-ones ran on the fields/The Lamb of God among them seen/And fair Jerusalem his Bride;/Among the little meadows green' (27.5–8: E170). Nor is it right to read the poem's warnings against Beulah's gentle enticements back into *Songs* or other early works like *The Book of Thel* (1789) or *Tiriel* (1791), both of which contain characters whose false child-likeness seems to suggest that prolonged innocence breeds stagnation. Though the world of Lilly, Cloud, Clod, and Worm in *Thel* is less robust than that of *Innocence* – has about it something of what Frye calls 'the rococo China shepherdess'[1] – it too identifies innocent virtues (selflessness, protection, health) with explicitly sexual or erotic experience. Thel's refusal to enter into it is a mistaking of false for true (and prolongable) innocence, rather than innocence for life or 'Vision'; Har and Heva, in *Tiriel*, are examples of what Thel will become.

Blake's treatment of a related issue – that of the subject/ object distinction – in other works aside from *Innocence* is no less problematic. Though in many passages he explicitly denies the independence of subject and object, a number of poems and designs imply a reality beyond or apart from the human imagination. Perhaps this results from the intractability of language itself, what Blake calls its 'stubborn structure' (*J* 36.59: E181). No poet can avoid dualist terms. But an argument of this sort clears up only some of our difficulties. Take, for example, the problems posed when we compare the final plates of *Thel* with those of *Visions of the Daughters of Albion*. Thel flees back to the vales of Har because she has been terrified by a voice from her own grave. That voice brutally denies the teachings of Lilly, Cloud, Clod, and Worm. Instead of a world in which 'everything that lives,/Lives not alone, nor for itself' (3.26–7: E5), and all creation is 'visited from heaven' by 'he that smiles on all' (1.19: E3), it speaks in sorrow of 'destruction,' 'the poison of a smile,' 'arrows ready drawn,' 'terror trembling and affright' (6.11–18: E6). Men are shown to be helpless victims of their five senses, incapable of closing out a world of misery and threat. But the voice we are hearing is Thel's, and the world it speaks of is a projection of her own fears and limitations rather than any objective or independent reality. The poem's conclusion is too perfect a fulfillment of Thel's 'virgin fears' for the reader to begin questioning the wisdom of

Lilly, Cloud, Clod, and Worm. Thel's tragedy is lack of vision, and we leave the poem feeling that the powers restricting her are within her control.

Visions also ends on a bleak note:

Thus every morning wails Oothoon, but Theotormon sits
Upon the margind ocean conversing with shadows dire.

The Daughters of Albion hear her woes, and eccho back
her sighs.

(8.11–13: E50)

Like Thel, Oothoon is left despondent and isolated. The poem's conclusion is especially disturbing because Oothoon is perhaps the most eloquent champion of vision in all of Blake's works. Having learned that 'every thing that lives is holy' (8.10: E50), she will no longer allow herself to be restricted by the empiricism that once 'inclos'd my infinite brain into a narrow circle./And sunk my heart into the Abyss, a red round globe hot burning/Till all from life I was obliterated and erased' (2.32–4: E46). Yet her world remains one of disunity and suffering, and the reader is left with the impression that Oothoon is subject to forces beyond her control.

The later works are hardly more consistent. What, for example, are we to make of Blake's notion of apocalypse in *Milton*? At times we are led to believe that 'whenever any Individual Rejects Error and Embraces Truth a Last Judgment passes upon that Individual' (*VLJ*: E551). Bloom claims that the poem justifies the ways of God to man because it shows 'that certain men have the courage to cast out what is not human in them, and so become Man, and to become Man is to have become God.'[2] Frye too suggests the possibility of an apocalypse for 'certain men': 'And if all art is visionary, it must be apocalyptic and revelatory too: the artist does not wait to die before he lives in the spiritual world into which John was caught up.'[3] But in the last plate of *Milton* Blake is at pains to distinguish between an individual apocalypse or revelation and the collective 'Great Harvest and Vintage of the Nations':

then to their mouths the Four
Applied their Four Trumpets and them sounded to the
Four Winds

Terror struck in the Vale I stood at that immortal sound
My bones trembled. I fell outstretched upon the path

A moment, and my Soul returned into its mortal state
To Resurrection and Judgement in the Vegetable Body
And my sweet Shadow of Delight stood trembling by my
  side

Immediately the Lark mounted with a loud trill from
  Felphams Vale
And the Wild Thyme from Wimbletons green and
  impurpled Hills
And Los and Enitharmon rose over the Hills of Surrey
Their clouds roll over London with a south wind, soft
  Oothoon
Pants in the Vales of Lambeth weeping oer her Human
  Harvest
Los listens to the Cry of the Poor Man: his Cloud
Over London in volume terrific, low bended in anger.

Rintrah and Palamabron view the Human Harvest beneath
Their Wine-presses and Barns stand open; the Ovens are
  prepar'd
The Waggons ready: terrific Lions and Tygers sport and
  play
All animals upon the Earth, are prepard in all their strength

To go forth to the Great Harvest and Vintage of the
  Nations.

(*M* 42.22–43.1 : E142–3)

These lines seem to suggest that Blake's vision is but a prelude to
true Revelation, an omen of things to come. Yet at the same
time, the last plates (as well as the poem as a whole) suggest that
Revelation is brought about by Blake's vision. Once the Last
Judgment is revealed to him, 'Immediately the Lark mounted.'
We leave the poem unable to tell for sure if its apocalypse is
collective or individual: a dilemma with obvious political
implications, and one frequently found by millenarians (or
millenarian types) in times of crisis.[4]
  Taken as a whole, *Innocence* implies that an individual

apocalyptic vision can transform the world. We, like Thel, have it within our power to alter those conventional modes of perception and understanding which alone keep us from a life of vision. Only a few plates suggest that the loss of vision is an inevitable and irreversible product of maturity, and even they seem less pessimistic when viewed in a larger context. For example, though the speaker in 'Nurse's Song' cannot stop the night from coming, other plates prevent us from taking as 'objective' her attitude towards it. Even the predatory beasts who search for prey among its shadows can be transformed into benevolent protectors if one has sufficient vision. 'Nurse's Song' sets limits to man's visionary capacity only when viewed in isolation. Nor should we forget that the intense moment of unity and inter-relation that slips so quickly from the nurse is the creation of an adult piper or poet. His visionary powers withstand the pressures of time and custom, even if hers do not.

Though the following plates are united by a common theme – the threatened loss of a newly awakened vision – they present us with characters whose reactions to it differ. Some reveal the disturbing consequences of a refusal to admit to loss; others accept what happens to them with a note of melancholy nostalgia that reminds us of the speakers in many of Wordsworth's poems; at least one character succeeds in breaking free of conventional habits of mind, retaining his vision through the dark night. All, though, even the most anxiously unsure, contrast strikingly with their bullying counterparts in conventional children's literature. We shall begin with 'A Cradle Song' because it provides a relatively straightforward account of the theme, and because the ambiguity of its concluding stanzas reveals a range of possible responses to the threat of vision's loss.

'A Cradle Song'

'A Cradle Song' traces a mother's thoughts and feelings as she sits beside her sleeping infant. Though the steady, unvarying rhythms of her lullaby are soft and reassuring, if we listen carefully to what she says, we shall detect the shadowy outlines of a deeper seriousness. Beneath the transparent simplicity of the mother's gentle repetitions lies a complex pattern of responses common to many Songs of Innocence. Her shifts in mood are extremely subtle, though, and are easily overstated. Even the slightest of Blake's lyrics – 'Infant Joy,' for example – repays close attention, but we must take care not to let our interpretations press too hard on what are only delicate suggestions.

In the first stanza the mother speaks of 'Sweet dreams' as if they were separate from her child. The 'shade' they provide reminds us of the protective enclosures formed over innocents by the sturdy oaks and elms of previous plates. (Other echoes are sounded by the actual content of the dreams: the 'pleasant streams' recall the river in which the sweeps bathed and the 'dimpling stream' that 'runs laughing by' in 'Laughing Song'; the 'happy silent moony beams' anticipate the mood created by the opening stanza of 'Night.') In the second stanza the mother speaks of 'sleep' as if it too were separate from her sleeping child. In line 5 it assumes the form of a bird ('with soft down'), in line 6 it becomes an 'infant crown,' and in line 7 an 'angel mild' hovering over the sleeping child. These rapid transformations (we barely have time to form one image before it flows into another) and the fact that 'sleep' and 'dreams' are made to occupy space, like objects, lends a strange, dream-like quality to the poem, as do the 'crooning, hypnotic rhythms' of the mother's lullaby, like 'the rocking of the cradle.'[5]

The mother's words suggest that she has slipped out of the world of everyday reality. Conventional distinctions between self and other are beginning to dissolve. When she tells us in stanza 3 that 'Sweet smiles in the night,/Hover o'er my delight' we are unable to tell whether she is referring to her own smiles or those of the child. She responds with such sympathetic intensity to her child's utterances that 'they become movements in her own soul,'[6] and in all of Nature as well. The words 'hover o'er' unite mother and child with the rest of creation. When 'absorbed in the present moment,' writes Hazlitt, 'There is often a local feeling in the air, which is as fixed, as if it were of marble.'[7] In this poem, the very air wears a smile. The mother's creative or visionary powers are responsible for the transformation of her world. We note that the verbs of the first three stanzas ('form,' 'weave,' and 'hover') can be imperative as well as indicative.

Though the smiles of lines 11 and 12 clearly emanate from the mother, when we move to stanza 4 we again lose our bearings. The 'Sweet moans' and 'dovelike sighs' that threaten the child's sleep can come from either child or mother. And when 'sweeter smiles' charm away ('beguile') the 'dovelike moans' we cannot tell if the child's moans have been replaced by its own smiles or those of its mother, or whether the mother's moans have been silenced by the sweet smiles of her child. The world created in the poem's first four stanzas is immune to the distinctions and identifications of 'adult' consciousness. With the child asleep and happy, 'All creation slept and smil'd,' an effect like that of Blake's evocation of the humanized pre-fallen world in *The Book of Urizen*:

> Earth was not, nor globes of attraction
> The will of the Immortal expanded
> Or contracted his all flexible senses.
>
> (3.36–8 : E70)

Line 18 relates the present charmed moment of sympathetic identity between mother, child and all creation to another time and another child. It also prepares us for the mother's weeping two lines later and for the explicit references to the Christ-child in the sixth stanza. The mother, we remember, speaks the line while watching her child sleep. Though the momentary disturbance of moans and sighs in the previous stanza has passed, she is soon overcome by a rush of tender feeling so intense that it causes her to weep:

> Sleep sleep happy child
> All creation slept and smil'd.
> Sleep sleep, happy sleep,
> While o'er thee thy mother weep

At this precise moment her visionary powers begin to fade. She cries because she senses an inextricable connection between the child's innocent beauty and its vulnerability. When Christ was born, Milton tells us, there reigned 'a universal peace through sea and land':

> The winds with wonder whist
> Smoothly the waters kissed
>   Whispering new joys to the mild ocean,
> Who now hath quite forgot to rave,
> While birds of calm sit brooding on the
>   charmed wave.[8]
> ('On the Morning of Christ's Nativity,' 11.64–8)

The sadness that tinges the beauty of these lines helps us to understand the mother's tears in Blake's poem. The peace Milton describes is but a prologue to the tragedy of Christ's maturity, and the mother weeps in line 20 because she sees in her child and in the silent smiles that seem to spread through all creation not merely the Holy Image of the Christ-child, but the inevitable pain and suffering that will come to her child as surely as it came to Christ. The earlier allusions to an 'angel mild' and an 'infant crown' suggest that thoughts of Christ have been with the mother from at least the second stanza, but only now does she begin to realize their implications.[9]

Once the thought of an historical Christ begins to surface in the mother's mind she loses touch with the present moment of unity and benevolence. Though all creation seems to be united with her child in happy sleep (just as it was on that distant morning when Christ was born) she herself feels vaguely isolated and unhappy. 'The effect of her tears,' writes David Wagenknecht, 'is to suggest that the mother is not a part of the sleeping and smiling creation but above it – herself godlike.'[10] The mother's only available comfort in her moment of isolation is the image of a forlorn and distant protector like herself – a mature Christ in heaven – watching and weeping over her, as she watches and weeps over her own child.

But the mother's fears for her child, and her sadness, do not last. Once the sight of the sweet babe's face intrudes upon her reflections (the line 'Sleep sleep, happy sleep' suggests that by stanza 5 she has receded into a world of her own thoughts), the image of an alienated and sorrowful divinity is gradually displaced by a truly Divine Image. The mother returns to vision in the poem's concluding stanzas, though the process as a whole is somewhat shadowy and mysterious:

> Sweet babe in thy face,
> Holy image I can trace.
> Sweet babe once like thee,
> Thy maker lay and wept for me.
>
> Wept for me for thee for all,
> When he was an infant small.
> Thou his image ever see.
> Heavenly face that smiles on thee.

Smiles on thee on me on all,
Who became an infant small,
Infant smiles are his own smiles,
Heaven and earth to peace beguiles.

In the last lines of stanza 6, after the mother has traced a divinity in her infant's face, she tries to explain what she has seen and to relate it to her fears for the future. There was a time, she claims, when she too was watched over and 'wept for.' The word 'once' points back to her sense of loss and alienation. But her image of God has already changed by line 24. The remote and sorrowful protector to whom she seemed to have likened herself in stanza 5 is transformed into a 'babe ... like thee,' 'an infant small.' Then, because her own child's face so forcefully reminds her of the face of her once youthful maker, it occurs to the mother that God's face must now be before her child. The 'Holy Image' she can trace in the child's smiling face must be a reflection of God's own face, and God must be smiling: 'Thou his image ever see./ Heavenly face that smiles on thee.' The word 'ever,' which, in this context, means 'now,' is one small sign of the mother's return to vision. More significant is the fact that 'Heavenly face' can refer to the mother herself. The child must be seeing a divinity in the face of the mother who bends over him, and by now the mother is undoubtedly smiling at the image of the divine content she can trace in the sweet babe's face. God returns to earth and shines forth in mother, child and all creation.

Bloom rightly complains about the 'supposedly inevitable movement from "Wept for thee for me for all" to "Smiles on thee on me on all." '[11] For though we can retrace the steps that have led the mother back to vision, we feel that something has been left out. She has moved too quickly from Christ the man of sorrows to Christ victorious. 'Beguiles,' the poem's last word, begins to arouse our suspicion. Might it not mean 'tricks, deceives' rather than 'charms away,' the sense we gave to it in stanzas 3 and 4? Though the mother seems to return to an eternal present, we are left with a disquieting sense that the moment is fragile, transitory. We know that in Christianity 'the joy symbolized by Christ is victorious over his meaning as the man of sorrows,'[12] and that the tense shift from 'Wept' to 'Smiles' indicates the mother's participation in that victory. But we cannot fully dismiss thoughts of future suffering and loss.

The designs, discussed in the opening chapter, feed our suspicions.

The problems posed by the concluding stanzas of 'A Cradle Song' suggest a range of possible responses to the loss of vision. If we admit our doubts and suspicions, then we can relate the mother to characters in other songs whose fears and needs cause them to close their eyes to suffering and retreat from the present moment. The design on the second plate may be Blake's hint that characters of this sort tend to become repressive figures. If we accept the shift from tears to smiles as a genuine restoration of vision, then the mother's response anticipates the triumph of the 'weary traveller' in 'Night.' It is also possible that the mother shares our doubts and suspicions. The word 'beguiles' may signal her own lack of trust in the permanence of vision. It resembles the last line of 'Infant Joy,' where hopes and fears are indistinguishable.

In 'Nurse's Song,' which we shall examine next, the speaker's response to the passing of a moment of insight is resigned and accepting. It seems to confirm our doubts about the authenticity of the mother's return to vision by implying that adults can expect no more than isolated glimpses of unity and inter-relation. Like other less extreme or pessimistic responses to vision's loss, it too has been hinted at in the concluding stanzas of 'A Cradle Song.'

'Nurse's Song'

We begin with a moment of complete harmony and inter-relation. Though the nurse refers to an objective reality 'out there' on the green and the hill, we can trace its contours in the description she gives of her own state of mind. When she says that 'everything else is still,' she may be referring either to the landscape (silent now save for the children's voices and laughter) or to her own 'heart' (or 'mind') which, though it hears the children, is also 'at rest.' The nurse, like the world around her, is 'at rest' and 'silent' because the day is ending, but also because the joyful sounds of her children assure her they are safe and happy. That the children's merriment is 'heard' not 'seen' hints at the nurse's calm. The guardian is as free of care as the guarded, and both seem to unite with all creation. In 'A Cradle Song,' a similar impression of unity and inter-relation was accented by the rhythms and repetitions of lullaby. Here the rhythms are more child-like. We are reminded of nursery rhymes such as 'Jack and Jill' or, more appropriately, 'Boys and girls come out to play,/The moon does shine as bright as day.'[13]

But the moment lasts only for a single stanza. The nurse is soon beset by anxieties that destroy the intense sympathy and peace she feels. In the stillness of line 4 and the space between stanzas she seems to have 'lapsed' into adult reflection. The sun is going down, she thinks to herself, and the 'dews of night' will soon be here with their threat of chill. (We are reminded of the dangers faced by the little boy lost as he wanders 'wet with dew' through fen and marsh.) Her sense of time past and time future blinds her to the reality of the present moment and causes her to impose her fears upon it. When she tells the children that 'the sun is gone down/And the dews of night arise,' she is no longer in touch with the world. Though birds fly above her and sheep cover the surrounding hills, she does not see them. Anxiety, not night, has blocked them out.

'Self-will,' writes Susannah Wesley, 'is the root of all sin and misery, so whatever cherishes this in children insures their after-wretchedness and irreligion; whatever checks and mortifies it promotes their future happiness and piety.'[14] Blake's attack on views of this sort begins with careful observation. Though there may be a touch of child-like egotism and calculation in the children's initial response to the nurse ('No no let us play' gently mocks 'Come come leave off play'), it would be wrong to call them wilful. They 'cannot [not will not] go to sleep'[15] because their energy and delight are still very much alive. We see this in their language. The directness and vivid clarity of a line like 'Besides in the sky the little birds fly' reminds us of 'Spring,' perhaps the most high-spirited of the Songs. The children are at one with what is being described, as in the lines 'Lark in sky' and 'Birds delight' from 'Spring.' Unhampered by anxieties born of the adult's reflective tendencies (darkness will bring dew and dew will bring chill), the children know (by being fully in touch with themselves and the world around them) that 'it is yet day.' They feel the daytime still within them ('we cannot go to sleep') and the arguments they adduce in support of their instincts – the birds are still in the sky and the sheep on the hills – do themselves demonstrate how awake they are. Hazlitt too has noticed this quality in children, in his essay 'On the Feeling of Immortality in Youth': 'Like a clown at a fair,' he writes, of being a child, 'we are full of amazement and rapture, and have no thoughts of going home, or that it will soon be night. We know our existence only from external objects, and we measure it by them.'[16]

The nurse's response to the children's request is delicate and complex. She allows them to stay out and play, giving way, in Hirsch's words, 'both to the arguments of the children and their trust.'[17] Once roused from anxious reflection she looks about her and realizes that the light has not yet faded away and that the dews of night pose no immediate threat. In giving in, the nurse acknowledges that she has lost touch with the present moment. But the tone of her acquiescence is calm and distanced: 'Well well go and play till the light fades away/And then go home to bed.' The note of quiet resignation in these lines is disturbing, however. The nurse cannot forget that the trust the children are now expressing will someday be tested by experience. Her tone points to a time to come in which, as Bloom puts it, 'the voices of children are no longer heard on the green, and the heart ceases to rest in their laughter.'[18]

Though the children have taught her to see again, returned her to the present moment, the nurse remains apart. The vision she attained in stanza I returns for a flash in the poem's penultimate line, only to fade away again. Her description of the children – they are ecstatic because allowed to stay out a little later – participates in their delight. There is the same sharp, vivid clarity and energy in 'The little ones leaped and shouted and laughed' as we noted in the lines spoken by the children in the previous stanza. And the word 'ecchoed' in the poem's concluding line also seems to suggest the nurse's return to vision. It does itself echo, and, like the word 'still' in line 4, it identifies the nurse with 'all creation' by making the children's sounds echo in her mind as they echo from off the surrounding hills. But the final impression it makes is hardly one of contented harmony and inter-relation. Its three syllables seem to recede, suggesting that the nurse is moving away from present joys. Perhaps, like the old folk in 'The Ecchoing Green,' she hears an echo of her own lost innocence in the joy of the children. Our sense that the echoes are dying out is meant to suggest both the nurse's lapse into memory and reflection, and the coming of night. The two are equated, which makes the loss of vision seem inevitable – the nurse having no more power to prolong a moment of insight than she has over the sun's setting.

Though it does not end on an optimistic note, the poem is

1 Giovanni Bellini, *The Madonna of the Meadow*

2 From Blake's Notebook (*c.* 1793–*c.* 1818)

3 'The Tyger,' *Songs of Innocence and of Experience*. Copy U

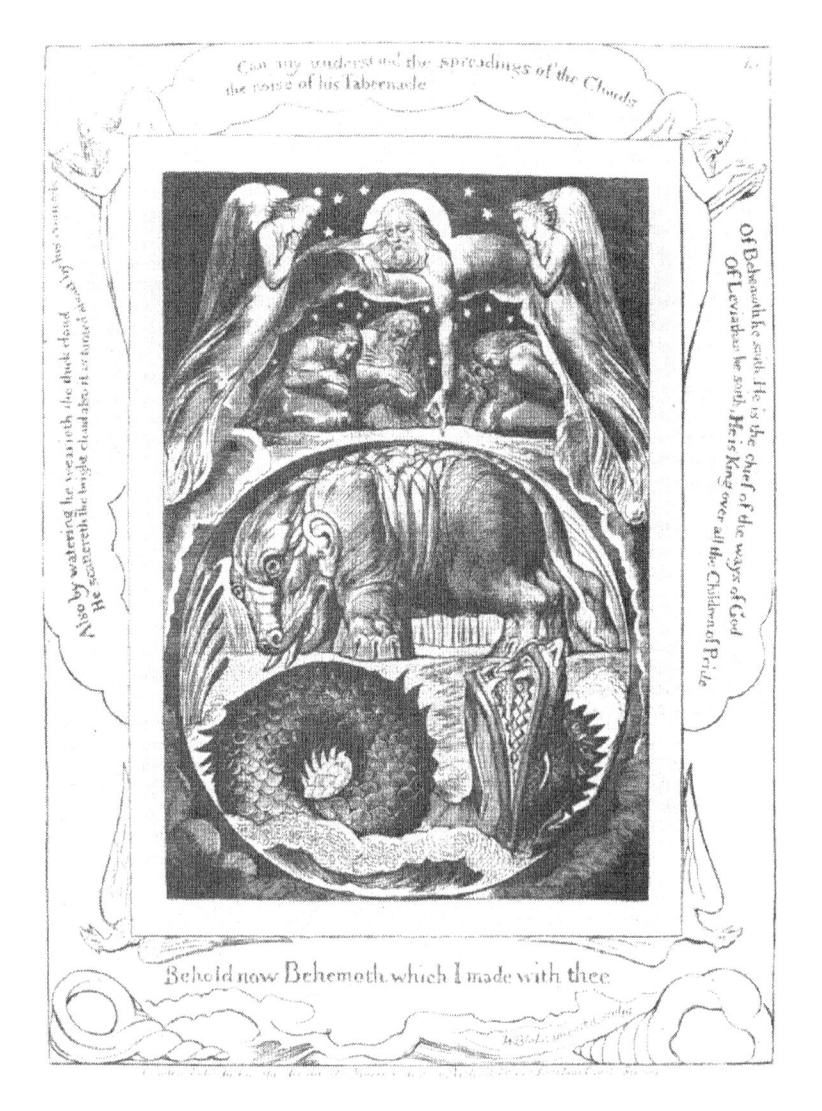

4 *The Book of Job: Behold now Behemoth which I made with thee*, line engraving, 1825

5 Blake's engraving of a Stothard illustration to Joseph Ritson, ed., *A Select Collection of English Songs* (1783), volume 2, plate 9

Here lads and laffes all repair,
And gather of this fruit fo fair ;
And thofe who gather moft will find
'Twill make them wife and feed the mind,
And five them from the birch behind.

6 Anon., *Mirth without Mischief* (c. 1780)

FABLES
IN
MONOSYLLABLES
BY
Mrs. TEACHWELL;
TO WHICH ARE ADDED

MORALS,
IN
DIALOGUES,
BETWEEN A

MOTHER and CHILDREN.

" Si la nature donne au cerveau d'un enfant, cette souplesse
" qui le rend propre à recevoir toutes fortes d'impressions ;
" c'est pour que toutes les idées qu'il peut concevoir, &
" qui lui sont utiles, toutes celles qui se rapportent à son
" bonheur, & doivent l'éclairer un jour sur ses devoirs, s'y
" tracent de bonne heure en caractères ineffaçables."
ROUSSEAU.

LONDON:
Printed and Sold by JOHN MARSHALL and Co. No. 4,
Aldermary Church Yard, in Bow-Lane.

Anne Elizabeth Whitbread
1788

The DOG.
(In Words of Four Letters.)

BOY.

I Love a dog.
Do not you?
MAMMA.
Yes sure.

7 Maternal care and instruction, from
   Lady Fenn, *Fables in Monosyllables*
   (1783)

8 Maternal care and instruction, from
   Lady Fenn, *Cobwebs to Catch Flies*
   (1783)

9 William Blake, *Christ in the Carpenter's Shop* (c. 1800)

10 William Hogarth, 'Evening,' plate 3 of *The Four Times of the Day* (the 1738 series)

11 Leonardo da Vinci, *The Virgin and Child with St Anne*

12 William Blake,
Illustrations to Young's
Night Thoughts
(*c.* 1795–7), Night IV,
page 5: no. 114

13 William Blake, *The Angel
of the Divine Presence
Clothing Adam and Eve*
(1803)

14 William Blake, *The Fall of Man* (1807)

15 William Blake, Illustrations to Gray's *Poems* (*c.* 1797–8), title-page to 'The Bard'

16 William Blake, *Age Teaching Youth* (*c.* 1785–90)

17 Jacques-Louis David, *Oath of the Horatii*, 1784 (Salon of 1785)

18 Jacques-Louis David, *Death of Socrates* (Salon of 1787)

19 Benjamin West, *Cleombrotus Ordered into Banishment by Leonidas II, King of Sparta* (1786)

Leaning against the pillars, & his disease rose from his skirts
Upon the Precipice he stood: ready to fall into Non-Entity.

Los was all astonishment & terror: he trembled sitting on the Stone
Of London: but the interiors of Albions fibres & nerves were hidden
From Los; astonishd he beheld only the petrified surfaces:
And saw his Furnaces in ruins, for Los is the Demon of the Furnaces;
He saw also the Four Points of Albion reversd inwards
Upon the valleys of Middlesex, Shouting loud for aid Divine.

In stern defiance came from Albions bosom Hand, Hyle, Koban,
Gwantok, Peachy, Brertun, Slaud, Huttn, Skofeld, Kox, Kotope
Bowen: Albions Sons: they bore him a golden couch into the porch
And on the Couch reposd his limbs, trembling from the bloody field.
Rearing their Druid Patriarchal rocky Temples around his limbs
(All things begin & end, in Albions Ancient Druid Rocky Shore.)

20 *Jerusalem*, Copy A, plate 46 (1804–20)

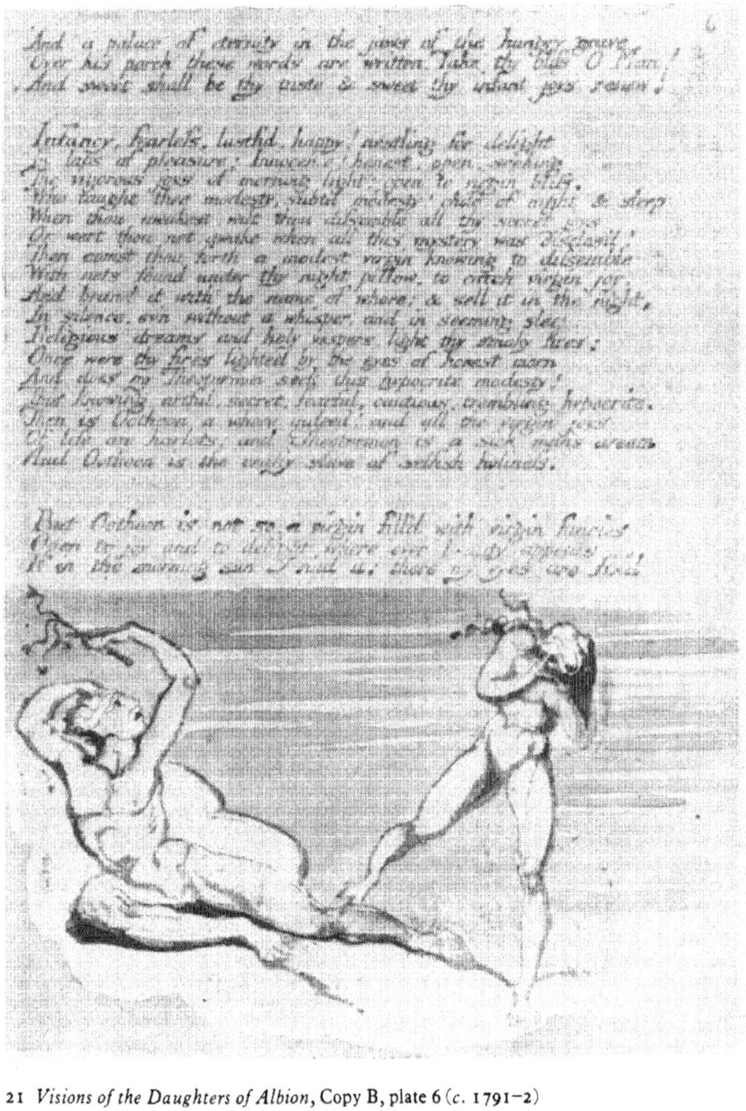

21 *Visions of the Daughters of Albion*, Copy B, plate 6 (*c*. 1791–2)

22 William Blake, Illustrations to Mary Wollstonecraft's *Original Stories from Real Life* (1791), plate 3, 'Indeed we are very happy! –,

23 William Blake, Illustrations to Mary Wollstonecraft's *Original Stories from Real Life* (1791), plate 1, 'Look what a fine morning it is. –'

Be calm, my child, remember that you must do all the good you can the present day.

Published by J. Johnson Sept. 1 1791

Oeconomy & Self-denial are necessary, in every station, to enable us to be generous.

Published by J. Johnson Sept. 1 1791

24 William Blake, Illustrations to Mary Wollstonecraft's *Original Stories from Real Life* (1791), plate 4, 'Be calm, my child, remember that you must do all the good you can the present day.'

25 William Blake, Illustrations to Mary Wollstonecraft's *Original Stories from Real Life* (1791), plate 6, 'Oeconomy & Self-denial are necessary, in every station, to enable us to be generous.'

hardly dark or depressing. The nurse, we must remember, is an exemplary guardian. Though sensitivity to children cannot return her to the life of vision she enjoyed in her own innocence, it can ensure that she will preserve and foster vision in others. She listens to the children and does not seek to impose upon them inflexible laws and prohibitions, nor does she demand immediate or mindless obedience. The children's spontaneity and close contact with the life around them does not frighten her or strike her as a rebuke, as it does the speaker of 'Holy Thursday.' She cherishes what beadle and wise guardian seek to repress. Like one of Chekhov's busy servants, she reminds us that we must do what we can, despite our awareness that loss and limitation are inevitable.

This is not an attitude we normally associate with the poet whose instinctive response to limitation was defiance ('less than All cannot satisfy Man,' Blake wrote in 1788, in the second of his two tracts entitled *There is No Natural Religion*), and who thought of his art as a means of ensuring 'That not one Moment of Time be lost' (*J* 75.8: E228). Though Blake would not have approved of the note of resignation in the nurse's tone, he saves his censure for characters who are incapacitated by their sense of loss and limitation. Thel, for example, laments the vulnerability of the infant worm, but does nothing to protect it. Though she sees that it is 'helpless and naked' (4.5: E5) and has 'none to cherish thee with mother's smiles' (4.6: E5), she allows it to remain exposed. When the Clod of Clay appears and immediately covers the Worm over 'In milky fondness' (4.9: E5), Thel's behaviour is made to seem selfish and indulgent. We reproach Thel, not for believing that children are 'born but to smile and fall' (1.7: E3), but for her indifference and self-absorption. The nurse shares Thel's belief that all things fade, but unlike Thel she behaves in a wholly admirable manner.

The shift of tense in the poem's concluding lines has bothered many critics.[19] It throws the action of the poem into an indefinite past, suggesting that 'When the voices of children are heard on the green' may not refer to the present moment, and that the dialogue in lines 5 to 14 may simply be the nurse's reconstruction. The structure of the plate reinforces this impression. The two branches of the tree on the left seem to encircle the text like the word-filled balloons cartoonists use to tell us what a character is saying or thinking.[20] That they branch out just above the nurse's head suggests that the top three-quarters of the plate constitute her thoughts. And when we take note of the book on the nurse's lap we may even consider the possibility that she is reading what we have just read, rather than day-dreaming it. An interpretation of this sort leads to dizzying complications. The nurse is shown sitting next to children playing merrily on a green. The sun seems to be setting and the green is bounded by hills. Once we imagine the nurse reflecting on an identical scene in some past time, we begin to feel as though we had entered a hall of mirrors.

The nurse's preoccupation with her own thoughts can be interpreted in several ways. Though we have taken it as a sign of her distance from the present moment, it also suggests that she is trustful and contented, like the children themselves. We are reminded of the design for 'The Lamb,' and the second plate of 'Spring,' where the complacency of the parent sheep suggests that guarded and guardian are united in trust. A similar ambiguity results when we attempt to place the nurse in relation to the dancing children: 'The children play their own game,' writes Erdman

> – not simply 'dancing merrily in a circle' (Keynes) but making a chain with their hands, led by two boys (the others alternately a girl and boy) to run under a kerchief held by a standing girl and boy – a version of 'London Bridge' perhaps, or 'Go in and out the windows.' Mary Lynn Johnson notes that the chain's opening near the nurse includes her in the visual circle.[21]

But *is* the nurse included in the circle? At first glance, the boy who leads the chain and stretches out his left arm, seems to be inviting the nurse to join in, but is she not too absorbed in her reading or her thoughts to notice the invitation? Even when we look more closely at the design, we are as likely to think the nurse excluded as included. If the children are playing 'London Bridge' or 'Go in and out the windows' then the boy who leads the chain points towards the kerchief, and the circle he is about to close will exclude the nurse. The design suggests that the nurse is both united with and apart from the children. The effect it has upon us is mixed, like that of the word 'ecchoed' in the poem's last line.

The green is enclosed in the foreground by two trees (an apple at left and a 'young elm'[22] at right) whose branches arch over it and seem to meet in the middle. Behind the low-lying hills the sky is lit a pale yellow, presumably because the sun is setting, though 'the shadows indicate high-noon.'[23] The absence of flowers, birds and lush foliage is a visual equivalent to the stillness remarked upon in the poem's first stanza. The empty, undifferentiated landscape (the sheep and birds the children speak of are nowhere to be seen) is vaguely disquieting, as in the title-page. Another ominous echo of the title-page is provided by the tree at the right, with its tightly encircling vine. These details help us to understand the nurse's tone in the poem's final stanza. When we look at the green and the empty hills behind it we cannot help but imagine the dangers they will hold once the light fades away. Nor can we prevent ourselves from associating the creeper-entwined tree at right with the several forms of constriction and encroachment to which the children will doubtless be subjected as they grow into experience. Like the nurse, we are forced to look beyond the graceful and energetic joy of the children at play.

Though the landscape at the bottom of the plate seems empty and undifferentiated, the marginal and inter-linear decoration of the text-block is filled with birds, tiny human figures, and swirls and curlicues of vegetation. At first we take its abundant and energetic life as a visual analogue to the exuberant delight of the children at play. But other, less pleasant associations are roused by the decoration. Erdman identifies the spiky green leaf above the 'S' of 'Song' and a leaf of similar color to the right of line four as acanthus. We last encountered leaves of this type on the plates of 'A Cradle Song,' where their unattractive shapes, together with the tangled and turbulent profusion of the surrounding decoration, struck us as ominous or threatening. A similar though less powerful impression is created by the decoration around the title and first stanza of this plate. The more we look at it, the more it resembles a 'jungle' or 'labyrinth,'[24] a visionary rendering of the nurse's premonitions of danger. Every thread of the poem's complex mood is woven into the text-block's decoration; even the calm sadness and resignation of the last stanza is figured in the delicately drooping branches of the weeping willow in the right margin.

We have seen this willow before. It appears on the second plate of 'The Little Black Boy,' where its melancholy presence in a supposedly Edenic setting has disturbing implications. To have it appear again on this plate may be Blake's way of suggesting a connection between the responses of nurse and black boy's mother to loss of vision. That it takes up only a part of the nurse's reflections, though, suggests that the mother's abandonment of vision for the precepts of Christian doctrine is but one of several possibilities for the nurse. At present, the nurse seems contented with the brief flashes of insight afforded her by contact with children. She accepts with quiet dignity the fact that she will never again lead a life of vision. 'The Little Black Boy,' on the other hand, shows us what happens when a character reaches conclusions similar to the nurse's but is unable to live with them.

'The Little Black Boy'

The teachings of the little black boy's mother suggest a deeply pessimistic response to life on earth. She shares with the nurse a belief that all things must pass away, that an adult's loss of a moment of vision or a child's loss of innocence is inevitable. But unlike the nurse, she bases her acceptance of loss and limitation on the promise of a heavenly reward. Though now we may be powerless to prevent suffering, we are only 'put on earth a little space.' Soon we shall be translated to a heaven in which all are united in God's love. Once our souls separate from our bodies, the mother believes, we will be free of loss and limitation.

'The Little Black Boy' offers a powerful but compassionate critique of the mother's teachings. Though it does not tell us how to regain vision, it gently discredits those who would have us look for an Eden beyond or outside this world. And by implying that the conventional Christian Heaven is a dangerous illusion, an 'allegorical abode' that perpetuates the suffering it was meant to counteract, it encourages us to seek true divinity on earth, in the behaviour of human beings.

In answer to – or perhaps in anticipation of – her son's queries about why his body is black when his soul is white, the mother tells him that God 'lives' in the sun, and that his love is transmitted to men through the sun's heat and light. Man is given a body because his soul cannot face a direct exposure to the heat of God's love. Only gradually does he 'learn to bear the beams of love.' That the bodies of mother and son are black suggests that they are much better able to receive God's love than is the pale English child.[25] But the implied superiority of black over white gives way in stanza 5 to a vision of eternity in which men's 'clouds' (that is, the bodies that protect 'like a shady grove' the more fragile souls within) 'will vanish.' Then black boy and white will come round God's golden tent and 'like lambs rejoice.' All will be equal in heaven, and there will be neither black nor white.

The mother's beliefs are hardly original: the image of the body as a cloud that shades the soul from light appears in both Plato and Dante, and the notion that earthly suffering is redeemed by divine favor can be related to the traditional doctrine of the 'fortunate fall.'[26] And just as traditional doctrine does not satisfy Blake, so the mother's explanations do not resolve her son's doubts. The black boy needs to know why there are color differences at all, and the mother's explanations avoid a direct answer to the question.

Wicksteed suggests that the mother's teachings reflect Blake's own point of view. Blake, it seems, is implying that black people are black because they have less vision than white people.[27] Though inferior, black people are nevertheless especially beloved by God because they protect those with greater visionary powers. But this is a difficult interpretation to accept. Not only does it legitimize slavery, which Blake hated, but it undervalues vision. Wicksteed's reading reduces vision to something like 'sensitivity,' when in fact Blake thought it the most valuable of all human and divine qualities. Man realizes God not through suffering and self-abnegating love, but through vision, and if the black boy has less vision than the English child, it is impossible for him to be closer to God's golden tent or better equipped to bear God's love. Those who accept Wicksteed's interpretation must place Blake alongside the anti-abolitionists of his day, men whose arguments are parodied in Bromion's speeches in *Visions* and then refuted and exposed by the enslaved Oothoon. If the black man is made to serve, it is not because of an inborn lack of vision, but because Urizenic forces have kept vision from him. The revolution of 'A Song of Liberty' will soon 'widen his forehead' (*MHH* 25: E43–4).

Other more explicit aspects of the mother's teachings distress us. Blake always distrusted those who denigrate the body ('When I from black and he from white cloud free') at the expense of the soul. In *Marriage* he tells us that 'Man has no Body distinct from his Soul for that called Body is a portion of Soul discernd by the five Senses' (4: E34); on page 5 of his illustrations to Night IV of Young's *Night Thoughts* (1797) (figure 12), he wittily depicts the soul's ascent as that of a naked body, and what Young's text calls 'this Mask of flesh' as mere clothing. And Bloom astutely points out that for Blake, 'to be free of the body's separation from the soul will not liberate us if the soul continues to be separate from the body.'[28] Also, if a black body is a consequence of bearing God's love, why should the black boy and his mother convey the impression that blackness is somehow not to be desired?

What the mother offers her son is hope. Though her answers are confused and inadequate, to condemn her for belief in the separation of body and soul (the doctrine of a corrupt church), and the establishment's interpretation of the black man's function (to protect the white child, to 'stand and stroke his silver hair,' and 'shade him from the heat'), would be as much a misreading of the poem as Wicksteed's unqualified endorsement of her teachings. We respond to the mother as we do to the advice of the elder sweep in 'The Chimney Sweeper.' Outrage and indignation are impossible given the pain and brutality of the sweep's life. We cannot strip from him the illusions he needs to make his life bearable, nor can we forget the potentially repressive consequences of Tom's pathetic dream of sweep-heaven or of the speaker's belief that 'if all do their duty, they need not fear harm.' In like manner, though we recognize that the mother's teachings are liable to make life easier for her son's master, we cannot condemn her. Sensing that her son is on the verge of losing his innocence, she wants to comfort and protect him against an experience that she feels will bring inevitable pain and suffering. She believes that nothing can be done to prevent his repression, and so she offers him the illusion that has sustained her. Instead of trying to transform the world through vision, she holds out the promise of a world to come.

The little black boy senses that the differences between himself and the English child have important and disturbing implications in experience: 'And I am black, but O! my soul is white,/White as an angel is the English child:/But I am black as if bereav'd of light.' The 'O!' is telling. It and the word 'bereav'd'[29] hint at the child's growing perception of his place in the world. Despite a belief that black skin signals God's great love, the child half realizes that it will bring him suffering, which is why we come away from the poem feeling that he wishes he were white.

Though comforted by what his mother says, the little black

boy's anxieties are never fully quieted. Perhaps he could not follow his mother's teachings? Perhaps he heard only the soothing sound of her voice? 'Having been instructed by confusion,' writes Bloom, 'the little black boy ends in that state. By his own logic he ought to say that the English boy will be like himself at the last, but instead he conveys the pathos of unfulfillable wish.'[30] The poem ends: 'And I'll stand and stroke his silver hair,/And be like him, and he will then love me.' The word 'then' in the last line does much to evoke in us the sympathetic response characteristic of *Innocence*. The mother's explanations – with their implied superiority of black over white – cannot wipe away the fears of his own inferiority that we have discovered in the words the child speaks in stanza 1. The superiority the little black boy has been taught to feel is eventually reasserted, but it has to compete with more deeply imbedded presentiments of inferiority. He is glad that, as his mother's arguments imply, he is God's favorite, but only because now the English child (who is white both inside and out, and who, one assumes, has not shown love for the black boy in the past) will learn to love him. The mother has only partly reassured her son; he still has fears of his own inferiority, and as experience advances – as we move from the end of the poem to the scene at the bottom of the second plate – he will find them substantiated.

The child's 'cloud' remains in copy Z. The black boy in the design on the second plate has been tinted a darker color than the English child and Christ.[31] Christ is thoroughly absorbed in the white boy – as the white boy is in him. The white boy is leaning 'upon our father's knee,' but the black boy is excluded and stands off to the side of the two figures. His right arm is extended and touches the white child's shoulder as if tentatively asking, or pathetically pretending, to be included in the spiritual and physical contact the others enjoy. Whether or not he is stroking the white boy's hair, as Erdman suggests,[32] Blake has managed to capture in the illustration all the pathos of the word 'then' in the poem's last line. Also, if the black boy's raised arm is an attempt to shade the white boy until he can bear to 'lean in joy upon our father's knee,' it is unnecessary, for the child is already there. If anyone is 'shading,' it is the white boy, who is keeping the light of God from the black boy by standing between the black boy and Christ.

Though it is true that the curve of the willow encloses the

three figures and unites them, once we look more closely at the design we realize that Blake has carefully separated the black boy from the two other figures. The line of Christ's staff or crook, for instance, is perfectly paralleled by the line of the white boy's body as he leans against Christ's knees, and the perpendicular angles of the seated Christ are echoed in the bent and outstretched arms of the praying white boy. The black boy, on the other hand, stands stiff, straight and apart – his sense of separateness mirrored in what I believe to be the troubled expression on his face.[33] There is a reason, then, for the picture or illustration to come after the poem rather than before it. The drawing is a continuation of the poem; it presents a context in which the black boy's doubts and fears, and the inadequacy of the mother's explanations, are given meaning. It marks the end of the child's innocence.

The black boy's mother has protected him up to this point. On the first plate, the child is able to raise his hand to a time of 'joy in the noon day,' because he is nestled in the shade his mother provides. The mother's back is bent, and its curve corresponds to the curve of the tree, which provides yet more protection. The sturdiness of the tree unites it with trees on the first plate of 'The Ecchoing Green,' the first plate of 'Spring,' and on the 'Laughing Song' and 'The Lamb' plates. All serve a common function: with their rich vegetation and thick trunks they provide ample protection for mothers, children and innocent, joyful play.[34] One loop of a vine swirls loosely around the tree, but unless one has seen other copies of the plate it is very difficult to identify in copy Z. Perhaps Blake took less trouble over it because he had already decided to strip all vegetation from the smaller tree at right whose branches arch over the rising sun. This tree provides a note sufficiently disquieting to balance the security of the scene at left. It also anticipates the willow of the second plate by arching over God the sun just as the willow arches over Christ. Its unpleasantly bare and withered appearance stays in our mind after we have turned the page.

The rising sun, with its fiery magenta radiance, is associated with God by the black boy's mother, but it can also be viewed as a sign of the passing of time. Already its beams stretch across the landscape, and soon, as the sun continues to rise, the rays will spread and bathe the hills, valleys and rivers in light, making them fully visible. It is characteristic of the most securely innocent scenes that they be enclosed, and when the distant landscape is fully in view it usually hints at the coming of experience or reveals a mature world of experience. On the first plate of 'The Little Black Boy' what lies between the mother, the little black boy and the sun is a landscape similar to the one seen in the background of the title-page, in 'Nurse's Song,' and more frequently throughout *Experience*. Its empty expanses seem alien or threatening to human life. Landscapes of this sort provide a sharp contrast to the scenes portrayed in front of them – mother and child, happy, carefree, dancing children. The mother's comforting words notwithstanding, what we see in the sun is less an image of godliness than of impending doom, or 'that sulphur orb that lights the darksome day' (*FZ* 2.28.18: E312); it reminds us, in other words, that the dark landscape will soon be revealed with the coming of the morning, the passing of time. Experience lies hidden in the background of the plate, and will soon force itself upon the little boy – even as he points eagerly to a time when the 'beams of love' will burn most fiercely.[35] The innocent vision is about to be lost, and again, as in the text, we are made to think of its loss as inevitable.

Yet the first plate of the poem remains rooted in Innocence, despite the lack of enclosure, the darkness, and the background landscape. The protective tree and the protective curve of the mother's back which enable the black boy to reach out with confidence (just as tree and mother enable a white child to reach out on the first plate of 'Spring') are not the plate's only grace notes. Innocence is also evoked in the border vegetation beneath the illustration. Although sapling and vine form a rather conservative border for the left side of the plate (they remind Erdman of the vegetative arch on 'The Lamb' plate),[36] the sprigs and branchings around the title and the squiggles and curves of the right border suggest a life and energy of the sort pictured on the 'Laughing Song' or the first plate of 'The Ecchoing Green.' At the space between stanzas 3 and 4 one sprig has begun to move among the words themselves. Though the bottom of the page is bordered by a dull green reminiscent of the landscape in the illustration,[37] swirling across it to connect with sapling and vine (and perfectly enclose the text) is a single spiralling growth. The presence of a tiny bird soaring with outstretched wings amongst the vegetation at the right is also characteristic of *Innocence*.

The black boy's fears and doubts are not fully realized until the second plate, where experience displaces innocence. The drooping willow[38] that bends Christ's back resembles no other sheltering tree in *Innocence*, but is found in the designs for 'Tirzah,' 'A Poison Tree,' and 'The Angel.' Though a traditional symbol of Christ (because, among other things, it 'gives away' its shoots and regrows them infinitely, like the sun with its rays), the tree, like *Experience* itself, seems to cage rather than protect, making men crouch instead of standing in a healthy, upright and assertive posture. What vegetation it has is drooping and sickly. The presence of roots is also disquieting. No other tree in *Innocence* has roots, but they are to be found in the 'Holy Thursday' of *Experience* and 'The Fly.' For Blake, the root is associated with repression.[39] Furthest from the leaves, branches and fruit of the tree, it moves downwards into the earth like a frightened secret. In 'The Little Black Boy' the roots (barely visible, if at all, in early copies; even those, like *In*.F, in which the black boy retains his color) are characteristically unpleasant. They creep like fingers over the grassy mound on which the tree rests, and, taken together, they form a claw. Erdman suggests that we compare this tree to the beautiful weeping birch of plate 7 of *America*, presumably because of the superficial resemblance in the curve and droop of branch and vegetation.[40] No two trees could be more different.

The river or stream that flows along the bottom of the plate is, again, unlike any other in *Innocence*. It is muddy and boggy, like that in 'The Clod and the Pebble,' a Song of Experience. It looks as if it had been 'mudded with feet of beasts' (*VDA* 2.19: E45) – probably those Oothoon mentions in *Visions* and Blake shows us in 'The Clod and the Pebble.' All the other streams and rivers in *Innocence* are clear. Nor is there any enclosure for the central grouping of Christ and children. Behind them we see empty stretches of landscape, and the bleak, undifferentiated blue-grey of the sky.

Details of this sort suggest that the picture the black boy's mother paints of Heaven is an illusion. The only true setting for her God is a world of experience. Even Wicksteed places the three figures on earth, taking special note of Christ's bared left foot. He claims that Christ has been drawn to earth by the loving tenderness and humility of the black boy,[41] but like Hirsch (who claims that the scene is set in a genuine Heaven),[42] he fails to comment on the more distressing aspects of the design, one of which is the physical appearance of the Christ figure himself.

If plate 2 presents us with a world of experience, then the figure of Christ must be given special attention. Is he to be implicated in the painful loss of innocence suffered by the black boy? Like the white boy, he seems oblivious to the black boy's presence. If this is the Christ who treats all men equally, the Christ the mother talks of, then why does he focus all his attention on the white child? This Christ is seen nowhere else in *Innocence*.[43] Only in 'The Little Black Boy' does Blake present us with a traditional Christ complete with beard and halo. A similar figure does appear, though, in 'The Little Vagabond,' a Song of Experience. He is 'God like a father,' not Christ, but it is only age – his long white Urizenic beard – that distinguishes him from the little black boy's 'father.' Hunched and kneeling, he draws a naked youth into the cave-like curve of his body.

Figures of this sort are perversions of true gods. Crouched, bent or weary forms rarely represent divinity or nobility.[44] Blake's Christ-like figures stand in *Innocence*: the Piper on the frontispiece is strong and erect; the shepherd, though at ease, is attentive and upright; and the child-shepherd in 'The Lamb' resembles both shepherd and Piper. In 'The Little Black Boy' not only is Christ's back bent over with weariness, but he lacks the sinewy muscles and bright healthiness which the other Christ figures possess. His robe ('usually uncoloured or White'[45]) is palest purple; his beard and his hair are straggly and droop like the vegetation on the drooping tree behind him. Hair like this, according to Hazlitt, writing of Coleridge's appearance on the occasion of their first meeting, 'is peculiar to enthusiasts ... and is traditionally inseparable (though of a different colour) from the pictures of Christ. It ought to belong, as a character, to all who preach *Christ Crucified*, and Coleridge was at that time one of those!'[46] Then there is the expression on Christ's face: tired and saddened, and possessing none of the calm benevolence and omniscient passivity of Blake's 'symbolic' pipers and shepherds. This, we begin to realize, is 'Creeping Jesus' (*The Everlasting Gospel*, 59: E511), the Christ not of Innocence but of Experience – a world where the traditional Christian virtues of Mercy, Pity, Peace and Love are transmogrified into pious-seeming parodies of themselves. This is the Christ of the church, of institutionalized religion. The men who create mandatory church attendance for the London poor in 'Holy Thursday,' and profess themselves Christians even as they construct a social system that has room for the sweep and the slave – these are the men who have created and who worship this Christ.

In its infancy the church opposed the pictorial representation of Christ.[47] The emphasis, as in the Gospels themselves, was on Christ's word not his image, and it was not until the fifth century, according to the art historian Arnold Hauser, that the church ceased to view depictions of Christ as dangerous lapses into idolatry. Hauser attributes this change to the reconciliation of church and state,[48] as does Northrop Frye, who believes that established authorities tend inevitably to create and worship idols and icons.[49] Once sacred art is officially sanctioned, it becomes subject to the authority and magistracy of the church. 'The sovereign interests of the faith are atthe matter,'[50] Jacques Maritain reminds us. When pictorial representations of Christ fail to conform to theological specifications, they must be censored or banned. Artists begin to depict Christ in accordance with the teachings of the church: He becomes a specific man in history, acquiring a set of well-known, easily identifiable characteristics.

The figures we see on the frontispiece, 'The Shepherd' and 'The Lamb' plates are images of Christ in men on earth. 'I am not a God afar off,' announces the Savior on plate 4 of *Jerusalem*, 'I am a brother and friend;/Within your bosoms I reside, and you reside in me' (18: E145). The bearded and weary Jesus of the second plate of 'The Little Black Boy,' in this and other late copies, is a particular man in history. He is a product of the church's insistence on a literal reading of Scripture – the man Jesus of Nazareth, the Christ of a dead past and a promised future. Centuries of tradition make it impossible for us to mistake his identity. He might easily preside over a Last Supper or deliver the Sermon on the Mount, like countless similar figures in Renaissance depictions of scenes from the Gospels. He differs from Blake's symbolic pipers and shepherds in that his appearance implies a divinity long since departed from earth. We are reminded of the Christ who 'once,' in some distant past, 'wept' for the mother of 'A Cradle Song,' and who enters her mind at the precise moment when she ceases to live in an eternal present. To believe in such a Savior, as the little black boy's mother does, one must have abandoned all hope of present divinity, or of a life of vision.

By revealing the confusions and potential dangers of the mother's teachings, 'The Little Black Boy' points the reader away from a false Christ. If we wish to find divinity, we must look for it in the here and now, in the child's loving trust and the mother's protective impulse. To search through a dead past or look towards a distant future is to pursue an illusion.

By exposing the mother's Christ Blake strikes a blow against forces that restrict vision. The control and assurance with which he does so implies that vision can be prolonged and maintained, that the loss of an illusion of this sort is a step towards the earth's transformation. But it is only a first step. In 'The Little Black Boy,' Blake attacks the notion that God creates and presides over a world of inevitable loss: nevertheless, though He may be an illusion, we are still left with the world as 'Vale of Tears.' We sense Blake's confidence and control, but we are not quite sure where it comes from. 'Infant Joy,' the Song we shall look at next, moves us closer to an answer by implying that the world of inevitable fading, of 'smile and fall' (*Thel* 1.7:E3), is itself an illusion. To free ourselves from it we must cease dividing time into past, present and future. Once we begin to see time whole, there can be no loss.

'Infant Joy'

In 'Infant Joy' we overhear a mother's imaginary conversation with her two-day-old child. The words we attribute to the child are projections of the mother's feelings, but since the child inspires those feelings, it is not wholly accurate to call their 'conversation' imaginary. The child speaks the first two lines and the mother responds in the third. The child then answers the mother's 'What shall I call thee?' in line 3 by declaring, 'I happy am/Joy is my name.' In the line that follows, the mother asks that 'Sweet joy befall' her child, perhaps because she is secretly worried that it may not. We are reminded of 'A Cradle Song' and 'Nurse's Song.' 'Experience' (or a sense of time and consequence) has begun to cast its shadow over the adult participant in an innocent scene. In the next line, though, the mother is returned to the present moment. Her child's radiant joy ('Pretty joy!/Sweet joy but two days old') dispels the gloom cast by thoughts of the future. As in 'Nurse's Song,' 'everything else is still' for the mother except for her sense of how attractive the child's joy is. Because the mother is so much at one with her baby, lines 7 and 8 resemble the spontaneous and unselfconscious exclamations of a child.

In line 9, however, the mother begins to drift back to

Experience. 'Sweet joy I call thee,' is not another exclamation like 'Pretty joy,' but a conclusion drawn from the two previous lines. 'I call thee sweet joy,' the mother is saying, 'because you are a "Pretty joy," a "Sweet joy but two days old." ' Though she still feels joyful herself, the intensity of the previous lines seems to have ebbed. Her words subtly suggest a return to an adult's way of seeing, and when she speaks of the child in line 9, a slight distance separates her from it. The difference between the lines 'Pretty joy!' and 'Thou dost smile' is that in the former no distinction can be made between the child's joy and what the mother feels, while in the latter, subject and object, 'Thou' and 'I,' are separated. When the mother says, 'I sing the while,' in the poem's penultimate line, we feel that her singing is as much a gesture of maternal protection as it is an expression of her own joy. The mother sings a lullaby to her child so that nothing will disturb its calm happiness. This is also what lies behind the closing refrain. Though the mother's song is 'Sweet joy befall thee,' which implies the return of adult anxieties, her singing is earnest of a determination to see that it will. This is why John Holloway believes that the mother's 'call for joy to "befall" her baby ... will not, in all likelihood, be empty.'[51]

But Holloway's reading seems to assume that the mother will always be there. It ignores the delicate suggestions of inevitable loss and separation that lie hidden beneath the mother's immediate joy, linking her to the speakers in 'A Cradle Song' and 'Nurse's Song.' The poem 'Infant Joy,' when taken alone, provides little assurance that the moment of unity a mother experiences with her child (and with all creation) can be prolonged or maintained. Once again, time is the enemy. It is only when the design is taken into consideration – and we no longer think of time in conventional terms – that the poem ceases to strike us as an isolated glimpse of divinity never again to be recaptured.

Two flowers, either anemones or parrot tulips,[52] dominate the design. The larger of the two has opened to form a huge carmine or scarlet blossom over the text, while the smaller droops, unopened, down the right margin. Both flowers come from the same plant and are supported by long, delicate stems bearing spiky, flame-like leaves. They completely enclose the text, framing or setting it off rather than constricting or stifling it. A similar frame is created by the large opened blossom. Its bright petals form a cradle for mother, child and winged figure, and, as in several other plates, the protective curve of the mother's back is reproduced by the outline of the flower in which she sits. Enclosures of this sort reinforce our sense that the poem's world is one in which innocents are shielded from danger or threat. The marginal character of the deep blue sky at the top of the plate creates a similar impression. The blossom seems to have crowded it out of the central scene, much as the text-tree does on the second plate of 'Night.'

The larger of the two flowers is an emblem of birth, and the flower at right suggests, simultaneously, a time before birth (it is a bud) and, because it droops so feebly, the decay of age. We can 'read' the design from right to left, with the bud becoming a blossom; or from left to right, with the blossom drooping into age. The vegetation traces the whole cycle of generation. The scene within the blossom itself also conflates past, present and future. The golden glow, halo and hands 'raised in awe'[53] of the winged figure to the right of mother and child suggest either angelic delight at Christ's birth, or (as Keynes and Hagstrum suggest) the Angel Gabriel.[54] But the more closely we look at it, the more problematic its identity becomes. If it is an angel of the sort found in scenes of Annunciation or Nativity, why are its wings short and spotted, like those of a butterfly? And why are they unlike the wings found on angels or angelic spirits on the 'Divine Image,' 'The Blossom,' 'Night,' and 'Spring' plates? Irene Chayes answers these questions by identifying the figure as Psyche: 'The wings, the hair, the suggested "Greek" line of the profile are all so faithful to traditional representations that the figure was surely intended to be recognized and to contribute her associations to the total meaning of the poem.'[55] Nor is this Blake's only depiction of the goddess. Chayes's article reproduces an engraving Blake made of Psyche after a design by his friend Cumberland. The figure on the 'Infant Joy' plate resembles not only Cumberland's Psyche, but other Psyches drawn by Fuseli and the illustrators of Jacob Bryant's *Mythology*, with which we know Blake was familiar.

Once we accept the figure as Psyche, our interpretation of other aspects of the scene within the blossom begins to change. Perhaps the figure's arms are less 'raised in awe,' than 'bent at the elbow and slightly raised, as though waiting for something to be put into them'?[56] Perhaps the child is about to be taken out of the care of its mother, in which case the scene depicts the Infant Joy's growth into what Erdman calls 'intellectual vision'[57]

(Psyche being associated with 'mind,' as in Keats)? Or, if one remembers the 'ardor' of Apuleius' Psyche, which we know Blake had read,[58] then the scene may imply a growth into sexual as well as intellectual awakening. Chayes points to the figure's hands and 'their stiffly spread fingers terminating in sharp points – points which visually rhyme with the pointed leaves of the anemone plant and the flame-like petals of the blossom.'[59] But Psyche is most famous as a symbol of metamorphosis and resurrection. Perhaps she is meant to translate the child into a heavenly realm beyond earthly existence? Halo and golden glow imply divinity, and the contrast between the earthly green worn by the mother and Psyche's heavenly gown of yellow-gold, is one Blake makes on 'The Blossom' and 'Divine Image' plates as well.

The ambiguous identity of the Angel-Psyche figure prevents us from limiting the scene within the blossom to any single phase of the life-cycle. Conception, birth, growth into maturity, death, and resurrection are all suggested. The design 'illuminates' the imaginary dialogue of mother and child by allowing the reader to see the mother's fears of inevitable loss as parts of a larger benevolent picture. The divinity of all phases of the life-cycle is suggested by the golden glow that surrounds mother, child, and angel. A similar impression is created by the decorative vegetation. The relation of blossom to drooping bud seems to confirm the mother's anxieties by suggesting that the beauty and fullness of the moment will not last. But once we view past, present, and future as parts of a larger design (the text's vegetative frame) we begin to realize that life itself is beautiful and benevolent ('protects' the poem it frames).

The design for 'The Blossom' uses similar techniques to make something of the same point.[60] The overarching flame-plant that extends up the right side of 'The Blossom' is Blake's attempt to envisage the energy instinct in all vegetation, and, by extension, in all material reality – to give form to the life-force Yeats saw in the chestnut-tree of 'Among School Children,' but which he could locate in neither leaf, blossom, nor bole. Though more energetic and sensuous than the two flowers of 'Infant Joy,' it is at least as beautiful. The enclosure it forms around the words frames them or sets them off, like more realistic decorative vegetation in *Innocence*, and its relation to the text strikes us as protective rather than threatening, despite its flame-like appearance.

Seven tiny human figures (six of them winged) cavort among the branchings above the poem's title. If read clockwise, they trace the life-cycle. The central winged and haloed madonna is dressed in a green robe in most copies[61] and we associate her with the world of generation. She is the 'Mother of my Mortal part,' providing comfort and protection but also posing a threat of restriction. The infant she cradles in her bosom is almost totally obscured in her embrace ('sulking,' no doubt, upon her breast, like the defeated child-speaker of 'Infant Sorrow'), and, as Wagenknecht points out, she faces 'against the direction of the circular process.'[62] Immediately to the left of the madonna a winged child seems to be reading from a book.[63] Still under the mother's influence, he is not yet free to join in the sports of the two somewhat larger, and probably older, figures above him. He reminds us of the two children on the title-page to *Innocence* who read from a book on their mother's lap. Though no longer helplessly restricted by swaddlings or mother's embraces, they too are clearly subject to adult authority. Above the infant with the book two figures fly towards each other, one with outstretched arms of joyful greeting, the other, perhaps, gesturing towards the madonna and child.[64] They are on the point of their first embrace, which encourages us to see them as a less mature version of the figures to their right. The wingless child at the far right is both the offspring of the embracing couple above the madonna – the tiny figures tracing the generative impulse or life-force from infancy to maturity to new birth – and the child of the flame-plant itself (the lines of his body mimicking those of the plant).

The wingless child points to the continuity of flame-plant and life-cycle and encourages us to see all seven figures as the flame-plant's offspring or 'flower.' Past, present and future again combine to form a single larger design. Blake's hope is that once we see time whole, we will no longer fall prey to thoughts of past and future. If we can return to a perpetual present, vision will again be ours.

The designs to 'Infant Joy' and 'The Blossom' imply that loss of vision need not be an inevitable result of time's passage, but neither shows us how to apply this knowledge to our own lives. As for the poems, 'Infant Joy' has a note of hidden anxiety that prevents us from attributing the design's wisdom to the mother, while in 'The Blossom' neither sparrow nor robin seems capable of altering its relation to the world.

Though the designs show us where we should be, neither they nor their poems show us how to get there. What we are looking for is another adult (aside from the Piper) who sees and understands the loss and separation entailed in time's passage and yet retains a sense of the unity and benevolence of all creation – whose vision survives the seemingly inevitable forces that overcome the speakers in previous poems. To find him, we must turn to 'Night,' the last Song we shall consider in this chapter, and one of the most complex and beautiful of Blake's creations.

'Night'

Despite a darkness lit by the supernatural glow of 'angels bright,' the world created in the first three stanzas of 'Night' is much like that of 'The Ecchoing Green' or 'The Shepherd.' All creation is united and at peace; all activity brings joy and delight; threat and danger are excluded by benevolent protectors. In stanza I the speaker tells us how the sun, the evening star, the birds and the moon have reached their proper night-time stations. He then informs us, 'a little tendentiously,'[65] that he too, like the birds, must seek out a nest. Speaker is likened to bird, moon to flower; the multiple inter-relations and identities recall the day-time stanzas that open 'The Ecchoing Green.'

But what sets the opening stanza of 'Night' apart from its day-time counterparts is its striking rhythmic structure. In place of the bright and skipping anapests of 'The Ecchoing Green,' each stanza of 'Night' opens with a ballad quatrain, modulates into three lines of iamb followed by anapest (though the feminine endings of 16 of the 24 lines involved might, it could be argued, force us to enjamb and assimilate the final syllable to the next line, making it anapestic), and concludes with a line of double anapests. 'The repeated alteration from stanza to stanza,' writes Alicia Ostriker, 'produces a sensation of hovering between waking and dreaming,' an effect that resembles the opening stanzas of 'A Cradle Song.' The four opening lines of the stanza form independent clauses that balance each other, while the four concluding lines move 'in a soft continuous flow of one sentence.'[66] We are made to glide along with the lines, effortlessly absorbing what they tell us. The gentle persuasive power of the poem's rhythms not only marks the differences between day-time joys and the softer, quieter joys of night, but helps us weave the more distressing aspects of the poem into a broader, more comprehensive understanding.

In stanza 2 we learn that the previous day was also suffused with delights. The speaker bids adieu to a world of healthy, life-giving 'green fields and happy groves,' before introducing the unseen angels whose silent ministry seems to ensure a continuation of delight ('joy without ceasing') and protection ('blessing'). That the angels tend both animate and inanimate nature ('bud,' 'blossom,' 'bosom') reinforces the impression of unity and inter-relation created in the first stanza. While poems like 'The Little Boy Lost/Found' take advantage of the conventional associations of night with danger or menace, the opening stanzas of 'Night' depict a world in which innocence thrives both day and night.

The angels' activities, described in stanza 3, are no different from those of natural guardians such as shepherds, nurses or mothers. Their soothing, calming influence comes over creation silently and imperceptibly, like night itself. The creatures visited by the angels are kept from harm because they are made to sleep in their nests and caves; 'weeping' is dissolved by a potion no more magical than the sleep night itself induces. By transforming night's influence into a vision of angels busily ministering to and protecting creation, the speaker implies the divinity of the natural realm. This is why angels who are 'unseen' can also be 'bright.' They are bright because the virtues they embody are divine; invisible because it is night and because those virtues are natural rather than supernatural.

Our half-conscious sense that the angels are the speaker's way of imagining night prepares us, to some extent, for their powerlessness in stanza 4. They can only 'pitying stand and weep,' merely 'seeking' to drive away the destructive thirst of wolves and tigers, because there are times when the weariness night induces is simply overpowered by the beasts' hunger. 'Night' makes no attempt to explain away or deny suffering. Like the rest of Blake's *Innocence*, it is neither other-worldly nor free from harm. That sheep are sometimes devoured by hungry wolves and tigers is a fact of life. It is also a fact that little boys find themselves alone at night in dangerous fens and bogs, or that grown men (like the speaker of 'Holy Thursday') are frightened by the exuberance of children and seek to repress and regiment them. Because the angels of 'Night' belong to the natural realm, their protective powers are limited, like those of human guardians such as the black boy's mother, the elder sweep, or the mother who weeps tears of pity over her sleeping child in the fifth stanza of 'A Cradle Song.'

As the speaker seeks out his nest, his meditations upon the night move from a sense of calm and soothing benevolence (the activities of the angels in stanzas 1 to 3) to an acknowledgment of danger and suffering. In light of previous poems we expect him to lapse from vision, but his tone remains unmoved. The initial mood of calm acceptance lives on in stanza 4, and we feel that night's soothing influence prevents him from becoming frightened or despairing. The second half of stanza 4, in which we discover the angels' influence still at work, even after they are shown to be incapable of preventing the dreadful rush of ravenous wild beasts, is the speaker's unconscious translation of his mood into vision. Though the angels are ineffectual, the speaker is himself still subject to the soothing spell of night, which is why he continues to speak of the angels, its visionary form, as 'most heedful.' He has no clear understanding of how their benevolent protection works (there is something shadowy about the way the angels 'Receive each mild spirit,/ New worlds to inherit'), but he still feels its presence. Though the night's traditional associations of loss and danger are well-founded, the speaker retains his innocent vision.

The heaven we encounter in stanza 5 is also part of the speaker's attempt to give visionary form to the mood night inspires in him. At first glance, the picture he presents us with is conventional – a lion lies down with a lamb. But the lion's eyes are 'ruddy,' and his tears (said to be 'of gold' for the same reason 'unseen' angels are said to be 'bright,' because they are instinct with the divinity of innocent virtues) are hard to account for. Perhaps they are attributable to the terrible fate suffered by the 'mild spirits' in the previous stanza? Or to the lion's sense of shame over his own participation in their savaging? If he can only weep 'there,' in a heavenly 'new world,' he must have behaved quite differently on earth. When in the next stanza the lion says, 'And now beside thee bleating lamb,/I can lie down and sleep,' the word 'now' carries the force of 'at last,' as though the lion's true feelings were distinct from the savagery of his earthly instincts. But what is especially interesting about the opening lines of stanza 5 is our sense that the lion's tears are not simply tears of remorse. He seems also to be crying out of pity for those 'mild spirits' already received into the heavenly fold.

Heaven, it seems, is a place of tears. The ruddy-eyed lion listening with pity to the lambs' tender cries reminds us of the weeping mother in stanza 5 of 'A Cradle Song.' Both are moved by a complex of powerful emotions the most prominent of which is a sense of the fragility of innocence. This is a perfectly natural response from a natural protector, but not from someone who lives in heaven. According to the lion, heaven is a place from which both 'wrath' and 'sickness' have been driven away. Why, then, do the 'tender cries' of sheep and lambs arouse his pity? And what is there to guard against? Is heaven a place of dangers as well as tears? When the lion describes Christ we are struck by the powers he singles out for praise; 'meekness' and 'health' will drive away 'wrath' and 'sickness.' These are the traditional attributes of Christ on earth, as embodied in the innocence of human figures like the child in 'The Lamb' or the adolescents on the second page of 'The Ecchoing Green.' The lion's savior bears little relation to traditional depictions of Christ triumphant or transcendent.

In stanza 6 the lion lies down beside the bleating lamb or is led by thoughts of Christ to 'grase after' it and 'weep.' His tears are for Christ as well as for the lamb – for the Christ who is a lamb. But the thought of Christ also moves the lion to 'grase after' the lamb, the immanent Christ being shepherd as well as lamb. We recall 'A Cradle Song,' where a mother cries with pity for the Christ whose lamb-like innocence is figured in her child's face, while Christ (shepherd to his flock) cries with pity over her. We also note that, though the lion is in heaven, he must content himself with mere thoughts of Christ. He sees Christ as he would see Him on earth, in the innocence of the lambs whose fold he guards. Nor can we help feeling, despite the allusion to Revelations, that the river of life in which the lion washes is earthly. To at least one other reader, 'Blake makes it very plain by the phrase "wash'd in lifes river" that ... the lion is not "out of nature." '[67] Though 'very plain' is somewhat too emphatic, by the time we reach the poem's concluding lines the lion has already been firmly associated with the innocent virtues of earthly figures from other Songs. To be washed in life's river is to have cared for and embraced life, to bring to it all that is implied in the line, 'Grase after thee and weep.' This is what makes the lion's mane 'shine like the gold.'

The poem's two final stanzas describe a heaven, but in

Gillham's words, 'Thoughts of God and Heaven are such that they turn innocent attention to the present moment.' The speaker's 'new worlds' are alive with the innocent virtues we value on earth: 'Even when heaven is thought of as a place where the dead go, they are translated in order to continue the enjoyment of their energies. They do not go there to receive a reward but in order to continue to fulfil obligations that are felt in this life.'[68] 'Night' only *seems* to be saying that this world must be transcended in order for the innocent vision to triumph. What it actually suggests is quite the opposite: we must look here on earth for our angels and heavens. Without knowing it, this is what the speaker in 'Night' does when he gives voice to his visions of an angel-studded darkness and a heavenly 'immortal day.'

The poem's designs reveal a similar discrepancy between surface appearance and reality. Both present a night-time scene, but the design on the first plate encourages us to find peace and security in the night through the influence of supernatural agents, while the second encourages us to see the virtues of those agents as natural. The ambiguities of the designs (is the lion on the first plate 'natural' or is he the lion who lies down with the lamb? are the five female figures on the second plate angelic or human?) prevent us not only from lapsing into an easy acceptance of an other-worldly heaven, but also from denying that there is something heavenly or divine in the innocent virtues of this world.

The design on the first plate of 'Night' is especially beautiful. The soothing rhythms of the text find their complement in a tall, slender tree whose trunk forms a right border for the text and then gently arches its branches across the top from right to left before curving up and back to cradle the title. The branches of the tree encircle 'Night' as loosely as the tree itself is encircled by a delicately spiralling vine. The soft flow of tree, branch and vine is extended by the flowing script of the title. The overarching protective tree is a motif that reinforces our sense, gained from stanzas 1 to 3, that 'Night' is also a part of Innocence.

A similar protective tree can be traced along the left side of the text, curving from left to right across the top of the poem. The right border is natural, the left supernatural. It is composed of brightly-lit, golden figures, some winged, others not, who stretch from the bottom of the plate up to the last lines of the first stanza. The gold of these figures is also found in four small stars and a tiny golden globe (the sun descending in the west) directly above the topmost angel, whose wings and arms are extended. This angel and the one below it seem to be reaching upwards. Their brightly-gowned bodies describe delicate curves, spiralling upwards like tree and vine, and encouraging us to look towards the top of the plate where we will find the 'angelic' brightness of the four stars and tiny moon. Nor does our eye stop here. Instead it continues over to the right, picking up the gold of the large oval moon that backs the title, the first of two small angels, sitting on a branch, and then the second, just above and to its right; a memory, perhaps, of that earliest of visions on Peckham Rye, 'a tree filled with angels, bright angelic wings bespangling every bough like stars.'[69]

Left and right borders contrast two forms of protective benevolence, anticipating the larger contrast of plates 1 and 2. Yet three small angels are woven into the natural border to the right of the text, and there is nothing particularly supernatural about the stars and sun at the top of the left-hand border, or the tiny round disc (a 'natural' moon without the golden glow of the larger moon behind the title) beside four more stars just by the feet of the second-highest angel.

Details of this sort complicate but do not invalidate the contrast between natural and supernatural. They are similar to the ambiguities that result from attempts to account for the golden lion sleeping at the bottom right of plate 1, or the golden text-block that seems to push the dark night sky to the plate's outskirts, softening it into a pale blue. The lion sleeps or rests in a cave-like green mound that curves over him, reminding us of other protective enclosures in *Innocence*. In copy Z it is impossible to tell whether the lion's eyes are closed, but it is clear that he is lying down rather than 'crouching' or about to spring, as Keynes suggests.[70] We can attribute the lion's peaceful rest to the protection afforded him by the cave and to the fact that, because it is night, he has quite naturally gone to sleep. (Blake forgets that cats are nocturnal hunters.) But his calm security may also be attributable to the tiny winged creature who hovers above him, presumably illustrating the lines of the third stanza just to its right.

A similar dilemma is posed by the lion's golden mane. Perhaps the charm cast by the angel not only calmed the lion but also lit it with a golden glow of divinity, in which case it belongs to the divine or supernatural realm. Yet a lion's mane is naturally gold, particularly if it has a stream or river in which to bathe, as this one does. Also, with the moon shining down upon it, the lion will light up naturally. So too with the text's golden glow: either it is lit by an other-worldly divinity like that of the surrounding angels, or by the natural light of a golden moon that, 'like a flower,' hovers among the branches of the tree at the top of the plate.

But what we notice first is the other-worldly brightness of the design. Supernatural aspects predominate, as in the text. (We only begin to question the angels in stanza 4.) This is the reverse of the impression created by the much darker second plate. In plate 1 the text is lit with gold, in plate 2 the background is mostly blue with a pale wash of yellow suggesting moonlight. The sky above and to the right of the text is a deep, dark blue studded with three white stars (not gold) such as we see scattered across an equally dark sky in 'Earth's Answer' in *Experience*. In place of the light delicacy of the slender tree on the right of plate 1 we are shown the right half of a much darker and rougher (more earthly?) tree that forms a left border for the text. We can just make out three figures, presumably angels, standing in the forks formed by tree-trunk and branches. At first they seem part of the tree itself. Though lighter than the rest of the trunk, they are nowhere near as bright as their counterparts on the first plate.

The five female figures strolling on the enclosed green below the text are much more human than the angels on the previous plate. They lack wings, their robes are only dimly touched with yellow-gold, and though their haloes are 'conspicuous,'[71] they are nowhere near as radiant as those of the angels on the first plate. Our initial impression is of young women out for a stroll, and only when we look more closely do we think they might be angels.[72] Their ease recalls the figures who lounge to the right of the sheltering oak on the first plate of 'The Ecchoing Green.' We are tempted to attribute their freedom from night-time fears to the protection afforded by the large sheltering tree and the low hedge that enclose the green. Blake takes care to match the speaker's vision of heaven with a design much less other-worldly than the one accompanying his vision of an earthly night. As in the text, the earthly is divine, the divine earthly.

If the weary traveller of 'Night' and the Piper who has created and illuminated *Innocence* can withstand the limited and limiting habits of mind that drag the speakers of 'A Cradle Song,' 'Nurse's Song,' 'The Little Black Boy,' and 'Infant Joy' away from a world of unity and benevolence, so too can we. Vision *can* be retained and prolonged. But the forces that restrict us, even in the sheltered world of the nursery and the green, are extremely powerful and deceptive. The Piper shows us the way in *Innocence* – teasing and coaxing us out of any merely passive understanding, forcing us to exercise our own imaginative powers – but soon, in *Experience*, we shall be on our own. Just as the child in the cloud vanishes when the Piper takes on a new way of seeing and speaking, so the Piper disappears once we begin to exercise our own visionary powers. The subtle and disturbing implications of the Piper's transformation into Bard immensely complicate our task. Though we have but newly acquired our capacity to attain and maintain vision, *Experience* quickly puts it to the test.

CHAPTER 5
ENTERING *EXPERIENCE*

I have taught the thief a secret path into the house of the just
I have taught pale artifice to spread his nets upon the
  morning
My heavens are brass my earth is iron my moon a clod of
  clay
My sun a pestilence burning at noon & a vapour of death in
  night

What is the price of Experience do men buy it for a song
Or wisdom for a dance in the street? No it is bought with
  the price
Of all that a man hath his house his wife his children
Wisdom is sold in the desolate market where none come to
  buy
And in the witherd field where the farmer ploughs for bread
  in vain

(*FZ* 3.35.7–15: E318)

Experience opens with four plates which form a narrative bridge
between the two volumes of *Songs*. The 'story' they tell is that of
the Piper's transformation into Bard. Getting this story right,
understanding the true nature of the Bard's character and
dilemma as it unfolds over the first four plates, is of utmost
importance to any reading both of *Experience* and of *Songs* as a
whole; much more so, I would argue, than speculation about
changes in Blake's attitudes and ideas between 1789 and 1794 (a

matter of considerable dispute)[1] or about his gradually evolving myth or system. That Blake changed is not in doubt: I simply think it best (and most in the spirit of this study, and of what it takes to be Blake at his best), to move from the text to the change, rather than from the change to the text. Once we have discussed the story and its larger implications, especially those which affect our reading of subsequent plates, we shall turn to several key poetic and pictorial motifs introduced in the opening sequence. The reader, it is assumed, moves directly from *Innocence* to *Experience*.

The frontispiece to *Experience* is dominated by figures we have seen before. Or at least we think we have. A child and a young man occupy the center of a pastoral scene, where sheep graze peacefully in the background. At first we identify these figures with the Piper and the child on the innocent frontispiece. But there are important differences. The Piper, now in green rather than pink, has lost his pipe. The child has sprouted wings and, in copy Z, a halo.[2] In the earlier frontispiece the Piper looks over his left shoulder at the child floating above him. The curves of his body echo the entwining trees on his left. The child's outstretched arms and legs suggest freedom and movement. The Piper's right arm and the pipe itself complement the diagonals of the child's body and the branchings of the background enclosure. In *Experience*, on the other hand, the shapes created by the arms of the shepherd-youth and the arms, legs, and wings of the child who sits squarely on his head are perfectly symmetrical. The graceful movement of curves and diagonals has been replaced by perpendicular angles and geometric forms.

Both child and shepherd-youth stare straight ahead. Gone is the human contact of the earlier frontispiece. Hagstrum calls the expression on the shepherd's face 'disturbed.'[3] To me it looks 'transfixed,' eerily calm and single-minded, as if charmed or spellbound. Neither he nor the child seem to be looking *at* anything, even us.[4] Though physically much closer to the child, the shepherd can no longer see him. If he could, though, as in the innocent frontispiece, would it still be a *human* child – the child of 'Piping down the vallies wild' – he was looking at? Were we wrong, we begin to wonder, to identify these figures with their innocent counterparts? What precisely is their relation to the earlier figures?

The title-page provides us with something of an answer. Two children, a boy and a girl, mourn the death of what we take to be their parents.[5] They remind us immediately of the similar, though younger and smaller, children who gather round their mother's or nurse's lap on the title-page to *Innocence*. Time has passed, the design seems to imply, and the children of the innocent title-page have grown into experience. Loss, isolation, and sorrow characterize their state. We return to the frontispiece, imagining a comparable passage of time. In *Innocence*, the figures on the frontispiece were identified by the first poem in the volume, 'Introduction.' When we turn to its experienced counterpart, 'Hear the voice of the Bard,' we cannot help but associate Bard with youthful shepherd. The Piper of *Innocence*, we realize, has grown into a Bard. Hence the absence of a pipe. He too, like the children of the title-page, has stepped into experience. His advanced foot, and the direction in which he faces, suggests that he is 'leaving behind him the flocks of Innocence.'[6] Hagstrum interprets the tiny patch of blue in the lower left corner of the plate as 'a suggestion of water' marking 'the frontier of Experience.'[7] Like the children of the experienced title-page, the Piper-Bard is in a new and more vulnerable position, having moved 'even further out of the sheltering woods.'[8]

Though the experienced 'Introduction' says nothing of the winged child, he too, presumably, is to be associated with a similar figure on the innocent frontispiece. How then do we account not only for the changes in his appearance but for his new and more intimate relation to the Piper-Bard? Erdman, Mitchell, and Hagstrum see the shepherd figure as a St Christopher, a 'Christ-bearer' who carries the child of Innocence (and all he stands for) into the world of Experience.[9] The Piper turned Bard, having embraced the truths of Innocence, becomes the child's helper and companion. In Grant's words, he 'accepts the perils of an activist creative life.'[10] That the child is no longer at a distance from him, as in the innocent frontispiece, is a sign of his commitment. Its wings and halo signal his realization, gradually acquired through an attempt in *Innocence* to enter into the child's world and way of seeing, that 'He who would see the Divinity must see him in his children.'

Why, then, does the frontispiece disturb us? Because in his urgency to proclaim the child's divinity, the Bard seems to have lost sight of its humanity. By giving it wings and a halo, he makes it look like an icon or totem. Man's god-like nature no longer emanates from an unmistakably human form, but from the iconic paraphernalia of religious tradition. What has happened, I believe, is that in his passage from innocence to experience, from Piper to Bard, the youthful shepherd has made a kind of religion out of the truths of innocence.[11] His prophetic 'message,' though wholly laudable, is subtly undermined by the manner in which he proclaims it: the winged child-god, image of man's divine potential, no longer looks human. A similar change is mirrored in the Bard's own face; its inwardness and impassivity suggest other-worldliness, the inhuman certainty and single-mindedness of prophet or seer.

The Bard's task, we learn from the experienced 'Introduction,' is to summon man to a realization of the divinity of his creative power and potentiality. The frontispiece shows him setting out on that task. His appearance, though, is disturbing, like that of the child he carries on his head, especially when we remember the divinely human children of *Innocence*, the little boy of 'The Lamb' plate, for instance, or the sleeping child in 'A Cradle Song.' Our uneasiness, though less intense, is of a piece with Earth's in 'Earth's Answer.' 'Introduction,' notwithstanding what I believe to be the Bard's good intentions, only feeds it. Our difficulties begin in line 3 with

> the Holy Word
> That walked among the ancient trees.
> Calling the lapsed Soul
> And weeping in the evening dew.

These lines, according to Frye, refer to Jesus, not Jehovah.[12] Blake has *Paradise Lost* in mind rather than Genesis 3:8, for like Milton (and 'all the anti-Nicene Fathers from Justin Martyr through Arius'),[13] he takes John 1:3 as proof that the Word, God's agent, is the Son, begotten before the Fall. In Genesis, moreover, Jehovah enters the Garden to punish Adam and Eve 'in the cool of the day' rather than 'in the evening dew,' nor is there any mention of his weeping, a distinctly Christ-like activity connoting sympathy and pity. Gillham also points to the note of regret in the Holy Word's voice, hardly a Jehovah-like quality.[14]

Yet still we think of Genesis. Though Frye's interpretation is attractive, especially in view of Blake's larger 'system,' it accounts for only some of our difficulties. Leavis's well-known reading is worth bearing in mind at this point:

'Present, past, & Future' suggests Fates, Wierds, or Norns – suggests, in fact, anything but a distinctly Christian sense of Time and Destiny. So that when the 'Holy Word' comes it enters into a strongly non-Christian context of associations, the total effect being something that (it might be said) is neither Christian nor pagan. The 'ancient trees' among which the 'Holy Word' walks, are, growing though they may in the Garden, Druid and are immediately evocative of a religious awe.[15]

Though this reading may indeed be based on ignorance not only of Blake's 'system' but of his views on the Druids,[16] its account of the poem's 'context of associations' strikes me as especially acute and perceptive. It also strikes me as an apt description of the effect the frontispiece has upon us. Though Blake's subtle departures from Genesis support Frye's reading, they never quite erase our initial picture of the Holy Word as a remote and mysterious presence rather than as Christ, especially if we move directly from *Innocence* to *Experience*. A presence of this sort is more in keeping with the stern, punishing God of Genesis 3:8, or with what Bateson calls 'the negative morality of the Decalogue,'[17] than it is with the Christ of the Miltonic or Christian version of the expulsion. Though the Bard's instinctive goodness (an inheritance from *Innocence*) makes him soften the qualities of the traditional Old Testament divinity – allows him to see Jesus-like qualities in the Holy Word – the message he accepts and helps to transmit is perilously close to that of a false God. When Gillham tells us that Blake 'is most interested in the God the Bard can utter,' we readily agree. What troubles us, though, is his claim that that God 'is known by the nature of man, the Divine virtues which yearn towards one another.'[18]

Frye and his followers, on the basis of Blake's practice elsewhere, simply assume that his vision of Genesis 3:8 would be the same as Milton's.[19] But on at least one occasion Blake depicted the Holy Word in the Garden as God the Father rather than as the Son. The tall, white-bearded and white-gowned divinity who dominates his 1803 watercolor of *The Angel of the Divine Presence Clothing Adam and Eve with Skins* (figure 13), is clearly a type of the stern tyrant God of Genesis 3:8. This 'Angel,' according to Damon, 'may take the form of an angel of light (II Cor. 9:14), and is often mistaken for God.'[20] In reality, though, he is Satan, as in Blake's second illustration to *Job*. To worship 'King Jehovah' (the Hebrew name Blake gives to the figure he calls 'The Angel of the Divine Presence' in the *Laocoön* plate (E455); the divinity who created the body, law, and hell) is to be a disciple of Satan. Jehovah or the Angel, writes Blake to Thomas Butts, 'cloth(ed) Adam and Eve with coats of skin.'[21] We might also note that the Angel of the 1803 watercolor wears an expression of sadness and pity rather than anger. Though weeping and regret are, as Frye suggests, Christ-like qualities, Blake frequently associates them, as does Earth in 'Earth's Answer,' with the false God Urizen or Nobodaddy, King Jehovah's prototype.

In other explicit treatments of the Fall matters are more complicated. The 1807 *Fall of Man* (figure 14) shows Christ leading Adam and Eve out of the Garden, but places King Jehovah above them in a position of control. Then there are related but less direct episodes: in 'My Spectre around me night and day,' a Notebook lyric of *c.* 1804, for example, we find the following exchange between a domineering and untrustworthy male voice, that of the 'Spectre,' and his suspicious and equally untrustworthy 'Emanation,' a female voice:

> [He] When wilt thou return and view
> My loves and them to life renew
> When wilt thou return and live
> When wilt thou pity as I forgive.
>
> [She] Never Never I return
> Still for Victory I burn
> Living thee alone Ill have
> And when dead Ill be thy Grave.
> (29–36: E467)

In the earlier *Book of Ahania* (1795), the eponymous heroine, Urizen's emanation, identifies her tyrannical lord in terms that even more clearly recall 'Earth's Answer':

> Cast out from thy lovely bosom:
> Cruel jealousy! Selfish fear!
> Self-destroying: how can delight
> Renew in these chains of darkness
> Where bones of beasts are strown
> On the bleak and snowy mountains

> Where bones from the birth are buried
> Before they see the light.
>
> (5.39–7: E88–9)

All of which is to say that arguments based on Blake's intentions, or on the authority of other works, must be approached with caution.

'Lapsed Soul' is no less troubling than 'Holy Word.' That 'Man has no Body distinct from his Soul' (*MHH*: E34) is as much as truth of *Innocence* as of *Marriage*. 'When man is raised,' writes Bloom of Blake's views on body and soul, 'he must be raised as a spiritual body, not as a consciousness excluded from energy and desire.'[22] That the Bard has begun to think otherwise is suggested not only by 'Introduction,' but by the appearance of the winged child on the frontispiece. Gone is the curving sensuality, freedom, and exuberance of the floating child of *Innocence*. Instead we find a divinity whose blank stillness suggests nothing so much as 'consciousness excluded from energy and desire.'[23] The Bard's dualism, moreover, goes hand in hand with what seems to be an equally orthodox attitude towards sin. Terms like 'lapsed' (we think immediately of Adam and Eve) and 'fallen light' (recalling Isaiah's 'How art thou fallen from Heaven. O Lucifer, son of the morning' (14:12)),[24] belong to a religious tradition in which energy and the awakening of the senses are thought of as evil. To the Piper, creator of such figures as the adolescents on the second plate of 'The Ecchoing Green,' or the sparrow of 'The Blossom,' they were virtues.

> Who it is
>
> That might controll
> The starry pole:
> And fallen fallen light renew

– whether Bard, Holy Word, or lapsed Soul – is, at first glance (and also, as we shall see, ultimately), impossible to tell. Whether the Bard or the Holy Word is the subject who calls and weeps in stanza 2, and cries out to Earth in stanzas 3 and 4, is equally uncertain. Later on we shall deal with the implications of confusions of this sort. For the moment we need only note that the Holy Word has become the Bard's inspiration, and that its message (whether reported or reiterated by his disciple) is as mixed in its implications as the winged child's appearance in the previous plate. Earth need only 'Arise' to free herself from the limits of 'floor' and 'shore.' But is the new 'morn' or 'break of day' about which the Bard-Holy Word speaks a metaphor for transcendence or transformation? To argue for the latter, which would place the Bard in company with the Piper, we must rely almost solely on our sense that the Bard is the Piper grown into experience. This we are encouraged to do, at least initially, by the designs. But then we must ignore lines like 'Arise from out the dewy grass,' and 'Rises from the slumberous mass,' which suggest a traditional Heaven above or after our world of body and matter (and so discourage us from reading 'Arise' as simply 'get up in the morning,' an innocent phrase like 'falling asleep' or 'falling ill'). This is harder to do; as hard, in fact, as it is to embrace the opposite extreme (i.e. to see the Bard as Earth's tyrannous, hypocritical 'Father of the ancient men'). That something is wrong with the Bard, from the perspective both of *Innocence* and of Blake's work as a whole, does not make him Urizen. He has become infected or corrupted in his passage from Innocence to Experience, but he is not, as we shall see, past redemption. Like Bloom, I should place him among Blake's 'Redeemed' rather than 'Reprobate' or 'Elect' classes.[25]

The term 'Bard' itself may offer us some clues to the Piper's new condition. The ancient Celtic Bards were minstrel-poets whose primary task was to compose and sing verses celebrating the achievements of chiefs and warriors. Their heroic narratives drew upon fact, legend, religious precept, law, genealogy, and prophecy in order, in Spenser's words, 'to set forward the praises and dispraises of men.'[26] In Blake's age, with its keen interest in native English alternatives to the heroes and legends of Greece and Rome, there was a good deal of poetry and prose written about Albion's ancient bards. Bards were thought of as prophetic artists of great antiquity and authority. Often they were associated with both Druid and Gothic cultures, since Dark and Middle Ages were frequently confused by those of Blake's contemporaries (Chatterton, Macpherson, and Smart, for example) most interested in promoting a native classicism.[27] 'The word "Druid," ' writes Frye of Blake's age, 'would be practically synonymous with "inspired bard" ';[28] hence young Wordsworth describing himself in *The Prelude* as 'a youthful Druid taught in shady groves/Primeval mysteries, a Bard elect.'[29]

Blake, of course, was no admirer of the Druids. Though on occasion he identifies them with an original, universal, pre-lapsarian culture of inspired 'Ancient Poets' ('All things Begin and End in Albion's Ancient Druid Rocky Shore' (*J* 27: E169)), the majority of his references are pejorative.[30] The Druids' history, like that of the Jews, was for Blake a type of the degeneration of poetic power or Divine Vision. Though at first they were 'naked civilized men, learned, studious, abstruse in thought and contemplation; naked, simple, plain in their acts and manners,' eventually they 'began to turn allegoric and mental signification into corporeal command' (*DC*: E533), transforming what were merely human creations, 'Fairies of Albion,' into 'Gods of the Heathen' (*FZ* 1.4.14: E397). Theirs is the story Blake tells in plate 11 of *Marriage*, one in which poets become priests and judges, and acts of creation are replaced by secret and restrictive practices, including human sacrifice.

Though Damon claims that Blake never shared his age's tendency to confuse Druids with Bards,[31] the evidence suggests otherwise. In plate 9 of *Milton*, for example, we are told how 'all Eden descended into Palamabron's tent/Among Albion's Druids and Bards, in the caves beneath Albion's/Death Couch' (1–3: E102). In *On Homers Poetry*, 'not Goths nor Monks' but the eponymous epic poet's works 'Desolate Europe with Wars' (E267), and in the accompanying design Blake depicts a Bard with harp standing under what Erdman identifies as an oak grove (oaks being sacred trees to the Druids). Also, in the eighth of his designs for Dante's *Inferno*, entitled 'Homer and the Ancient Poets,' Blake again associates epic poet as Bard (and war-monger) with Druid oak grove.[32] Finally, in *A Descriptive Catalogue*, Blake describes the following scene from his painting (now lost) of 'The Ancient Britons':

> The dead and the dying, Britons naked, mingled with Armed Romans, strew the field beneath. Among these the last of the Bards who were capable of attending war-like deeds, is seen falling, outstretched among the dead and the dying; singing to his harp in the pains of death.
>
> Distant among the mountains, are Druid Temples, similar to Stone Henge. The Sun sets behind the mountains, bloody with the day of battle.
>
> (E536)

This is not to suggest that Bards and Druids (in their degenerate state) were always the same for Blake. There is little Druid-like about the Bards of *The Song of Los* and the opening plates of *Milton* (though both sing to Eternals). Nor is it to suggest that the Bard of *Experience* is either a war-monger or an advocate of human sacrifice. It is only to point out that for Blake, as for his contemporaries, Bards were associated not only with antiquity, poetic high-seriousness, and prophecy, but with a Dark Age of religious and military barbarism. Even when Blake's Bards are at their most noble, they still carry with them disturbing and unpleasant associations, write with 'iron pens the words of truth' (*Samson*: E434). Though Blake's illustrations to Gray's *The Bard*, for example, go even further than the poem in identifying poets with true kings, they also make the Bard himself doubly violent and vengeful, elicit our sympathy for Eleanor and Edward (even while recalling their crimes), and cast doubt on the ultimate value of the poetry inspired by war-like Elizabeth. Blake also gives his Bard a long white beard and a starry gown, which makes him look like Jehovah or an Old Testament patriarch (figure 15).[33]

'Bard,' I am suggesting, was not, either to Blake or to his age, a neutral term, one whose associations were indistinguishable from those of, say, 'artist,' 'singer,' 'poet,' or 'minstrel.' Nor was its connection with secret religions and war-like cultures its only troubling association for Blake. Bards address nations not individuals. Their songs are stern and serious, containing messages so urgent that often they seem to stand out from the surrounding lines as if italicized. 'Mark well my words,' cries the Bard whose Song opens *Milton*, 'they are of your eternal salvation' (2.35: E96). Urgency of this sort, an insistent pointing of meaning, telling rather than singing, the assumption of authority – these, in part, are the qualities (and dangers) of prophetic verse; symptoms of the sort of thing Lawrence had in mind, in his essay on Poe, when he called Blake 'one of these ghastly, obscene "knowers." '[34]

Now the Bard of *Experience* is neither ghastly nor obscene (nor for that matter is Blake, even at his most 'prophetic'), but he is, like Lawrence himself (hence the vehemence of the epithets), a 'Knower.' Not always or unremittingly, but often. And as a knower, he is constantly in danger of violating the very principles and ideals which animate his outrage. The Bard is a prophet of the imagination. His object, like that of the Piper who once he was, is the liberation of man's divinely creative powers, of the 'Poetic Genius' within us all. The Bard's songs, like those of an Old Testament prophet, are works of social criticism; they speak of his age's brutal and tragically misguided suppression of divinely human potentiality. But they do so in bardic or prophetic terms – terms which slide all too easily into what they oppose. The Bard decries authority, yet speaks from it; has, like a prophet, 'heard the Word.' His songs lament the violation not of individuals, the 'minute particulars' of *Innocence*, but of 'the Individual.' Their outrage and compassion, though properly placed, are generalized, directed towards the nation, the culture, mankind. Often, as we shall see, they are expressed in the form of propositions, statements, assertions. Even when a song poses insoluble dilemmas ('The Clod and the Pebble,' for instance, or 'The Tyger'), the manner in which those dilemmas are posed – the sharp clarity of the alternatives they offer us – point to a prophetic or Bard-like certainty.

When prophetic habits conflict with visionary ends, the result for the reader is a disquiet similar in kind, if not in intensity, to that produced by the frontispiece. And this brings us to a central problem not only in our interpretation of *Songs*, but in any assessment of Blake's work as a whole. There are two Blakes: Blake the poet-artist, and Blake the bard-prophet; Blake the lover of the Psalms and the Song of Solomon, and Blake the disciple of Ezekiel and Isaiah; Blake-Los and Blake Los's creator. In *Jerusalem*, writes Leavis, Blake

> can represent Los, human creativity in the fallen human condition (for 'fallen' put 'rising'), as working creatively though unpossessed of any vision of an ultimate goal. But as prophetic poet with Swedenborg, Boehme, and Milton behind him, he can't help feeling that he must himself aspire to a clarity and certitude of such vision. Yet the idea of possessing an achieved knowledge of ultimate solutions and ultimate goals is not for poets or artists, or for those among us who, figured by Los, know that their business is to get the conscious and full human responsibility that the crisis of the human world calls for awakened and vindicated.[35]

Leavis's unfortunate association of Swedenborg, Boehme, and Milton ought not to distract us (though it is just the sort of thing he himself would pounce on in another context): the conflict he points to between poetic and prophetic modes is, in Blake's case at least, a real one. To say, for instance, as does Gillham, that Blake was 'not much interested in abstract statements, however much apparent truth they may contain,'[36] simply will not do. Blake loved the prophetic mode, a mode which tends towards aphorism and abstraction. Yet abstraction was his enemy. 'To generalize,' he generalizes, 'is to be an Idiot' (Annotation to Reynolds: E630).

That Blake himself was aware of this conflict, at least in the 1790s and 1800s, is clear not only from *Milton*, the literal subject of which is the betrayal (and ultimate regeneration) of poetic powers by prophetic indignation, or from his explicit reference to Urthona's spectre as a 'Spectre of Prophecy' in the concluding lines of *The Four Zoas* (9.138.6: E392), but from the following episode from plate 12 of the *Marriage*:

The prophets Isaiah and Ezekiel dined with me, and I asked them how they dared so roundly to assert that God spake to them; and whether they did not think at the time that they would be misunderstood, and so be the cause of imposition.

(E37)

The prophets answer these questions, if at all, only obliquely. Isaiah is the first to respond:

I saw no God, nor heard any, in a finite organical perception; but my senses discovered the infinite in everything, and as I was then persuaded, and remain confirmed, that the voice of honest indignation is the voice of God, I cared not for consequences but wrote.

(E38)

This is much like Blake's own 'Every honest man is a Prophet he utters his opinion both of private and of public matters Thus if you go on so, the result is so' (Annotations to Watson's *Apology for the Bible*: E606-7). But it skirts the question of 'imposition.' Ezekiel's response is somewhat more to the point, though also more disturbing:

The philosophy of the East taught the first principles of human perception; some nations held one principle for the origin and some another. We of Israel taught that the Poetic Genius (as you now call it) was the first principle, and all the others merely derivative – which was the cause of our despising the priests and philosophers of other countries, and prophesying that all gods would at last be proved to originate in ours and be the tributaries of the Poetic Genius. It was this that our great poet King David desired so fervently and invoked so pathetically, saying by this he conquers enemies and governs kingdoms. And we so loved our God, that we cursed in his name all the deities of surrounding nations, and asserted that they had rebelled; from these opinions the vulgar came to think that all nations would at last be subject to the Jews.

'This,' said he, 'like all firm persuasions, is come to pass, for all nations believe the Jews' code and worship the Jews' God, and what greater subjection can be?'

(E38)

Though Ezekiel may hope to avoid the sorts of mistakes his predecessors made in the name of 'true prophecy' (by which is meant the identification of God and Poetic Genius) *how* he plans to do so we never learn. All we are left with is a story of lamentable decline, one which only confirms those doubts which inspired Blake's original question. Prophecy leads to imposition; prophets become (or beget) priests; Moses the visionary and deliverer becomes Moses the law-giver.[37]

'I heard this with some wonder,' says Blake of Ezekiel's speech, 'and must confess my own conviction' (E38). Why 'must confess'? And what, precisely, made Blake 'wonder'? Might he not be registering something more than simple astonishment at Ezekiel's appearance? Might he not be feeling something of the same uneasiness Ezekiel's words rouse in us? That the question of prophetic imposition reappears in the work's penultimate 'Memorable Fancy' seems to suggest as much. After Blake-as-devil exchanges visions with his angelic antagonist in plates 17 to 20, the Angel complains to him that 'Thy phantasy has imposed upon me and thou oughtest to be ashamed,' to which Blake answers: 'We impose on one another, and it is but lost time to converse with you whose works are only Analytics' (E41). This exchange not only raises the same questions as do the opening lines of plate 12, but provides a similarly unsatisfactory answer. Blake-as-devil avoids an outright acknowledgment of imposition. We understand and sympathize with his 'honest indignation,' his sense that devilish imposition is trifling in comparison to the restrictions of Angelic or 'Analytic' imposition, but we still feel, if only for a moment, that the Angel has grounds for complaint. The Angel, it is true, deserves what he gets, and it *is* for his own good. Still, Blake-as-devil seems almost to gloat, in a manner like that of the sons and daughters of Luvah (in Night 9 of *The Four Zoas*), whose job, to tread down 'Human Grapes' in an apocalyptic 'Wine Press,' is also, disconcertingly, their delight (136.5–27: E389). And he *does* treat the angel roughly. When, therefore, the word 'Opposition' appears immediately following the Ezekiel passage at the end of plate 20, what we hear in it are traces of something other than 'true Friendship': 'imposition' too echoes within it. The righteous indignation of Blake-as-devil, in other words, like that of many a prophet (Ezekiel and Isaiah were frequently cited by prophetic radicals of Blake's day, in part because of their denunciations of kingly power), shades all too easily into the 'indignant self-righteousness' (*J* 1.7.73: E149) Los condemns in his spectrous self. Prophetic habits compromise visionary ends.

In *Songs*, though, Blake puts this conflict or contradiction to work, framing it, as we shall see, within the larger dramatic context of the Piper's growth into Bard, and the Bard's gradual realization of the dangers and deficiencies of the prophetic mode. It becomes his subject. *Songs* is, therefore, like so many of the great works of its period, autobiographical; another of Blake's several attempts to order and account for the conflicts and crises of his own life and art. The pattern or story it discloses is that of his mythic *alter ego*, Los, in *Urizen* and *The Four Zoas*: an artist becomes what he begets in the act of illuminating or defining – and so saving – a fallen world. In *Songs*, though, Blake brings to this story a self-knowledge only intermittently present (one thinks of the high-flown parodistic rhetoric, self-consciously 'Bardic,' of *Urizen* or bits of *Milton*) in the works which succeed it.

Yet even in *Songs* Blake is not always or everywhere in control of the conflict between poetic and prophetic impulse, and at times it breaks out in ways characteristic of later and less tightly organized books. 'The Divine Image' of *Innocence*, for example, asserts (a word whose awkwardness only underlines the sort of conflict I am discussing) the humanity of God's image; talks or tells us of it. At the same time, the 'Image' it depicts is, in Bloom's words, 'a monster of abstractions.'[38] At the very center of the poem, in stanza 3, lies a divinity with 'Mercy' for a heart, 'Pity' for a face, 'Love' for a body or form, and 'Peace' for a dress. Each of its attributes, the poem *tells* us, is 'human,' but the picture we are presented with, the image we try to construct, is not. Even if we think of 'Mercy,' 'Pity,' 'Peace,' and 'Love' as 'modes of the divine image and not its elements,'[39] the inhuman anatomy and appearance of the image remain in our mind. Not only does 'The Divine Image' teach us what rather than how to see, but its third stanza prevents us from creating the human God it 'insists,' with all the solemn certainty of a 'Knower,' is there. Though discrepancies of this sort are rare in *Innocence* (quite out of keeping with the Piper's character and function) they serve to remind us that the Bard's dilemma was also Blake's.

How, then, do the Bard's deficiencies become the subject of his Songs? If the Bard is to *Experience* as the Piper is to *Innocence*, then he is the creator of its Songs. *Innocence*, we remember, opened in 'Introduction,' with the Piper's report of an encounter with a floating child. The encounter took place some time before the poem was composed ('On a cloud I *saw* a child./And he laughing *said* to me'), and serves to explain the origin, purpose, and character of the Songs that follow. A similar encounter takes place at the beginning of *Experience*, though Blake spreads it over two poems, introducing it somewhat differently. We are in it, in 'Introduction,' before we know where we are. *When* the encounter took place (again, sometime in the past) we discover only at the beginning of 'Earth's Answer.' 'Earth rais'd up her head,' we realize, introduces the Bard's report of the lapsed Soul's reaction to his call. 'Introduction' turns out to have been the Bard's dramatic recreation of a past event, an event which explains the Songs that follow. For just as the Piper's initial song, his carefree piping, was altered (his 'Songs' inspired and shaped) by the encounter with the child, so Earth's reaction to the Bard's initial call not only provides us with the 'story' of *Experience*, but helps to explain the character of its Songs.

Songs of Experience is the Bard's attempt to come to terms with – to understand and account for – Earth's bitter and painful rejection of his call. It is also his answer to Earth's own call. If the Piper's Songs are a response to the floating child's 'Pipe a song about a Lamb,' *Experience* is the Bard's response to Earth's anguished 'Break this heavy chain.' The world the Bard depicts in the plates that follow is Earth's world, a world of manacles and chains, secret joys, selfish, cruel fathers, and thwarted virgins. By seeing through Earth's eyes, the Bard hopes not only to discover the forces that hold her down (or make her hold herself down) but to free her from them. Through prophetic wrath and insight the activist Bard hopes to dissolve mind-forged manacles. What he does not immediately realize, though, is that he himself is implicated in Earth's repression; that her initial, fearful rejection of his call was neither wholly groundless nor misguided. Only gradually does he learn that he too has been infected; that the intensity of his outrage and the fervour of his prophetic certainty have begun to make him sound much like the figures he most abhors. Like many a prophet, he is in danger of 'Generalizing Art and Science till Art and Science is lost' (*J* 38.54: E183). 'What is the price of Experience,' asks the epigraph to this chapter. 'All that a man hath.' As the Bard will discover, his has become a voice of Experience, despite the true divinity of its message and the justice of his indignation.

We, though, can sense this from the start. When Earth mistakes the Bard-Holy Word ('That walk'd among the ancient trees') for 'The Father of the ancient men,' we know exactly why she does so, even if we think her wrong. We even understand why she identifies it with 'Starry Jealousy,' since on the previous plate the cloud-couched poem itself (the Bard-Holy Word's 'call') emanates from a dark, star-studded sky – comes, that is, from Nobodaddy's or Jehovah's realm.[40] Erdman thinks the naked haloed figure lounging in front of the poem is male, the Holy Word in human form.[41] If he is right, our doubts deepen. Even if we think this figure female (and hence Earth), as do Keynes and Grant,[42] we still leave the plate associating the Bard-Holy Word's call to 'Arise' with a world 'up there' among clouds and stars. Our doubts are thus aroused by the design as well as the text.

The story, then, as it unfolds over the first four plates, describes two sorts of entry into experience. On the one hand, the Piper turned Bard steps forthrightly into Earth's dark vision. In this sense, he knows exactly what he is doing, knows what is wrong with the world he has entered, and sets out, by exposing its evils, to mend it. At the same time, though, and without knowing it, he enters into experience in quite a different sense: by falling into the very mental habits he seeks to expose in others. The Bard is like Los in *The Four Zoas*: 'terrified at the shapes/Enslaved humanity put on he became what he beheld,/ He became what he was doing he was himself transformd' (4.55.21–3: E331). To understand what Blake means by 'Experience,' therefore, we must look beyond the specific evils indicted by individual poems and designs to the manner in which those indictments are framed. How the Bard expresses himself will be as important to our understanding of *Experience* as what it is he has to say.

At this point, before moving beyond the opening sequence, we must turn to several key poetic and pictorial motifs not yet mentioned in our discussion of the Piper's growth into Bard. The first concerns the manner in which Earth describes her oppression, in particular the prominence she gives to its sexual dimension. Bateson believes Blake originally intended 'Earth's Answer' to follow a different poem. In 'Introduction,' he writes,

> Earth is not woman but 'the lapsed Soul,' i.e. Adam (or perhaps Adam and Eve), and the 'break of day' is not a sexual millenium but a political or religious one. And so the appeal 'O Earth, O Earth, return!', which is clearly addressed to mankind in general, really requires a different answer from the one it gets. A general issue is reduced to a particular one.[43]

This reading strikes me as unnecessarily (and uncharacteristically) narrow. Sexual shame or self-consciousness is Jehovah's first punishment in Genesis. Body itself becomes a badge of divine exclusion to Adam and Eve. When, therefore, Earth emphasizes the sexual nature of her wished-for liberation, subtly assimilating sexual and non-sexual (though still earthly) creativities (sowing and ploughing, the growth of buds and blossoms, the joys of spring), she is attacking a very large issue indeed – that of the exclusively transcendent nature of divinity, of fealty to Nobodaddy and all he stands for. Jehovah's opposition to earthly sexuality, his denigration of the body, of man's God-like power to bring forth life, is a symbolic dismissal and discrediting of all earthly creativity. Divinity or the creative power resides in God alone; that is what the guilt of our first parents – the eagerness, in Genesis, with which they cover their newly awakened bodies – is meant to signify.[44]

The disfiguring consequences of Jehovah's success become a recurrent theme in *Experience*. Again and again, in poems like 'The Sick Rose,' 'The Angel,' 'My Pretty Rose Tree,' and 'A Little Girl Lost,' we are shown precisely what happens when 'delight' is 'chained in night.' At the same time, though, whenever the Bard bodies forth Earth's objections to Starry Jealousy – takes up her outrage and indignation – he does so in terms which disturb us. Think, for instance, of 'The Clod and the Pebble,' the first of the plates to follow the opening sequence.

'The Clod and the Pebble' affects us in much the same way as do the two previous plates taken together. The clod presents us with views which seem at first glance to be instinct with innocent truth and virtue. These views are then immediately countered by a cynical, though not particularly embittered, voice of experience. In broad structural terms, the clod is to the Bard-Holy Word of 'Introduction' as the pebble is to Earth in 'Earth's Answer.' Once the pebble has had its say, we begin to question the wisdom of the clod, just as 'Earth's Answer' raised doubts about the Bard-Holy Word's call. We also begin to reconsider our identification of the clod's views with the virtues of innocence. Earth, in rejecting the Bard-Holy Word, was spurning a call she had ample reason to distrust. Similarly, in this poem, there is much about the clod and what it has to say, which subtly twists the innocent vision. Though at first we may think of the poem as describing 'the two states of *Innocence* and *Experience*, as expressed in unselfish and selfish love,'[45] or see 'the clod of three-fold vision' in contrast to 'the pebble of single vision,'[46] gradually we begin to wonder.

How, for instance, are we to reconcile the image of a totally yielding and pliable selflessness ('Trodden with the cattle's feet') with the impression of strength and assertiveness created by such figures in *Innocence* as the shepherd on 'The Shepherd' plate, the Piper and child on the innocent frontispiece, or the child on 'The Lamb' plate, all of whom are meant to embody innocent love? How can we forget the healthy sexuality of their bodies, our sense that they are not only capable of but made for physical pleasure and gratification? In *Innocence*, we remind ourselves, care and reverence for others went hand in hand with respect for, rather than denigration or denial of, one's humanity. As

Adams suggests, the clod's position 'tends towards what Blake would call the "religious" view. It leads to a rejection of sensual pleasure, perhaps to a desire for martyrdom.'[47] Though there are figures in *Innocence* whose love seems wholly selfless (the mothers in 'A Cradle Song' and 'Infant Joy,' for example), even they differ from the clod in important respects. Gillham is especially perceptive on this point: 'The liveliness of the speakers in the innocent songs,' he writes, 'is increased by their ability to participate wholeheartedly in the situation of the moment and to sympathize. This sort of self-forgetfulness leads to a heightening of individuality and not, as in the case of the clod, to a squashy plasticity.' The mother in 'A Cradle Song,' 'observes her child intently and is sensitive to the silent wind that blows between them; she is most perceptive and without dogmatism, but only because she is capable of active enjoyment.'[48]

It is this more complex vision of innocent love which the Bard seems to have forgotten, mistaking for it the sort of innocence found in the world of Har and Heva in *Tiriel*. For the Bard, the opposition of clod and pebble is one of innocence and experience. By setting it out as he does, he hopes to show how easily innocence is overcome by experience (the powerlessness of innocents being a recurrent theme in *Experience*). But the experienced perspective, we realize, is hardly restricted to the pebble's point of view. We can also see it in the way the Bard structures his poem; in what I have called the starkness or sharpness of the alternatives he offers us. The inadequacy of these alternatives is suggested by the design in the top half of the plate, where sheep (ram as well as ewe) and lambs stand side by side with cattle. Both species of animal drink from the brook, muddying its waters by treading upon the clods which form its banks. Innocence as well as experience, the design seems to suggest, belongs to the physical world; sheep too, the very symbols of innocence, must feed and drink. Though the clod, paradoxically, denies love its 'earthiness,' innocence, as the top half of the design (as well as *Innocence* itself) suggests, *includes* body, which is why sheep and cattle are placed together, and why both are shown drinking intently.[49]

The clod's view of a spiritual love without body is as inadequate as the pebble's breezy, soulless 'binding.' The Bard seems to have lost touch with the delicate unity of 'The Ecchoing Green' plates. He can no longer restrain himself from reaching after that 'eternal sunrise' which innocence only appears to offer. Instead, impelled by his new penchant for abstraction, he moves from one inadequate alternative to another. Once again, therefore, as in the two previous plates, the reader finds himself in a difficult position. He can neither accept the Bard's call in 'Introduction,' and his view of innocent love in 'The Clod and the Pebble,' nor can he reject them, as do Earth and the pebble. We are on our own in *Experience*, and our capacity to retain a unified vision is as much threatened by the Bard's simplistic optimism as it is by the pessimism which inevitably ensues from it. At the same time, moreover, we must resist the temptation, inspired by seemingly insoluble problems of the sort 'The Clod and the Pebble' pose, to 'yield up moral questions in despair.'

The sharp dichotomies of *Experience* return us to the world of the children's book, with its equally clear and unambiguous choices: saved and doomed, good boy or bad. The Puritans set the pattern, of course, as in, for example, Robert Russell's *A Little Book for Children and Youth* (1693–6?), with its descriptions of 'who they are that are good children; and also who they are that are Wicked Children, With a Dialogue between a Good Mother and Naughty Girl; also a Dialogue between Good Children and Naughty Children'; or Benjamin Keatch's *War with the Devil; or the Young Man's Conflict with the Powers of Darkness* (1673), one half of the frontispiece to which depicts a 'youth in his converted state aetat. su. 16,' dressed in Puritan costume, striding along a 'narrow' way oblivious to the fire of gun-toting devils, while the other shows him dressed like a Cavalier, moving along a 'broad' way towards a flaming lake.[50]

Nor were sharp black-and-white divisions of this sort restricted to Puritan authors. Newbery's publications, for example, though influenced, or rather protected, by Locke's *Education*, and conceived in a spirit quite unlike that of most 'Good-Godly' books,[51] nevertheless continued to depict life for its readers in terms of clear-cut and perilous alternatives, as in *The History of Tommy Playlove and Jacky Lovebook: wherein is shown the Superiority of Virtue over Vice* (1783). Day's *Sandford and Merton*, though founded upon the progressive principles of Rousseau's *Émile*, is similarly uncompromising in its structure. It too presents us with an almost wholly 'wicked' or 'naughty' child, the ill-mannered, sickly, spoiled Tommy Merton, and contrasts him with the sturdy, kindly Henry

Sandford, the epitome of all virtues, a kind of Anglicized Émile. Tommy's ultimate conversion at the hands of his tutor, Mr Barlow, is pure Rousseau, but the initial contrast between good boy and bad is clearly inherited from an older Puritan tradition. When, therefore, Blake planned a 'Gates of Hell' to accompany his first children's book, the 'Gates of Heaven,' or contrasted studious with freedom-seeking child, in the *c.* 1785–90 watercolor, *Age Teaching Youth* (figure 16), or coupled *Experience* with *Innocence*,[52] he may well have been remembering and playing upon the sharp black-and-white contrasts of contemporary children's books and theories of childhood.

The visual equivalent of the Bard's tendency in poems like 'The Clod and the Pebble' to simplify and abstract complicated issues, is found in a delicate stylistic shift from what might be called the predominantly 'Gothic' forms of *Innocence* to what Blake calls 'Grecian' or 'Mathematic Form' (*On Virgil*: E267). This, I am aware, is itself an enormous simplification;[53] but it is Blake's, not mine, and one he makes throughout his career (not just in the more dogmatic assertions of the 1800s), in spite of obvious affinities to the linear Neoclassicism of Flaxman, Cumberland, and Mortimer. It is also one of which modern art history would not be wholly scornful. To E. H. Gombrich, for instance,

> That procession of styles and periods known to every beginner – Classic, Romanesque, Gothic, Renaissance, Mannerist, Baroque, Rococo, Neo-Classical and Romantic – represents only a series of masks for two categories, the classical and the non-classical.[54]

When Blake thought of the classical in these terms, as a norm, he was against it, invariably transforming his share of the age's retrospective nostalgia and prospective utopianism to a native and/or Hebraic rather than classical antiquity. The 'Gothic' belonged in his mind to that native tradition, from as early on as his first works as Basire's apprentice, to the Dante designs with which his career closed.

The shift from Gothic to Grecian in *Songs* is especially pronounced in the opening sequence of *Experience*, particularly in the first two plates. On the frontispiece, for instance, there are only two trees, neither of which twists or twines as do those on the first plate of *Innocence*. The tree in the right foreground (so massive we can see only part of it) lacks supple human curves like those of the innocent frontispiece, and though its vegetation forms a canopy over the heads of shepherd-Bard and winged child, organic richness and intricacy are hardly its prime qualities. What Goethe called 'meaningful and rugged,' bounding lines like those of the tree-top foliage on the innocent frontispiece, has been replaced by the 'insignificant and smooth,' a single ordered and controlled line forming a neat Romanesque arch over the heads of the two symmetrically arranged figures below.[55] (Greek and Roman or Romanesque forms were equally suspect to the Blake of broad, Gombrich-like classical/non-classical distinctions: 'Rome and Greece swept Art into their maw and destroy'd it' (*On Virgil*: E267). 'We do not want either Greek or Roman Models if we are but just and true to our Imaginations' (*M* 1: E94)).

On the next plate, the title-page to *Experience*, the shift in style is even more pronounced. Gone is the rich exuberance of curving, curling, bursting decorative foliage, the sweep of branch and volute. In its place we find the stark, unbroken horizontals of church wall,[56] marble bed or bier,[57] and supine, pillowed bodies. The lettering of the title creates a similar impression. Erdman likens the word 'Experience' to an iron fence.[58] Keynes describes it as 'set like a bar across the page.'[59] 'Songs' is similarly unadorned (at least in comparison to its innocent counterpart), and so too is the lettering at the bottom of the plate. In copy Z, moreover, Blake turns the ground upon which the female mourner stands into a kind of step or rectangular platform, yet another geometric form. Even the few curves and diagonals the design does possess are carefully patterned. The backs of male and female mourners, for instance, are identically bent. The male and female sprites ('the true human forms of the mourners below')[60] on either side of the word 'of' help to form a neat triangle around it, their arms and legs similarly placed. Only the rich, rainbow-colored sky, with its asymmetrical patches of blue, pink, and yellow, and the faint swirls and squiggles of decorative vegetation (about which we shall soon be talking), relieve the larger impression of stark order and control. In *Innocence*, objects merge one with another, edges are softened, corners rounded. Here, all is stark simplicity, each object or plane discrete, distinct, self-contained, reminding students of late eighteenth-century art, not only of the unadorned geometric idealism of the revolutionary French architecture of Ledoux and Boullée in the 1780s and 1790s, or of the formal austerity of David's most famous canvasses of the same period (figures 17 and 18), but of the less politically conscious historicism of earlier English artists; of Benjamin West (figure 19), Gavin Hamilton, and Nathaniel Dance. In Ledoux's architecture, writes Rosenblum, 'the most elementary geometric components [were] ... arranged ... by a system of juxtaposition rather than fusion, much as the figures in the *Horatii* [of David] asserted a new independence and isolation of parts.'[61]

Abstract severity of this sort goes hand-in-hand with anti-erotic bias; the sexual and the amorous being associated with the decadent rococo of Louis XV and the *Ancien Régime*. Blake, of course, would hardly have approved this sort of starkness: to him, the sober monumentality of radical or heroic Neoclassicism, so unlike the rich sensuality of the Neoclassicism of, say, Winckelmann on Greek sculpture, or the voluptuous nudes of Canova, would seem to deny the body its needs and pleasures. It also, of course, as in the *Horatii*, idealized martial virtues: stoicism, death, sacrifice. The classical in this sense – severely rational, abstract, anti-erotic, militarist – was Blake's enemy, despite its affinities to the radicalism of Godwin's England and Robespierre's France.

Qualification, though, as I have suggested, is essential: to call the hieratic postures of Bard and child on the frontispiece to *Experience* classical, as we have done, and the *contrapposto* of their innocent counterparts Gothic, makes little sense, as Bindman points out, if one takes, for example, the effigies of Westminster Abbey as representatively Gothic. So too, if symmetry is thought of by Blake as a sign of rigid, 'Mathematical' form, to his age (this is also Bindman's point) it was a *rejection* of the norm, a sign of conscious primitivism.[62] Moreover, the closest of Blake's contemporaries, Flaxman and Cumberland, were among the first of many in his age who sought to blend Greek classicism with the late Gothic of Masaccio, Ghiberti, Giotto, and other artists of the Florentine Quattrocento.[63]

Still, contrasts of the sort I have been adducing do bring us closer to understanding precisely what Blake means when he says 'Grecian is Mathematic Form: Gothic is Living Form' (*Virgil*: E267); or why, because he thinks Gothic churches 'representative of true Art' (*VLJ*: E549), he flanks the eponymous heroine of *Jerusalem* with Westminster Abbey and her fallen anti-type, Vala, with what looks like St Paul's (figure 20). Grecian or Mathematic form (in Blake's eyes if not always in his work) grows out of and reflects a world of isolated subjects and objects, of discrete and distinct forms. Its appropriateness to the second volume of *Songs* lies, in part, in our sense that *Experience*, in John Holloway's words, is 'a universe of disjunction and non-relation,' a world of 'universal turn-away.'[64] Gothic forms, on the other hand, with their often delicate interlacings and rich profusion of swirls and curves aptly characterize the harmonious one-ness, interrelation and exuberance of the innocent vision.

Holloway's description of *Experience* as a world of 'universal turn-away' grows out of his discussion of the experienced 'Introduction,' a poem which, together with 'Earth's Answer,' its sequel, is filled with ruptures and rejections; with an Earth 'lapsed' from its maker, and a maker calling upon it to arise 'from *out* the dewy grass.' But the phrase 'universal turn-away' applies equally well not only to these and other poems in *Experience*, but to many of the designs as well, both to their figurative and iconographic as well as their formal properties. The scene at the bottom of 'The Clod and the Pebble' plate (a perfect complement to the pebble's coldly impersonal, rebarbative vision of love) provides a case in point. Like Erdman, I find it hard to credit Keynes's reading of this scene as a kind of food cycle.[65] (Only the frog at the far right seems to be 'preying' on anything, and the object of his attack is by no means clear.) To me, the design seems to stress the *absence* of contact between animals. Each creature is isolate and mechanical as it goes about its business; as oblivious or indifferent to its neighbor as the pebble is to the flowing waters of the brook.

Isolation and self-absorption of this sort, prefigured in the disturbingly vacant expressions on the faces of Bard and winged child on the frontispiece, in the grief-stricken mourners (heads buried in hands) on opposite sides if the death-bed on the title-page, recurs throughout the designs to *Experience*. In the very next plate, for instance, 'Holy Thursday,' a mother looks *away* from her children (one of whom hides his own face in despair), totally absorbed in her own weariness and misery. In 'Nurse's Song' and 'The Fly,' brother and sister seem wholly oblivious to each other's activities; in 'The Sick Rose,' neither of the 'rosy buds forlorn'[66] in the top half of the plate is aware of the other's existence. The 'virgin queen' of 'The Angel' looks away from and holds off her lover even as she caresses his cheek, and like the lovers in the design to 'My Pretty Rose Tree,' seems lost in moony, miserable self-absorption.

In *Innocence*, characters stand and reach out to one another. In *Experience*, they crouch or huddle or stretch flat upon the ground, heads buried in arms and hands, faces vacant, abstracted.[67] Their isolation and self-absorption is a kind of iconographic equivalent of the separateness, the sharp clarity and distinctness, of the designs' 'Grecian' or 'Mathematic' forms. Only the child who leads the old man on the 'London' plate, and the naked children on the third 'Lyca' plate, reach out to others in ways which appear genuinely helpful or positive. The embrace of old man and naked youth on 'The Little Vagabond' plate is, as I suggested in the previous chapter, a kind of smothering. The outstretched arm and poised comb, with sharp-pointed teeth, of the nurse in 'Nurse's Song' suggests threat and restriction. The mother or nurse on 'The Fly' plate who 'holds the child in an iron grip and obscures his vision with her body'[68] reminds us of the shepherd-Bard on the frontispiece. (Her instruction, like the Bard's steadying, suggests 'hindrance to ... freedom.')[69] The outstretched arms of the child in 'Infant Sorrow' and the female form of the rose at the bottom of 'The Sick Rose' signify fear and resistance rather than joy and communion.

Even figures who aspire to what seems like genuine communion, such as the male and female sprites in the top half of the title-page, find their way blocked. Think, for instance, of what Erdman calls 'The relationship of the serpent to the grapes, far above his head' in the design to 'Earth's Answer' or of the Angel's attempt to caress the virgin queen on 'The Angel' plate.[70] *Experience*, we quickly discover, is filled with such images of failure and disjunction – with figures separate and apart, isolated by external obstacles such as the sharp-pointed decorative vegetation on the title-page, or by their own despairing self-involvement.

Mention of the vegetation on the title-page brings us to the more general question of differences in decoration between *Innocence* and *Experience*. Earlier, in chapter 2, we touched upon the apparent similarities in pictorial style between the two volumes. *Experience*, I argued, only seems to be identical in pictorial style to *Innocence*. When we look closely, subtle and significant differences appear. What ought by now to be clear, is that this apparent identity functions as a kind of test, a visual equivalent to the problems posed by the seeming or surface innocence of the Bard's words in 'Introduction.' Once again, therefore, we have to be on our guard: in this case, against the sort of generalization which equates decoration *per se* with exuberant life and health. For example, the massive lightning-scarred tree[71] to the right of the Bard on the frontispiece is 'decorated' by vegetation which, at first, we think of as softening its stark outlines. This vegetation, though, looks like ivy, which, unlike the vines of *Innocence*, can bear neither fruit nor flower. Ivy, we realize, is found nowhere in *Innocence*, though it reappears several times in *Experience*.[72] It differs in appearance from the decorative vegetation of *Innocence* in the sharpness of its pointed 'scourge-like' leaves with their somewhat more geometric, triangular or rectangular shapes. Keynes calls these shapes 'unpleasant,'[73] though his reasons for doing so only become clear in the next few plates. Even in copy Z, where the decorative sprigs and branchings which separate the two sprites on the title-page look less like ivy than do those on other copies (in part because no attempt has been made to color them green), the shapes of the leaves as well as the decidedly 'unpleasant' spikes which tip them, clearly echo the decoration on the frontispiece. They are like the thongs on the 'cat' or 'scourge' Theotormon holds on plate 6 of *Visions* (figure 21). On the next plate, these shapes reappear as stars; symbols, according to the poem they 'illuminate,' of a power man no longer controls, of a light that, its height in the heavens notwithstanding, has 'fallen.' In *Innocence* vegetation metamorphosed into red-gold flame; here it is transformed into something quite different. Swirling, energetic profusion is replaced by small, spiky, distinct patches of color; heat and flame give way to the cold light of distant stars.

Of course, not all decoration in *Experience* conforms to this pattern. As in *Innocence*, Blake varies his larger motifs in order to create smaller, local contrasts. On the title-page, for instance, 'Songs' is surrounded by and gives off leaves and flowers, while 'Experience' is unadorned. Erdman rightly sees this contrast as a kind of tug of war in which 'the "of" and the ivy connecting the two halves lifts Experience into Songs or pulls Songs down ... conditional upon our reading.'[74] Neither word, though, is particularly attractive or welcoming. 'Songs' is itself relatively sober and unadorned, at least in copy Z, where its surrounding foliage is uncolored and, in places, hard to distinguish. In Z, it is the gold background as much as the surrounding decorative vegetation which creates an opposition between the two words.

Even the brightest of experienced plates ('The Clod and the Pebble,' for example, or 'Holy Thursday,' or 'The Fly') – plates which look, at first glance, much like those of *Innocence* – give off quite different impressions, begin to change and darken, under closer inspection. In *Innocence*, this darkening process was used to qualify and complicate essentially or predominantly positive plates (one thinks of the purple storm cloud of 'The Lamb' or the spindly trees just outside 'The Ecchoing Green'). Here its effect is more radical. The 'Holy Thursday' plate, for example, presents us with an initial impression of health and fruitfulness which is almost wholly undermined by closer inspection.[75] Once we have noted the two dead or dying children – sole fruit and flower of a supposedly (and superficially) 'rich and fruitful land' – pillowed among its lush greenery, we go on to note a host of lesser, though similarly disquieting, details, visual equivalents of the 'eternal winter' described in stanza 3. Not only are the distant mountains (snow-capped in copy Y), 'bleak and bare,' but so too are the branches of the oak tree which arches over the appalled mother and her tiny, dead or dying infant. The roots of this tree, moreover, are clearly visible, and its massive trunk (we remember the tree on the frontispiece) is unadorned, even by ivy. Erdman suggests that we think of the oak leaves in the lower right margin as having fallen from the tree,[76] a further sign, if not of winter itself, at least of its imminent arrival. The spear grass which grows behind the oak leaf at bottom right reminds us of the thorns mentioned in line 11. It also reminds us of several other long, pointed shapes in the opening sequence: the sliver-like breaks in the text-cloud of 'Introduction,' for instance, or the snaky foliage on 'Earth's Answer.' When vegetative strands or fronds (as opposed to the more patch-like shapes discussed earlier) appear in *Experience*, the impressions they give off are almost always unpleasant. If the acanthus of 'A Cradle Song' is unsettling, how much more so, for example, the thin, finger-like swirls of decoration to the right of the last three stanzas of 'Earth's Answer,' or even the leafless, spidery branchings which stretch across the 'Holy Thursday' text, isolating rather than tying or weaving its stanzas together.

One last important aspect of *Experience* we have not yet dealt with in our discussion of the opening sequence is the sheer difficulty – the obscurity and complexity – of many of its poems and designs. No contrast between *Innocence* and *Experience* is more pointed than that of the former's 'poetic lucidity' and the latter's 'prophetic obscurity.'[77] Prophets, of course, despite their penchant for the declamatory mode, are notoriously obscure (think of Ezekiel and Isaiah), especially when, like the Bard, they themselves are confused. Nor is the Bard's task (or ours) made any easier by the literal darkness 'dread and drear' of the world he means to expose and reform. The only comfort we can take in our confusion is a sense of its thematic appropriateness. In *Innocence*, the transparency of the Piper's songs – the ease with which we grasped their surface meanings – was matched by the effortlessness of his communications with the floating child. In *Experience*, our failure to make sense of what we read, even syntactical sense, matches the Bard's own failure to communicate with Earth, or Earth with him.

On occasion, though, this very 'obscurity' can point us back to the Bard's lost innocence. Take, for example, the question of who it is in 'Introduction' 'That might controll/The starry pole:/And Fallen fallen light renew!' Blake's erratic punctuation provides three possible candidates: the Holy Word, the Bard (or the Bard as the Holy Word's agent), and the lapsed Soul. If we take Holy Word as the antecedent of 'that' in line 8, there are two possible explanations for his (or His) lack of 'controll': either the Holy Word needs Earth to rise up if he is to control the starry pole, or he could control it if he wanted to, but chooses not to until Earth rises. Both meanings, of course, provide evidence for a host of possible interpretations of the Holy Word's character, either as Jehovah or as Christ. If, on the other hand, we take Bard rather than Holy Word as the antecedent of 'that,' the reading 'might control if he wanted to, but chooses not to until Earth rises,' makes little sense. In this case, only one possibility seems plausible: the Bard's *ability* to control the starry pole depends upon Earth's rising. Finally, if we take lapsed Soul as the antecedent of 'that,' only Earth's unwillingness or inability to rise prevents it (if the speaker is to be trusted) from controlling the starry pole. The interesting point about these possibilities is that, though there are no sure grounds for choosing one over another, each, in its own way, reveals a single, shared assumption: that the lapsed Soul, either directly or in league with the Holy Word and/or Bard, retains the capacity to alter or control her world. Though the second stanza's ambiguities signal genuine and dangerous confusions, they also point to the Bard's essential or underlying innocence. They suggest that his vision, though compromised and obscured by disquieting 'lapses' into experienced terminology, remains that of the Piper: which is why, in part, we resist Earth's identification of him with Jehovah.

Experience, as this brief survey of its prevailing motifs suggests, requires of its readers a tenacious and resourceful commitment to innocent virtues. It asks us to beware of simplifications that sacrifice individuals for 'the Individual'; to resolve seemingly insoluble dilemmas by rejecting the mental habits which frame them; and to temper Earth-like indignation with a deeper and more far-reaching perception of underlying innocence. Its largest and most unexpected demand, though, is that we redeem or rescue its 'author,' our nominal guide; that we learn to extend tolerant understanding to those who, like the Bard in 'The Voice of the Ancient Bard,' 'wish to lead others when they should be led.'

CHAPTER 6
FALSE INNOCENCE

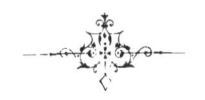

The discrepancy in *Experience* between prophetic means and visionary or poetic ends takes several forms in the later plates, mostly in the poems rather than the designs. I intend, in this chapter, to isolate and identify those forms, carefully disentangling the end or endorsed object from the righteous or complacent endorsement. Once we have examined the nature and extent of the Bard's infection – the often quite subtle symptoms of his own unwitting 'lapse' – we shall then turn to the several sorts of false innocence in late eighteenth-century children's books from which, in large measure, those symptoms were, I believe, drawn. The focus, in other words, will be on the second of the two sorts of entry into experience mentioned in the previous chapter. Relatively little will be said about plates such as 'The Angel' or 'The Poison Tree,' for example, which tell us more about the Bard's findings than about his own character and dilemma. *What* the Bard sees, the subject of most earlier studies of *Experience*, will take second place in these readings to the way he sees and the way he reacts to what he sees.

In many plates of *Experience*, large social injustices are exposed and attacked at the expense of particular truths or individuals. The experienced 'Chimney Sweeper' provides a case in point. To Rossetti, 'there can be no comparison between the first "Chimney Sweeper," which touches with such perfect simplicity the true pathetic chord of its subject, and the second, tinged somewhat with the commonplaces, if also with the truth, of social discontents.'[1] The 'truth' Rossetti refers to at the end of this passage is not that of the sweeps' sufferings (something the innocent version amply documents, for all its stress on the minimal comforts and self-sustainings of imaginative fellow feeling). Rather it concerns the context in which that suffering is placed, the 'use' to which the activist Bard puts it. Our sense that the Bard is using his speaker, and that the poem has a palpable design upon us, is communicated in two ways. First in the manner of the sweep's introduction:

> A little black thing among the snow:
> Crying weep, weep, in notes of woe!
> Where are thy father and mother? say?

What bothers us about this opening is the unnamed speaker's obliviousness to the feelings of the actual child in front of him. The phrase, 'A little black thing among the snow,' is hardly calculated to do the child, to whom it seems to be addressed, much good. The speaker's pity for the sweep is generalized, offers no immediate sustenance. Similarly, when the speaker asks the sweep where his parents are, we feel that his concern is less to return the child to them, than to elicit precisely the sort of answer he receives. 'Say,' says the speaker, as if priming the child for a set response. There is something contrived about the opening of this Song. The misery of the child's situation, we feel, is being shown off to us. The speaker treats it and him as a kind of example – an example of some larger 'social discontent.' We think back to the easy commerce between Piper and floating child in the innocent 'Introduction,' and try to imagine the former asking a similar question in a similar way. Whereas the Piper's encounter with the child struck us as sensitive and spontaneous, this speaker's strikes us as calculated and manipulative – both of the child and of us. It reminds us of pictures of concerned politicians talking with ghetto children.

That the sweep himself is no more genuine or spontaneous only increases our sense of design or contrivance. His reaction to his situation is hardly what we would expect from a child, even from a stylized Blakean child. Instead of confusion, fearful anger, or fatigued indifference – all believably child-like reactions to the miseries of a sweep's lot – we find reasoned analysis and understanding, not just of parents (compare the dispirited blankness of the innocent sweep's 'When my mother died I was very young,/And my father sold me ...') but of

society as a whole. What the child says is, of course, absolutely
right. The social injustice he condemns is real, and so too is his
perception of 'God and his Priest and King' as the true enemy.
But his combination of child-like artlessness ('They are both
gone up to the Church to pray') and analytical sophistication and
self-awareness (note the syntax of the following stanzas, their
formal register) strikes us as false:

> Because I was happy upon the heath
> And smil'd among the winter's snow:
> They cloth'd me in the clothes of death,
> And taught me to sing the notes of woe
>
> And because I am happy, and dance and sing,
> They think they have done me no injury.

'I could observe, in little pieces, as it were,' said David
Copperfield of his child self, 'but as to making a net of a number
of these pieces, and catching anybody in it, that was, as yet,
beyond me.'[2] Where, we wonder, did the sweep gain the strength
and sophistication to make such connections, to see through his
parents' self-deceptions? The design depicts as woebegone a
'little black thing' as the poem's opening, so it won't do to talk
of this sweep as older or more mature than his innocent
counterparts. The answer is simply that the Bard has sacrificed
or distorted a particular, individual truth in order to register a
larger 'truth of social discontent.'

His reasons for doing so are made clear in stanzas 2 and 3, the
aim of which is to point out the dangerous consequences of those
very moments of imaginative fellow-feeling celebrated in the
earlier version. Singing and dancing on the heath (perhaps in the
traditional May Day dance of sweeps and milkmaids in London,[3]
in which case the poem comments on the innocent 'Holy
Thursday' as well), can, warns the speaker, lead parents or
onlookers into thinking their children 'uninjured.' But this, of
course, is something we already know: it is precisely what gives
such power to the line 'So if all do their duty they need not fear
harm' in the earlier poem. Why make the point again, and so
directly? Because the Piper has become a Bard, and no longer
trusts the poetic indirection of piped song. There must be no
mistake about these rationalizations and self-deceptions, the
experienced 'Chimney Sweeper' seems to insist, nor about the

network of institutions which make them possible. And so we get the false, or rather generalized, pity of the opening lines, and the implausible knowingness of the lines' prophetic urgency and directness victimize even as they seek to save.

'Holy Thursday' provides us with another, though slightly different, example of the Bard's tendency to simplify and distort. Its unnamed speaker sees through the hypocrisy of its celebration right from the start. How, he asks in the poem's opening line, can we call a procession of this sort 'a holy thing to see'? The children's true condition must be our concern, and neither their brightly colored uniforms nor their 'innocent faces clean' must be allowed to obscure it. What the speaker sees when he looks at the children is the reality of their everyday lives, and his outrage at the evils of their condition is, no doubt, only fanned by their present appearance.

His outrage, though, as we quickly discover, is born out of abstract sympathy. Though the speaker cries out for the redress of shameful wrongs, he does so in a manner which suggests that he has lost touch with their particular or individual victims. He never really focuses on what upsets him. *We* have to set the scene, reminding ourselves that he is reacting to a specific event, a procession of children into St Paul's. Though his opinions and attitudes, sparked by meditation on the scene, are laudable, they are also remote and generalized. We react to them as we do to those of many speakers in *Experience*: by agreeing, while at the same time noting a disquieting tendency towards exaggeration and self-righteousness. We also note a disturbing affinity between this speaker's imagery and that of the Bard in 'Introduction.'

The word 'Babes' in the third line of the poem strikes the first unsettling note. These, obviously, are the charity-school children of the innocent poem, the 'boys and girls' whom the earlier speaker referred to as 'flowers of London town,' and whom the Piper depicted above and below the text. That they are 'babes' here rather than 'boys and girls' may simply signal the intensity of the speaker's sympathy and concern. But it might also suggest a kind of emotional calculation, a playing upon feelings, both our own and those of the speaker himself, especially in view of several subtle but affecting exaggerations in the lines that follow.

The 'cold and usurous hand' which reduces the babes to misery is that of the 'wise guardians' society employs to feed them. It is 'cold,' a word which reminds us of the earlier poem's 'wands as white as snow,' because it feeds without affection; 'usurous' because, in M. G. Jones's words, those who ran the charity schools 'lined their pockets with money saved from the children's rations';[4] or, as Gillham suggests, because caring for poor children was thought of as a means of keeping them from crime, and hence as a 'good investment': 'The hand that feeds the child is usurous because the hope of a return is the only effective incentive to charity that can be at work in a wintry world.'[5] The line 'Fed with cold and usurous hand' shows the Bard, or the Bard through his speaker (a problem we shall soon be discussing), at his best. Though our focus in this chapter will be largely on the Bard's failings, a line such as this one reminds us just how deep and penetrating his insights can be. When the Bard is at his best as an activist poet, he is the best sort of prophet, one whose function, in Paley's words, 'is not to predict the future but to expose the otherwise hidden motives and consequences of human decisions.'[6]

The speaker of the innocent 'Holy Thursday' describes the sounds of the singing children as a 'hum of multitudes,' 'a mighty wind,' 'Harmonious thunderings.' His experienced counterpart hears only 'a trembling cry.' Both speakers half create what they hear. The guilt of the innocent speaker accounts for the ominous echoes of retribution in his imagery. The experienced speaker's insistence that we look more deeply into the truth of the children's condition accounts for the enfeebling of their song. 'One should be hard-headed with a hard-headed poem,' Hirsch rightly insists, 'several thousand voices, even of deprived children, do not produce a trembling cry.' The experienced speaker 'falsifies by exaggeration what was true in the earlier conception.'[7] The source of this exaggeration is the speaker's powerful sense of the brutalities visited upon the children. His indignation, like that of the speaker in the opening lines of 'The Chimney Sweeper,' is genuine, but it is also generalized — and abstract as well. Children so brutalized, reasons the speaker, simply cannot sing a song of joy; so it is not a song of joy they are singing. To an activist such as the speaker, tactics determine reality:

> Is that trembling cry a song?
> Can it be a song of joy?
> And so many children poor?
> It is a land of poverty!

Line 7, 'And so many children poor,' is rhetorical sleight of hand. The speaker means us to think of it as 'proof' of the suspicions of lines 5 and 6.

We must never, insists the speaker, lose sight of the children's suffering. Our silence only lends tacit support to their continued impoverishment. Not to hear their song as a 'trembling cry' is to do them an injury. The speaker, in short, is a polemicist, a prophetic activist prepared to sacrifice the truth of some present reality for a greater good. His exaggeration is a distortion, a calculated appeal, whether conscious or unconscious, to the emotions. Through it the speaker hopes to rouse a 'rich and fruitful land' to much-needed reform. The reform, we acknowledge, *is* much-needed; yet still, and this is what makes complaint so difficult, we are made to feel like the Angel of plates 17 to 20 of the *Marriage*: imposed upon.

In stanza 3 the speaker loses sight of the present scene completely. His concern now is with that 'land of poverty' mentioned at the end of the previous stanza. 'Land of poverty' refers, of course, not only to the children's material state, but to the spiritual and emotional impoverishment of society as a whole. It is a land without sun, with wintry fields 'bleak and bare,' and ways 'fill'd with thorns.' No rose can withstand the rigors of a climate of this sort. Without sun there can be no growth and blossoming. Hence line 12, 'It is eternal winter there,' the finality of which reminds us of line 8. The difference between this line and line 8, though, is that the latter is clearly a response to a present reality: to the 'holy thing' of line 1. Line 12, on the other hand, comes right out of the speaker's head; it is a product of reason and reflection, a necessary conclusion drawn in the abstract. Given such poverty in a rich and fruitful land, the speaker seems to be saying, this world must necessarily be one of 'eternal winter.' The conclusion is inevitable, and no first-hand knowledge of the poor need lie behind it. That it is not strictly true does not bother the speaker (though it bothers us); its ultimate effect – that of rousing a rich and fruitful land – is all that counts for him.

The utopian vision of the final stanza follows from line 12. The speaker posits a world warmed by the sun, its fields fed by rain. The fruit of the fields alleviates the babe's literal hunger, while the sun's beams, and the life-giving rain provide symbolic nourishment in the form of love (see 'The Little Black Boy') and spiritual energy. The 'mind' which is 'appalled' (so whitened and pallid that the world seems a perpetual winter, 'bleak and bare,' as if bleached of color; or shrouded, like the winter sky) by the poverty of the last line, can be either the babe's or the wise guardian's. It can also, of course, refer to the guiltless speaker and his audience, outraged by the anomaly of needless suffering in a rich and fruitful land.

This artful multiplicity of meanings reinforces the innocent truths of mutuality and inter-dependence. It also hints at a dominant theme of *Experience*: the blighting effect victimization has on victimizers as well as victims. Why, then, do stanzas 3 and 4 leave us vaguely troubled and unsure? Because, in Hirsch's words, they

> imply that the social arrangement that has produced charity schools and usurous hands has gone wrong because it has gone against nature. It is unnatural for the sun never to shine and for winter to persist forever. ... What makes this poem ... more vulnerable than its predecessor is its failure to recognize that if 'eternal winter' is unnatural, so is 'eternal spring.'[8]

In his prophetic fervor, the speaker of the experienced 'Holy Thursday' substitutes an unreal and unrealizable vision for the more complex paradise of innocent songs like 'Night' and 'The Ecchoing Green.'[9] He speaks metaphorically, of course, but his metaphors, like those of the Bard in 'Introduction,' suggest transcendence rather than transformation. Innocent speakers rigorously resist the attractions of 'eternal spring'; experienced speakers seem constantly to succumb to them. In doing so they become like Urizen, their enemy, who explains his withdrawal from Eternity in the following terms:

> I have sought for a joy without pain,
> For a solid without fluctuation
> Why will you die, O Eternals?
> Why live in unquenchable burnings?
>
> (*U* 4.10–13: E70)

By implying that winter or the 'dewy grass' ('Introduction') of body will be excluded from a 'future age' ('The Little Girl Lost') or 'truth new born' ('The Voice of the Ancient Bard'), the speakers of *Experience* ally that truth with the heaven sought for by Urizen and his priest and beadle.

Not that they intend to, of course. The speaker of the experienced 'Holy Thursday' would be shocked by our reading, as shocked as was the Bard by Earth's rejection of his call. But they do, and in ways we find impossible to ignore, especially if we come to *Experience* directly from *Innocence*. Though their intentions are good, the reforms they aim at laudable, such speakers simplify and distort particular truths. In resisting their simplifications, we put our recently acquired innocent beliefs, the lessons we have learned, to work: 'minute particulars,' we remind ourselves, must not be sacrificed to generalities, however high-minded; 'using' others, even for their own good, cannot but weaken respect for the Divine Humanity.[10] We neither reject nor condemn the aims of the speaker of the experienced 'Holy Thursday.' Rather we see them for what they are – passionately caring, but deeply flawed, and potentially dangerous. A response of this sort is characteristically innocent. It is, in fact, identical to our response to the speaker of the innocent 'Chimney Sweeper.'

Songs of Experience like 'The Chimney Sweeper' and 'Holy Thursday' reinforce our doubts about the Bard's character and call in the opening sequence. They also help to provide a context for similar though more subtle ambiguities of response elicited elsewhere in *Experience*. Think, for example, of the critical controversy surrounding 'Ah! Sun-flower' and 'The Lilly,' two of the three flower poems on the plate immediately following 'The Tyger.' To Bloom and others, the love offered by the 'Lilly white' (we shall be looking at 'Ah! Sun-flower' in a moment) is genuine – an openness which is its true purity.[11] Holloway, on the other hand, calls it 'not love but "love"': the cant term that would have been dear to the love-mouthing but murderous priest in ... "A Little Boy Lost." '[12] The heart of the controversy lies in the lily's traditional associations with the Virgin Mary 'meek and mild.' We see the poem, in Grant's phrase, either as an 'ostentatious' revision of tradition,[13] a sort of exercise (in the diabolic manner of the *Marriage*) for the more fully developed iconoclasm of Blake's treatment of the Virgin in *Jerusalem* (61.5–13: E209) and *The Everlasting Gospel* (i.1–6: E794); or as an ironic restatement of those religious attitudes ('love' in Holloway's sense of 'cant') which thwart genuine desire. The Bard's, or speaker's, good intentions, his desire to set Earth free, shine through both readings, and evidence can be adduced in support of either interpretation. That the Lilly 'Shall' (as opposed to 'doth') 'in love delight' suggests to Hirsch 'the biblical ring of rewarded righteousness.'[14] To Grant, the Lilly's 'delight' serves to distinguish it from 'the long-suffering clod' of 'The Clod and the Pebble.'[15] Holloway, on the other hand, rightly asks us to recall 'the traditional notion that the abandonment of virginity goes with a "stain" on whiteness which could be likened to the "modest" (the blushing) rose,'[16] while Erdman notes the lifelessness, in terms both of line and color, of the Lilly's appearance not only in copy Z but in almost all other copies.[17]

For every argument, we quickly discover, there is a counter-argument, and recourse to other works only provides further grounds for disagreement. The controversy is impossible to resolve without ignoring evidence, and to ignore evidence is to imply lack of control on Blake's part. Now Blake, as we have seen, is not without his lapses, even in *Songs*, but before we attribute our difficulties to the poet himself, we ought first to remember 'The Chimney Sweeper' and 'Holy Thursday' – or rather the initial dramatic or narrative context they help to keep alive. If 'The Lilly' leaves us with unresolvable doubts, are these not attributable to the Bard himself rather than to Blake, especially since the Bard's confusions or lapses often center on precisely the sort of difficulty we find here (i.e. the use of a conventionally religious vocabulary to express radically unconventional views)? The problems of interpretation posed by 'The Lilly,' I am suggesting, not only cannot but ought not to be resolved, since they form part of a larger pattern in *Experience*.

Much the same is true of 'Ah! Sun-flower,' where our inability to accept either a pessimistic-sardonic reading of the sort advocated by Bloom or Wagenknecht (one in which the poem's 'sweet golden clime' is an illusion, and 'aspire' means 'fail to attain'), or a more straightforward, unironic interpretation such as Hirsch's, again seems part of a larger design.[18] What William Keith calls 'the essential ambivalence' of the poem is simply all too familiar.[19] The problems it poses about transcendence versus transformation are found not only in poems like 'Holy Thursday' but in the introductory sequence as well. Like 'The Lilly,' 'Ah! Sun-flower' represents a sympathetic response to Earth's cry for sexual liberation. Its aim is to expose the insidious hypocrisy of the forces which hold Earth down. This it does, however, in two quite distinct ways:

first through its tale, and second through our inability to decide what that tale means, to resolve, that is, the contradictory signals it sends out. This second form of 'exposure' brings the tale's teller, the Bard, into the picture; in this respect, again 'Ah! Sun-flower' and 'The Lilly' resemble each other. Only in 'My Pretty Rose Tree,' the first of the three flower poems, do the Bard's character and dilemma play no part. Though its speaker's personality is every bit as problematic as those of the speakers of 'Ah! Sun-flower' and 'The Lilly,' we think of it as 'part of the tale,' part of what the Bard intends us to see. This is what makes the poem less 'prophetic' than its companions, both of which pretend to a voice of impersonal authority.

One important difference between *Experience* and *Innocence* is the frequency with which the former tells us about rather than depicts (on a conscious level, at least) the evils it condemns. There are, for instance, many more unnamed speakers in *Experience* than in *Innocence*, and most of them, like the impersonal poetic voices of 'Ah! Sun-flower' and 'The Lilly,' address us directly, in tones of Bard-like authority. Moreover, those speakers in *Experience* who are clearly not the Bard, often function as mere illustrations or examples of the maxims with which a Bard-like voice introduces them. This, of course, is most obviously true in 'The Little Girl Lost' and 'A Little Girl Lost,' where introductory 'prophetic' stanzas are clearly marked off (by a serpent-entwined branch of foliage in the former, non-italic script in the latter) from the poetic narratives which succeed them. But a similar structure of statement and proof, maxim and illustration, underlies many other experienced Songs. 'The Human Abstract,' for example, opens with six lines of 'doctrine' followed by an allegory which ironically 'illustrates' them. In one draft version, Number 8 in the Notebook, lines 1 to 6 are spoken by an 'angelic' (i.e. devilish) 'Devil.'[20] Here, though, the break between the poem's two parts is somewhat harder to distinguish, in part because the allegory itself is abstract and sententious (an all too familiar complication at this point). The opening lines of 'The Chimney Sweeper,' to which we have already referred, provide another example:

> A little Black thing among the snow:
> Crying weep weep in notes of woe!
> Where are thy father and mother? Say?

The sweep's condition is communicated to us directly, before the child himself actually speaks. To think of these lines as directed at any real child is, as we have seen, extremely difficult. The poem's speaker, like the Bard in the introductory stanzas to the two little girl poems, seems to be looking or talking beyond the child: we, his readers, are his true audience. The child is there merely to exemplify and amplify general truths and attitudes already implied in the lines which introduce him. He and his suffering become an 'illustration.'

Divisions of this sort between maxim and illustration are characteristic of *Experience* in two ways: first, in the simple fact of their frequency, and second in the Bard's frequently ambiguous relation to them. When they are found in poems spoken by characters obviously tainted by Experience, we treat them as 'evidence,' as a part of the Bard's findings. Structuring arguments in this way, the Bard seems to be saying, is a characteristic mental habit of Experience, the implications of which (turning individuals into 'examples') are dangerous and unpleasant. When the Bard himself employs such distinctions, though, either directly, in poems like 'A Little Girl Lost,' or indirectly, in a poem like 'The Human Abstract,' he once again exemplifies, as in his penchant for telling rather than depicting, or his use of religious language, the very habits he seeks to expose and overturn in others.

'A Little Boy Lost,' the next Song of Experience I want to consider, introduces another key discrepancy between poetic or innocent ends and prophetic or experienced means. This poem too, after a fashion, is divisible into maxim and illustration, beginning in a manner which reminds us immediately of the prophetic introductions to the two little girl poems. Its opening stanza is composed entirely of maxims and separated from the rest of the text by a bracket of foliage. In stanza 2, though, when the logical consequences of these maxims are spelled out, we realize that they come from a character within the poem, the little boy of the title. Though part of the poem's 'story,' they stand out from it in much the same way as do the opening lines of 'The Human Abstract.' That subsequent lines 'illustrate' them (though not in the sense their speaker intends) is, moreover, all too painfully clear.

If the manner of the first two stanzas – declamatory and logical – is pure experience, its matter is wholly innocent. The child uses reason in the service of its enemies. All creatures, he argues, are equally holy; the only God we can know is the God within, it being impossible 'to Thought/A greater than itself to know'; God and his priests are both likened to and loved like (i.e. in the manner of) 'the little bird/That picks up crumbs around the door' (an innocent ambiguity that recalls the line, 'Birds delight,' in 'Spring'). The child's instinctive innocence, the poem implies, turns even reason to good use.

Yet his argument is that of a Deist, as the murderous Priest implies (Gillham aptly compares stanzas 1 and 2 to passages from Hobbes, Pope's *Essay on Man*, and Locke);[21] and Deists, like all those who 'set reason up for judge,' invariably deny children the imaginative freedom *Innocence* celebrates (cf. Locke's *Education*). We are left, then, in all too familiar a dilemma: unable to side with 'most holy Mystery,' yet deeply disturbed by the little boy's rationalism. Like so much else in *Experience*, the poem's opening stanzas win a local battle by risking a larger and more important one. Their mode is that of poems like the experienced 'Chimney Sweeper,' the 'logical structure' of which, according to Holloway, may be expressed ' "because" A, therefore B and C, and *in the same way*, "because" D, therefore E and F,' or 'The Fly,' which concludes with a mock-syllogistic 'for ... if ... then.'[22] They remind us that reason too is a temptation as well as an enemy to the Bard and his creations.

'A Little Boy Lost' has not fared well with the critics, most of whom consider its indignation heavy-handed. To Gillham, Blake's attack on priestcraft in stanzas 2 to 6 'has no finesse about it whatever and his victory is easily taken.'[23] Bloom complains that 'Blake does little to guard himself against his own indignation.'[24] Hirsch refers to the 'heavy artillery'[25] of the concluding stanzas. One consequence of this heavy-handedness is that it curbs our reactions to the way the little boy speaks in stanzas 1 and 2. Elsewhere in *Experience*, as we have seen, the twin themes of social injustice (what happens to the little boy) and the subtle and unwitting corruption of would-be reformers (his experienced manner) smoothly intertwine. Here they clash. Our sympathies are so strongly enlisted in the child's favor by the concluding stanzas that complaint about his rationalism seems churlish. Yet it is impossible to ignore the priest's accusation. Even Wicksteed, who rarely sees discrepancies between manner and matter in *Experience*, thinks Blake's sympathies 'by no means entirely with the child's argument, however strongly they may be with the child himself.'[26] Like other readers, though, Wicksteed drops his point as soon as he makes it. The poem offers him no choice. Though 'A Little Boy Lost' exposes the corruptions of victim as well as victimizer, the latter's violence embarrasses us into silence about the dangers posed by the former.

It also leads us, again because we are embarrassed, to find excuses for the child, to see his argument as another sign of victimization. Someone, we begin to suspect, must have taught this child to argue, to sound so like a little adult. That his words are like those of a Deist is not his fault. First his child-likeness is taken from him, then his life. Though other poems in *Experience* present us with children or child-like speakers corrupted by adult modes of thought, none focus our sympathies as strongly as 'A Little Boy Lost' on the immediate victim. 'The Little Vagabond,' 'The Schoolboy,' 'The Fly,' and 'The Garden of Love,' for example, all leave us vaguely suspicious of their speakers. Though others may be responsible for the subtle corruptions of their seeming innocence – the unsettling note of calculation, the unwitting lapse into logic or religious orthodoxy – our sympathy for them takes second place to a sense that we are being misled. The subtle seductiveness of these speakers – a seductiveness cancelled in 'A Little Boy Lost' by the child's violent death – makes us think of them as threats rather than victims.

Experience is filled with characters whose individual identities are compromised by, or sacrificed to, the causes or ideas they espouse. Some seem knowingly to participate in the compromise, as does, for example, the speaker of 'The Fly,' who is either an adult affecting a child-like innocence, or a child trying to sound like an adult.[27] Others, like the little boy of 'A Little Boy Lost,' seem to have that identity thrust upon them. Usually, as in 'The Chimney Sweeper,' we think the Bard blind to the falsenesses or failings of his characters. The baldness of line 15 of 'A Little Boy Lost' – 'One who sets reason up for judge' – marks it off as an exception.

The faintness or subtlety of the false notes struck by many of the Bard's speakers, particularly the unwitting ones, makes what bothers us easy to overlook. To do so, though – to slide over what strikes us as contrived or calculated or disingenuous – is both dangerous and wrong; for it gradually wears away the complexities of true innocence, replacing them with a false and ultimately restricting vision. Since true innocence is, moreover, so easily mistaken for the sentimental and conventional (think back to the risks Blake took in innocent Songs like 'The Shepherd' and 'The Lamb'), the more subtly it is falsified, the greater the dangers it poses.

Take, for example, the problems posed by that most seemingly straightforward of experienced Songs, 'The Garden of Love.' On the surface, no poem could be simpler (the design is a different matter, as we shall see). What had been a place of 'joys and desires,' becomes one of 'Love' in the lily's religious or institutional sense; a chapel and graveyard disfigure the green of innocent sexual play found in plate 2 of 'The Ecchoing Green.' If the poem invites us to share its speaker's baffled dismay, the values he implicitly endorses make such sharing possible. That his 'Garden of Love' was originally a place both of innocence and of 'gratified desire,' is especially reassuring; clearly his is no Clod or Lilly-like innocence. What holds the speaker down, 'binding with briars' his 'joys and desires,' is external: the 'priests in black gowns' who serve Earth's 'Father of the ancient men' and 'Free love with bondage bound' in 'Earth's Answer.' All the qualities of Earth's enemies – secretiveness, mystery, and compulsion ('walking their rounds' suggests soldiers on guard) – surround the chapel and its servants, preventing the speaker from enjoying those 'sweet flowers' that *Innocence* and certain experienced plates ('The Sick Rose,' for example, or that of the three flower poems) have taught us to associate with sexual love. At first glance, then, the poem seems a simple attempt on the Bard's part to recreate a moment like that of Earth's initial subjugation. This, the Bard seems to be saying, is how Earth first found herself 'Prison'd on watery shore.'

Yet something bothers us about the poem's simplicity. Bloom, for instance, finds its bitterness so much 'simpler and poetically less effective' than that of other Songs dealing with similar themes that he calls 'The Garden of Love' 'the poorest of the *Songs of Experience*' and even wonders if it 'might perhaps have been better left in the Notebook.'[28] Simplicity, of course, is not in itself what bothers him or us. Rather it is a sense of something artful about the poem's artlessness. The wide-eyed child-likeness of the second line's 'saw what I never had seen' seems contrived. There is also something too pat, too predictably deplorable about the objects of the speaker's indignation in the final stanza (the neat internal rhymes in lines 15 and 16 play some part in creating this impression). We feel sympathy and outrage at first, but after them comes something quite different: a vague sense that we are being played upon. The speaker's (moral) victory, as in 'A Little Boy Lost,' is too easy.

The poem's allegorical implications lie at the heart of our distrust. Not because they point to any supposed incompatibility between sexual fulfilment and the speaker's child-like manner (that would make ours a very Lilly-like complaint) but because of the suddenness of the garden's transformation. That external institutions rob the speaker of his joys (or loves) is the main burden of his song. These institutions are both real and powerful. That they appear so unexpectedly, though ('saw what I never had seen'), without, for example, any of the intermediate darkening which creeps into the innocent sweep's voice, disturbs us. How, we wonder, can love, in Gillham's words, be 'made sinful, and so a reminder of mortality,'[29] wholly by external agency? The speaker is not like Ona in 'A Little Girl Lost,' a bud blasted before it reaches maturity. Because the speaker has loved and lost, he must himself bear some responsibility for what has happened, since the 'joys and desires' bound by the priests in the last stanza are his own (i.e. they emanate from him) as well as the objects of his love. Once we remember what the garden's transformation stands for, neither the suddenness of the speaker's fate nor his helplessness is wholly believable. The child-like way in which the speaker tells his tale, though, makes us think of him simply as victim. It bothers us, therefore, because it seems an attempt to mask or play down his responsibility.

The relationship between text and design only augments our doubts. The poem itself lies under the ground, beneath an open grave beside which kneel a priest and his young charges. Unpleasant, squiggly flourishes divide the stanzas. One, at the bottom, fattens into an earthworm as it climbs the right border. Another, above it, has been painted red, reminding us of the flesh-like acanthus on the first of the two 'Cradle Song' plates in *Innocence.* The volutes which grow out from the title are similarly unpleasant. Some are spiky, like thorns – others look like roots. 'All grow downwards,' notes Erdman.[30] Decoration of this sort, I believe, implicates the text itself, not just the priests in its story. That the speaker's words sprout thorns, grow out of roots, lie buried in the ground, ought to put us on our guard.[31] It ought also to make us take seriously an interpretation of the sort

Gillham proposes, one which sees 'The Garden of Love' as 'a realm of the mind.' 'If it is despoiled,' writes Gillham of the garden, 'the only person who can effect the damage is the individual concerned. If the speaker once enjoyed love that has now become degraded by religious and social pressures, it is he who has given way to the pressures.'[32] The speaker's indictment of established institutions, we realize, subtly undermines an essential truth of Innocence: the liberating power of vision. The Bard has so entered into Earth's way of seeing that he has forgotten the initial truth which lay behind his unfortunately phrased call in 'Introduction.' By giving his speaker a child-like simplicity, the Bard seeks our sympathy for him, but he also obscures not only the speaker's responsibility for what has happened, but his capacity to put it right – to regain the love he has lost. So eager is the Bard to communicate the evils of religious and social compulsion, that he falsifies both his speaker's character and the vision he aims to serve.

The eponymous speaker of 'The Little Vagabond' provides another and perhaps clearer instance of the sort of right-minded complacency that strikes us as false in 'The Garden of Love.' He too displays all the right opinions – ale-house over church, joyousness over sober-sided piety – while neatly attacking the church's failings: its hypocrisy, for instance ('*modest* dame Lurch, who is always at Church'), the viciousness of its compulsion ('Would not have bandy children nor fasting nor birch'), its implacability, jealous hoarding of divinity, and tendency to abstract good and evil (all implicitly repudiated in the concluding stanza). For Gillham to complain that the vagabond's vision is too earthy ('He places too much emphasis on a mood of insistent pleasantness, and a Church of drinking parsons and elated congregations does not seem more responsible or mature than one of "fasting and birch" '[33]), seems to me quite wrong. If we are to fault the speaker, it is surely not for views repeatedly endorsed by *Innocence*. Though his ideal religion is conceived in terms of the comforts he lacks (remember 'sweep heaven' in the innocent 'Chimney Sweeper'), it is hardly one of 'very private and limited satisfactions.'[34] His concern, after all, like that of the children who suffer in *Innocence*, is for the comfort not only of himself and his mother, but of the Parson, Dame Lurch's children, even God himself.

Why, then, do we find ourselves resisting his appeal, unable to believe in his innocence as we did in that of, for instance, the innocent sweep or the little black boy? Because his victory, like that of the speakers of 'A Little Boy Lost' and 'The Garden of Love,' is too easy, the enemies he attacks too obviously evil. His acuteness, though structured in adult terms of cause and effect, 'if' and 'then,' is tricked out with the designedly endearing awkwardnesses of the *faux naif* or child actor. The poem's metrical irregularities, its half rhymes, and *rime riche*, are all too obviously intentional. Lines like, 'And we'd be as happy as birds on the wing,' or 'We'd sing and we'd dance all the live long day,' sound stale and formulaic. Again, David Copperfield provides a useful contrast: 'I look from Mr Chillip, in his Sunday neckcloth, to the pulpit; and think what a good place it would be to play in, and what a castle it would make, with another boy coming up the stairs to attack it, and having the velvet cushion with the tassels thrown down upon his head.'[35] The difference between this passage and "The Little Vagabond" is young David's speedy and unconscious entry into his fantasy, the flying cushion so vividly imagined that any hint of calculation or analytic distance seems out of the question.

The distinction between true and affected innocence is, I am aware, a fine one. Why, for instance, balk at the more sentimental lines of 'The Little Vagabond' and not at 'Little lamb who made thee' or 'How sweet is the shepherd's sweet lot'? Context plays its part: the simple fact that the former come from *Experience* is important. It matters, for instance, that so many adult speakers in *Experience*, the Bard included, are not to be trusted; that their words are often circled by or seem to grow out of unattractive decorative vegetation of the sort found on 'The Garden of Love' plate; that the little vagabond's 'God the Father' looks like Earth's 'Father of the ancient men,' or the monstrous old man on 'The Human Abstract' plate. Why else, for example, should 'The Schoolboy' strike us as a simple protest against social compulsion in *Innocence*, and something quite different in *Experience*?[36] Though at first, when we read it in *Experience*, we think its eponymous speaker a true innocent, closer inspection reveals disquieting similarities to characters like the little vagabond and the child speaker of 'A Little Boy Lost.' Lines like, 'How can a child when fears annoy/But droop his tender wing' strike us as distanced and calculating, much too knowing to be truly innocent. This, we think to ourselves, is hardly the way the Piper or one of his speakers register their protests. Their songs are much less direct or black and white.

Nor would we be wrong, despite our knowledge of the place this plate originally held in *Innocence*. 'The Schoolboy' was shifted from *Innocence* to *Experience* not just because it is a poem of protest but because its overt social concern is unmitigated by the sort of sympathy and insight the innocent 'Chimney Sweeper' and 'Holy Thursday' (both 'protest' poems) show for victimizers as well as victims. The protests of true innocents – the speaker of the innocent 'Chimney Sweeper' or the little black boy – are tentative and implicit. The schoolboy's 'argument' is explicit, like those of the eponymous speakers of 'The Little Vagabond' or 'A Little Boy Lost.' It is also experienced in structure: 'O! father and mother, if buds are nip'd/ ... /How shall the summer arise in joy.' Contrast this with the children of the innocent 'Nurse's Song' who *cannot* go to bed.' Think also of the calculation, the palpable design (reinforced by the insistent rhyme, a common feature of these poems) of 'Under a cruel eye outworn,/The little ones spend the day,/In sighing and dismay'; and then contrast it with the elder sweep's more muted and effectual concern for little Tom Dacre. That Blake saw none of these differences when he first composed the poem does not really matter (except to reinforce our sense of how personal the Bard's dilemma was for him). It is enough, for our purposes, that at some point he removed it from *Innocence*. In *Experience*, he must have realized, the fact that the schoolboy's innocence seems compromised by the explicitness of his protest – that prophetic urgency and fervor falsify the genuinely child-like – fits into a larger, organized pattern. Its flaws become the Bard's not Blake's.

2

'The Schoolboy' is one of several plates in *Experience* which deal directly with the educational or instructional issues raised and implicitly commented upon by *Innocence*. Others are 'The Fly' and 'Nurse's Song,' the designs to which depict the dispiriting and isolating consequences of adult instruction (note the lassitude and passivity of the nurse's charges in the latter; the implied transition from learning to walk to the casual violence of the young girl's 'thoughtless' game in the former; the separation of children in both). It is the texts, though, and precisely those which reveal discrepancies between poetic ends and prophetic means, which keep the educational debate talked of in chapter I before our eyes. The schoolboy, I suggested earlier, sounds like a child-actor, a *faux naif.* The same could be said of the speakers of 'The Little Vagabond,' 'A Little Boy Lost,' 'The Chimney Sweeper,' 'The Garden of Love,' and 'The Fly.' All strike us as too good, too knowing, too calculatedly appealing in their artful combination of innocent vulnerability and wisdom. They are like the 'good' or 'model' children in late eighteenth- and early nineteenth-century juvenile books, especially those to whom I think we should now turn, whose creators were influenced by Rousseau.

The *Émile*-inspired model child owed his existence, in part, to Rousseau's notion of the sort of useful or practical information applicable to small communities of farmers and craftsmen, not to an England in which the industrial revolution was already under way. 'In a highly complex society,' writes Muriel Jaeger of the problems facing Rousseau's late eighteenth- and early nineteenth-century English disciples, 'the information that can be reinforced by practical experiences is too limited.'

What a 'naturally educated' child knew he knew well; it was a part of himself; but it was not really enough for a citizen of nineteenth-century Britain. Moreover, as Edgeworth himself had found, the method throws a greater strain on the educators than most of them are willing to undergo and costs more than they can afford. ... More and more the teachers gravitated back to books, which Rousseau had entirely ruled out for children under ten. They remained, however, books from which every imaginative stimulus had been carefully removed. The child, like Émile, learned only facts (or whatever were then believed to be facts) but not only, nor even chiefly, facts that it could see and handle. Rousseau's bar on reasoning with children was also inevitably discarded when they no longer learnt only by experience.[37]

The terrible irony of this state of affairs cannot have escaped Blake. Instead of freeing and respecting children, the educational progressives robbed them of what he considered their most cherished qualities.

That Rousseau's educational followers found themselves, like

Lockeans, turning to reason as a mode of instruction is not, finally, surprising (though it must have been immensely disappointing to men like Blake); Rousseau himself had ambivalent feelings about what E. J. Hobsbawm calls 'reason as against "feeling." '[38] For Rousseau, writes Erdman, 'there is a dilemma in the fact that the growth of reason corresponds to the degeneration of the species, for reason is to Rousseau man's potential capacity for perfecting himself.'[39] No wonder, therefore, that when Mary Wollstonecraft, in her Preface to *Original Stories*, apologizes that 'These conversations and tales are accommodated to the present state of society; which obliges the author to cure those faults by reason which ought never to have taken root in the infant mind,'[40] we cannot tell whether her apology is that of an apostate or a believer.

The tutor's role in *Émile* also led to distortions, both of Rousseau's theories and of the voices of the children who were to exemplify them. It too, like Rousseau's attitude to reason, was somewhat ambiguous to begin with. On the one hand, the child was to teach himself, through personal experience. On the other, the tutor was to prevent him from avoiding or skirting over the displeasing effects of undesirable behavior. Though the child was to be as free as possible, the tutor was to be in constant attendance, firmly but tactfully drawing the lessons of experience, even when they entailed suffering. This is why parents, though the most 'natural' of guides, are, in practice, unable to fulfil the tutor's role. That the ideal tutor would be difficult, if not impossible, to find, Rousseau knew full well.[41] In the juvenile fiction of Blake's day, though, he was everywhere. By the 1780s the omniscient *Émile*-inspired teacher, friend or parent had become a stock figure in children's literature. Characters like Mr Barlow in *Sandford and Merton*, Mrs Mason in *Original Stories*, the fathers in *Harry and Lucy*, or in Aiken and Barbauld's *Evenings At Home; or The Juvenile Budget Opend* (1792–6), Rosamund's mother in 'The Purple Jar,' or Mr Gresham in another of Maria Edgeworth's stories, 'Waste Not Want Not,' knew everything, could and did explain everything, and quickly turned each new experience – 'from the consumption of a plate of cherries,' complains Dickens of that 'instructive monomaniac,' Mr Barlow, 'to the contemplation of a starlight night'[42] – into a profitable lesson. 'For this unnatural growth,' writes Wordsworth of the model child, 'the trainer blame,/Pity the tree.'[43]

Especially galling was the manner in which fictional tutors expressed their wisdom, as in the following passage from Wollstonecraft's *Original Stories*. While Mrs Mason and her charges are out for a walk, a storm breaks:

The children were terrified; but Mrs. Mason gave them each a hand and chatted with them to dispel their fears. She informed them that storms were necessary to dissipate noxious vapours, and to answer many other purposes, which were not, perhaps, obvious to our weak understandings. But are you not afraid? Cried the trembling Caroline. No, certainly, I am not afraid. – I walk with the same certainty as when the sun enlivened the prospect – God is still present, and we are safe. Should the flash that passes by us, strike me dead, it cannot hurt me, I fear not death, I only fear that Being who can render death terrible, on whose providence I calmly rest; and my confidence earthly sorrows cannot destroy. A mind is never truly great, till the love of virtue overcomes the fear of death.[44]

The fictional children cared for by Mrs Mason and her like spoke in no less pompous and 'unnatural' a fashion, particularly those whose role it was to provide 'correct' responses in a given model situation. Take, for example, six-year-old Henry Sandford, the English Émile, who, when invited to dinner by Squire Merton, ex-planter father of his friend Tommy, criticizes his adult host for the extravagance of the meal, observing that 'it is not fit that we mind what we live upon, but we should take what we can and be contented, just as the beasts and birds do, who lodge in the open air and live upon herbs and drink nothing but water and yet they are strong and active and healthy.'[45] Like Wordsworth's model child, or the vagabonds and chimney sweepers of *Experience*, Henry is 'Innocent himself, withall, though shrewd/And can read lectures upon innocence.'[46]

Nor was it only in fiction that impossibly 'model' children like Henry appeared. Though Edgeworth's educational experiments on his own son (approved by Rousseau himself on a visit to Paris in 1777) had finally to be abandoned, those of Benjamin Heath Malkin lasted right up until his unfortunate child's death at the age of seven.[47] Malkin, subsequently headmaster of Bury Grammar School, and a man of 'advanced' educational views, published a biography of his son in 1806, four years after the child's death. Blake was commissioned by Malkin to design and engrave a portrait of the child for the frontispiece, and seems to have become something of a spiritual comforter to the bereaved father.[48] In the Preface to young Thomas's biography Malkin protests that his child's extraordinary achievements (infant Thomas knew his alphabet at age one and a half, could read at two, write at three, and master any English book at four) were the products of personal initiative, rather than parental prodding.[49] His insistence that his son's talents were natural and naturally developed, and the pride he took in the extraordinary amount of information the child managed to absorb in his young life, were typical of progressive, *Émile*-oriented English educational theorists.

As for the child himself, he seems to have taken Henry Sandford as a model, adopting a style in his letters clearly calculated to please moral-minded adults:

> The months of the year are January, February, March, April, May, June, July, August, September, October, November, December. Civilized nations, in January, they in general agree to begin reckoning the new year from the first of that month.
>
> – Water is, when frozen, expanded; that is, takes up more room than before. ... My Latin Dictionary is very useful to me, so is my stool. ... The Calendar of Nature is very useful to me; and I think it was very good in Dr Aiken and Mrs. Barbauld to write these employing books for little boys instead of grown people.
>
> (Letter of October 30, 1800, to his mother)

> I hope you will trust that the great and good God will make us both [Thomas and his younger brother Benjamin] better still, though I assure you I have this morning had very serious thoughts of being much better now I am six. However, I still think there is much room for improvement in us both, especially me. ... I hope that you think all this about improvement is a very good subject. ... Ben, I trust, will read and spell to me well; for you know, the better he does it, the more improvement he will gain by it, and the more useful it will make him. He seems to me to be a very good little boy.
>
> (Letter of October 30, 1801, to his mother)[50]

These, the accents of a self-consciously 'ideal' or 'model' child[51] – the sort Wordsworth, Lamb, and others deplored – we have been listening to in *Experience*, not just in its improbable children, but in the false naiveté of obviously adult speakers. The characters of *Experience*, like Henry Sandford or Mrs Mason's charges, have, that is, been sacrificed to the larger principles of their 'creator,' in this case the Bard. Blake's *Songs*, though especially sensitive to the cruelties and limitations of Lockean and Calvinist conceptions of childhood, are no less attentive to the falsifications and sentimentalities of progressive theory and practice.

This is true in other respects aside from the depiction – or rather 'violation' – of character. Take, for example, the Bard's tendency to declaim and assert. Liberal or Jacobin children's books, like many Songs of Experience, tend to 'state' rather than to embody or depict their themes, or to embody or depict them only after they have been stated. First Mrs Mason lays down a law or maxim, then she provides, or has provided for her, an incident which illustrates it. This structure of maxim and illustration, statement and proof, is, as we have seen, characteristic of *Experience*. What also reminds us of *Experience* is our sense that the illustrative episodes in books like *Sandford and Merton* are false and forced. Rousseau himself had realized, in *Émile*, how difficult it would be, even when the child was brought up in the country, where the course of nature is less frequently obstructed, for tutors to contrive the simple situations that alone would teach cause and effect. Many of these situations, Muriel Jaeger reminds us, 'had to be secretly contrived by [the] tutor, who must, one fears, have had to pay out quite large sums of money to induce other people to play the parts assigned to them.'[52] 'Such is the method of *Émile*,' writes Fuseli with unmixed approval, 'insinuating virtue, without giving one single precept.'[53]

Insinuating and contriving, though, often defeats the purpose it means to serve – manipulating children in the name of liberty, patronizing them in the name of respect. David Williams, for example, tells of having cured one pupil of lying, by secretly enlisting the help of another, getting him to fight with the first youth, and then disbelieving the liar's story when he came, quite legitimately, to complain. He even went on to ask the second youth's help in getting the first to learn truthfulness, inducing in one the very habit he sought to discourage in the other.[54]

Even when Nature alone is the teacher, as is often the case in late eighteenth-century progressive juvenile literature, the implausability of its just proceedings strikes us as contrived and patronizing. In 'The Orange Man, or the Honest Boy and the Thief,' in the Edgeworths' *Harry and Lucy* series, for example, honest Charles fights wicked but stronger Ned in order to protect some oranges he has been given by an orange man. At a crucial moment in their struggle, a conveniently right-minded horse trots by and helpfully kicks Ned.[55] Though the story does not patronize its young readers by preaching to them, it does present them with a falsely simplified picture of the world, one intended to 'do them good.' Blake, as the Songs of Experience we have been examining imply, was acutely aware of the disrespect for childhood and innocence implicit in simplifications of this sort. Is it not precisely what disturbs us about the experienced 'Chimney Sweeper,' for example, in which the eponymous speaker's words perfectly conform to the expectations raised by the Bard-like (that is, authoritative as well as compassionate) voice which introduces them?

The extremity or exaggeration of the introductory formulations of a Mr Barlow or a Mrs Mason also remind us of *Experience*. They too positively invite us to think up exceptions, as we do, for instance, when we encounter a phrase like 'eternal winter' in *Experience*. Finally, like many experienced Songs, progressive juvenile books of the late eighteenth century frequently, and often at highly inopportune moments, lapse into the very habits – of diction, structure, and tone – they are meant to oppose. The old 'Good Godly' black/white divisions shine through the surface tolerance; the 'rational' voice of the omniscient tutor takes on the harshly impersonal tones of a Keatch or a Janeway; the child's world, like a Calvinist's, is governed by predetermined events.

Blake's consciousness of the dangers of this sort of progressive manipulation must have derived in part from his contact with the progressives themselves. The man who in later life was to complain of Rousseau that he 'thought men good by nature ... but found them evil and found no friend' (*J* 52.45–6: E199),[56] was unlikely to have overlooked the manner in which so many of the advanced educationalists of his, as of any, age tended in the name of liberty, to lose sight of the particular children on whom they experimented. While Mary Wollstonecraft was a teacher, one of her biographers tells us,

'Her letters, which discuss neighbors, callers, servants, and lodgers freely enough, do not so much as mention the name of a pupil, although the ideas she had begun to acquire about education, filtered down from Rousseau and Thomas Day, required close and constant supervision of each child.'[57] Day himself, an unswervingly loyal disciple both of Rousseau and of liberty, could see his way to bringing up two foundling children with the express purpose of eventually picking the more 'correct' of the two as his wife (judged, in part, by their reactions to tests of endurance such as the dropping of hot wax on bare arms or the unexpected firing of pistols close to their ears).[58] Blake lived in the world of these men and women. He knew Malkin. He also knew and worked with Mary Wollstonecraft, and though we have no proof that he actually met Day and the Edgeworths, he was on close terms with Johnson, the former's publisher, and with Stothard, the illustrator of the first edition of *Sandford and Merton*. Blake also knew and worked for Thomas Wedgwood, whose proposed 'Centre for Child Study and Controlled Development' aimed to spread the theory, radical in its own fashion, if not quite in Rousseau's, that pupil and tutor should be shut *away* from nature ('the child,' writes Wedgwood to Godwin in 1796, 'must never go out of doors or leave his own apartment'). That Wedgwood could be as obtuse or insensitive as the next theorist is also suggested by his once having considered William Wordsworth for the Wardenship of the Centre.[59] As for Godwin, who also wrote and published children's books influenced by Rousseau, and whose views on personal relations were at least as 'theoretical' as Day's, Blake seems to have found him singularly unsympathetic.[60] In sum, while Blake shared many of the political and social sympathies of Rousseau and the educational progressives, he must, at the same time, have been profoundly dismayed by the part their juvenile books and educational treatises played in transforming a genuine faith in the nobility of childhood into the sort of educational system even a Mrs Sherwood could approve. He must also have connected this transformation to an equally gradual and unintended betrayal in the political sphere: that of the Revolution in France, suggestions of the corruption of which began to appear in the Illuminated Books as early as 1792–3.

Blake's disenchantment with progressive educationalists, though, is hinted at even earlier, in the 1791 illustrations to Mary Wollstonecraft's *Original Stories*. Plate 3 (figure 22), for example, bears the caption 'Indeed we are very happy,' but depicts a singularly *un*happy and uncomfortable recipient of Mrs Mason's charity, honest Jack the Fisherman; plates 1, 4, and 6 (figures 23–25), on which Mrs Mason and her two girls, Mary and Caroline, are depicted, suggest, in Cornelia Meigs's words, that Blake was 'entirely on the side of the children.'

> Although he has presented Mrs. Mason as slim, lissome, and goodlooking, one sees her always in a studied pose, the conscious teacher, while the children look wistfully out from the page as though glancing surreptitiously at that wider and more natural world which their conductress will not allow them to enter.[61]

Blake's use of almost exactly the same design – that of a vine-strewn doorway, with adult female in the center and children on either side – to illustrate both the 'Nurse's Song' of *Experience* and the frontispiece to *Original Stories* only confirms the reading.

Experience, then, despite the prominence it gives to questions of adult love and sexuality, continues, like *Innocence*, to allude to – to echo, parody, and expose – key motifs and presuppositions of late eighteenth-century children's books and educational theory. Its focus, though, is less on the traditionalists, the followers of Locke and Calvin, than on their supposed antagonists. The problems its speakers pose for us are precisely those raised by progressive children's books. The same 'Yes, but ...' characterizes our reactions to both. *Experience* teaches us to guard against the sorts of simplifications and sentimentalities propounded by right-minded educational innovators. It also teaches us to take seriously the dangers they pose.

CHAPTER 7
THE BARD REDEEMED

In chapter 1 I argued that Blake's greatest debts to children's literature were structural and functional in nature: that *Songs* was at once alphabet and guide to doctrine (*Innocence*), and reader or workbook (*Experience*). The tests *Experience* poses the newly initiated visionary (the reader, that is, who comes straight from *Innocence*) are often subtle and difficult. But they are also, as I have tried to suggest, meant to be recognized and overcome. The ultimate source of the most difficult of these tests is the Bard himself, a guide who unwittingly lapses into the very experienced tendencies he means to expose and overturn in others. The problem I want now to examine is that of the Bard's own fate. Does his story – that of an artist's growth into innocent visionary and subsequent lapse into experienced prophet – contradict the visionary aspirations excited and tested by *Songs* as a whole? Is the reader to succeed where the Piper-Bard fails? Is the Bard throughout *Experience* a victim to the confusions betrayed in the opening sequence?

To answer these questions we must look first to those later plates in *Experience* in which the Bard appears *in propria persona*. The first of these is 'The Little Girl Lost,' the opening stanzas of which echo the confusions of 'Introduction':

> In futurity
> I prophetic see,
> That the earth from sleep,
> (Grave the sentence deep)

Shall arise and seek
For her maker meek:
And the desart wild
Become a garden mild.

Here again we have a call to Earth, a promise of future bliss, a proposed rejection of the here and now – and ominous echoes of Genesis 3:8. When the earth 'shall arise' from sleep to meet its 'maker meek,' the 'desart wild' of our present earthly existence will become a 'garden mild.' Since 'desart,' 'wild,' and 'sleep' take on specific symbolic meanings in succeeding lines, the full impact of the Bard's words can only properly be understood in light of what follows. Lyca's story – that of a symbolic sexual awakening (see chapter 2) – must be looked at closely.

When first we meet Lyca she is alone 'in desart wild.' All we know of her past (aside from the fact that her parents are distraught at her disappearance) is that she 'had wander'd long/ Hearing wild Birds song,' which suggests either that she 'wandered after' the song, like Keats following the song of the nightingale, or that the song somehow accompanied – was associated with – her wanderings. Throughout *Songs*, in both text and design, wild birds in flight are associated with freedom, delight, realized aspirations, energy, and assertion. They are also associated with open and untrammelled sexuality. We think back to the bottom half of the first plate of 'The Ecchoing Green' where a golden bird darts 'swift as arrow' ('The Blossom') towards ripe grapes; or to the 'painted birds' of 'Laughing Song' whose voices, echoing those of attractive young revellers 'with ... sweet round mouths,' swell the poem's exuberant chorus of delight. This is the song Lyca hears in 'The Little Girl Lost.' It is a song heard by all young maidens who, from an experienced perspective, 'lose their way.'[1] In *Innocence*, it sanctifies, as in plate 2 of 'The Ecchoing Green,' where the girl in green is haloed as she reaches, like the golden bird of the previous plate, for a bunch of grapes; in *Experience*, as in 'A Little Girl Lost,' it leads to vicious reaction on the part of adult authority.

In stanza 5 Lyca, wearied by her wanderings, calls out to 'sweet sleep' in the manner of a lover. Given the serpent whose tongue hisses out between stanzas 2 and 3, the 'Tree' under which she lies, and the pun in the poem's fourth line (as well as several other suggestive details referred to in chapter 2), we associate 'sleep' with the realization of those desires awakened or signalled by her wanderings in 'desart wild.' From her first appearance in line .12 Lyca has been seeking sleep. What prevents her from attaining it are memories of her parents. She begins to imagine what they must be feeling, sees them weeping over her disappearance, fretting over where she will sleep. Line 20 implies that the parents simply cannot conceive of their daughter sleeping anywhere except in her bed at home. Sleep entails trust, comfort, peace, qualities they think they alone can provide for their daughter. If Lyca can sleep in 'desart wild,' it suggests that she is 'at home' in her freedom and independence; that she trusts her desires and impulses, 'wild' though they may be. (The 'desart' she feels at home in need not be a place of barren sands or sterile expanses. As Hirsch reminds us, Blake is probably using the term 'in its root meaning: an uninhabited and uncultivated tract or country, a wilderness.'[2] The designs on plate 2 suggest as much.)

In lines 21 to 22 Lyca imagines telling her parents of her situation. Though she means to comfort them, her words ('Lost in desart wild/Is your little child') are hardly reassuring. Rather they suggest that complex of painful and often contradictory emotions – the need to defy, even hurt the parents one loves – which invariably attend a child's growth into independence. When Lyca goes on to ask her mother and father in the next two lines how they expect her to rest if her mother weeps, she is being both considerate and manipulative. Hirsch calls lines 23 and 24 'a kind of loving blackmail.'[3] Though genuinely upset at the thought of her mother's misery ('Psychologically ... she will be unable to descend into experience because of a sense of guilt at abandoning the parents, if the parents weep over her'),[4] she is also fearless, determined to use all her emotional resources to free herself from parental guilt. There is something touchingly heroic about Lyca's attitude towards her situation. It is not the 'desart wild' against which she must struggle, but her own ultimately life-denying impulses to return home – impulses which her parents probably fed before she left, and which the image of their weeping embodies.

Lyca is 'lost' only to her parents. Nothing in her tone suggests that she is anxious about her state – nothing, that is, except the thought of her parents' anxiety. Though Lyca calls the night 'frowning' she is not afraid:

> Frowning frowning night,
> O'er this desart bright,
> Let thy moon arise,
> While I close my eyes.

She closes her eyes in trust that night will answer her request and let itself be lit by the moon. We are touched by her openness and vulnerability, as well as by her determination to enter into experience. It is, we feel, her trust which has made the desert 'bright,' just as her attitude towards sexual experience will hallow the ground upon which she embraces it in the stanzas that follow.

In stanza 7 Lyca had shown innocence of another sort. If her mother insists on weeping (taking 'her' in line 25 to refer to the mother's heart), then because Lyca is loving and dutiful, she will not sleep; or, in symbolic terms, will hold herself back from entry into experience. (If 'her' refers to Lyca's own heart the result is the same.) Like Adams, I believe that a withholding of this sort would be 'tragic,'[5] a life-denying act equivalent to Thel's retreat, or Har and Heva's withdrawal, or Oothoon's having remained in Leutha's vale, or the Lady's return to her parents in the last of Blake's illustrations to Milton's *Comus* (two versions: c. 1801, c. 1815). In Lyca's case, though, it is genuine feeling for her parents rather than timidity which prompts her to contemplate a retreat. She is a dutiful daughter, but she is also a newly independent person, with a clear sense of what she wants and needs. Her intention in stanza 7, gently pursued, is to shame her parents into the calm that will set her free. We are made to feel towards her what parents feel when their daughters enter into marriage. For all her innocence, fragility, and inexperience, Lyca, like the blushing bride of popular tradition, seems to know and look forward to what awaits her.

What happens to Lyca in the rest of the poem confirms her innocent faith and trust. The wild beasts who undress her and carry her away are like the lions of 'Night': tender and caring, yet still 'wild.' The 'couching lion' who becomes 'A spirit arm'd in gold' in 'The Little Girl Found' is, for Blake, the true Christ; his love is human, earthly, energetic, not 'holy' in any disembodied 'cant' sense. The fierceness of his attack and his gentleness go together, validating Lyca's attraction to and trust in all that 'wild birds song' represents.

That the two poems end with Lyca asleep and her parents 'In

a lonely dell' need not undermine what has gone before. Though left with 'all the sorrow Parents feel' (*FZ* 5.62.10: E335), Lyca's Mother and Father have at last adjusted to their daughter's independence, no longer fearing for her safety as though she were a child; doing so, though, has left them alone. For them, Lyca will always be 'asleep.' The Lyca poems, like their designs, remind us of 'Night.' Though filled with mystery and what looks like mysticism, their concern is with the here and now, with a phenomenon no more magical than that of a child's growth into adulthood, and her parents' consequent attempts to adjust to the loss. What makes these poems special, though, and what accounts for their original inclusion in *Innocence*, is the golden glow, at once sober and approving, cast over the whole process, which sanctifies it without ignoring the pain it entails. In this, they are like traditional fairy tales, whose effect, in Bruno Bettelheim's words, is 'to enable [the child] to accept the problematic nature of life without being defeated by it, or giving in to escapism.'[6]

What, then, are we to make of the Bard's opening words; words which seem almost an interpretation of Lyca's story? We associate Lyca with the 'earth' the Bard refers to in line 3 (thanks to the female Earth of the opening sequence), and think of the Bard as calling for her to wake and quit the desert for a 'garden mild.' But in the final plate we realize that Lyca's desert *is* a garden. What could be 'milder' or more beautiful than the concluding design? Lyca has already transformed the 'desert wild,' not by rising from it, but by seeing it right. Her story places wholly different values from those of the Bard on words like 'desert,' 'meek,' 'sleep,' and 'transcendence.' Lyca embraces the very world of body the Bard calls Earth to reject. Yet as in 'Introduction,' the Bard's words are only in part disturbing. Though his language echoes that of the oppressor God, and though he asks earth to arise, he also speaks of the desert 'becoming' a garden mild rather than being abandoned for it. Still, though, earth-Lyca, he insists, must wake; and waking, given the symbolic value of sleep in succeeding stanzas, would mean abandoning this world for the supposed pleasures of an 'allegorical abode.' The difference, then, between the Bard of these plates and the Bard of the introductory sequence is very slight, a matter of degree. If anything, our doubts about him deepen.

Whereas the 'Lyca' poems feed our suspicions about the

Piper's lapse into Bardhood, 'A Little Girl Lost,' the next poem in copy Z in which the Bard appears undisguised, dampens them. The 'love' the Bard speaks of in the opening stanza belongs, for instance, clearly to this world; is a sort Lyca and Oothoon would approve. Nor is the indignation with which he laments its repression coupled with calls to 'arise' or with disconcerting references to 'lapsed Souls' or 'makers meek.' The Bard of 'A Little Girl Lost' strikes us as a wholly sympathetic ally and defender of the Earth of 'Earth's Answer.' His aim is to corroborate her account of the forces ranged against her, to expose the cruel hypocrisy of those who 'hold her down.' Ona's tyrannous, 'hoary,' 'father white,' with his 'loving look/Like the holy book,' reminds us immediately of Earth's 'Father of the ancient men,' 'Starry Jealousy.' He also reminds us of the 'Holy Word' of 'Introduction,' since the place from which he bans his daughter (with 'dismal,' and no doubt weeping, care) is a garden. Only the second stanza's reference to an 'Age of Gold/Free from winters cold' troubles us, calling to mind the implied eternal spring of 'Holy Thursday.' The rest of the stanza, however, associates holiness with a wholly natural light ('sunny beams'), one which sanctifies nakedness and delight, and quickly puts our doubts to rest. So, too, does the initial impression of 'immense libidinal energy'[7] made by the design (all those swirling tendrils, soaring birds, the squirrel arching towards a bunch of grapes). In short, the Bard of 'A Little Girl Lost' strikes us as a trustworthy guide, one whose path through *Experience* is lit by a vision of true innocence. Our doubts, accordingly, diminish, even as our confusion about the degree of control Blake exercises over his meanings grows.

'The Voice of the Ancient Bard' does much to resolve that confusion – in any copy of *Songs*, even, it could be argued, those in which it appears under the innocent heading. It also opens a whole new chapter in the Bard's story. It is the last plate in *Experience* and the third, not counting the opening sequence, in which the Bard appears *in propria persona*. The effect it has on other plates in *Experience* is immensely important (again, no matter which half of *Songs* it appears in: though in copies of *Innocence* issued separately from *Experience* the effect is, of course, quite different). No other experienced plate in copy Z does more to re-confirm our initial doubts about the Bard, or to justify our discomfort with seemingly straightforward plates.

It does so if, that is, we are prepared to accept its speaker as the Bard of previous plates: as an older and wiser version of the figure we have followed from carefree piping to prophetic indignation, from growth into and out of innocence. This, though, is precisely what poem and design encourage us to do. Once again, as of old, the Bard begins with a call. Once again he speaks of a new day, an 'opening morn.' *This* opening morn, though, begins today, right away. 'Truth new born' is no longer relegated to some distant future or golden past. 'Doubt *is* fled,' along with all the other impediments to wisdom encountered in previous plates: 'clouds of reason' of the sort that befogged the child-like speakers of 'The Fly,' 'The Chimney Sweeper,' and 'The Little Vagabond'; 'Dark disputes' of the sort encountered in 'A Poison Tree' or 'My Pretty Rose Tree'; 'artful teazing' of the sort found in 'The Angel' or 'The Lilly.' Folly's 'endless maze,' its ways filled with 'tangled roots,' reminds us of the journey we ourselves have just taken – *Experience* being a kind of maze, its paths, like the borders of its designs, strewn with root-like tangles. 'How many have fallen there,' sighs the Ancient Bard: and we remember the 'wanderings' of lost little boys and girls, of the speaker of 'London,' of the many isolated and mournful figures in the designs.

'Fallen,' though, disturbs us, as does the femininity of 'Folly' (it makes us think immediately of Lyca, as if wandering in 'desart wild' were folly). The image of a regenerate Bard, freed from infection, begins to recede. But only for a moment. The next line, 'They stumble all night over bones of the dead,' makes us associate 'Folly' with 'clouds of reason' rather than with a Lyca-like (to her parents at least) 'fall.' Our hopes return, and are further buoyed by the poem's concluding lines: 'And feel they know not what but care:/And wish to lead others when they should be led,' which must, we feel, refer to the Bard himself, or rather to the Bard of previous plates. The lines not only confirm our earlier doubts about the Bard, but help us to understand why he now refers to himself as 'Ancient.' In the course of his wanderings, the Bard has grown old (when the plate appeared in *Innocence*, 'Ancient' may also, or primarily, have meant 'of former (prelapsarian) time'). The same thing happens to Urizen in *The Four Zoas*: his 'hideous pilgrimage' through a newly fallen world leaves 'bright hair scattered in snows his skin barkd oer with wrinkles' (6.74.10–11: E344). Though the Bard's tone is subdued, saddened by the many false turns he has taken, he retains his innocent faith in the possibility of a *present* 'truth new born.' Like Los in *Jerusalem*, he has 'kept the Divine Vision in times of trouble' (95.20: E252). His is a tone we have heard before: in the concluding stanzas of 'The Ecchoing Green,' 'Night,' and the 'Lyca' poems, those most 'experienced' of innocent Songs. What gives this poem its special poignancy, though, is its note of personal loss – a note which, together with the design, opens up a whole new species of hitherto unnoticed self-references in earlier plates. At the last, the Bard sees himself aright: as a guide in need of guidance, a mental traveller whose prophetic certainty and optimism has been so undermined that 'care' threatens to be his only knowledge.[8]

The design to 'The Voice of the Ancient Bard' is equally poignant. The Ancient Bard, garbed in blue,[9] with long white beard and hair, occupies center stage. Ranged round him are youths and young children, all of whom remind us of earlier figures from both volumes of *Songs*. Though listeners need not look directly at musicians or speakers, this grouping forms a particularly inattentive audience, recalling (though this is hardly a scene of comparable brutality or moment) the 'youth of England' in *Europe* who are 'compell'd' to listen while 'Aged ignorance preaches canting,/On a vast rock, perceived by those senses that are clos'd from thought' (12.7–8: E63). The couple at far left, reminding us of the lovers on the first plate of 'The Little Girl Lost,' are totally absorbed in their embrace, backs turned to the Bard; the girl kneeling in the right foreground looks away from the Bard to the three friends behind her. These friends, an amalgam of the three strollers on the second plate of 'Night,' and the three youths idling at the edge of the green on plate 1 of 'The Ecchoing Green,' give the Bard, at best, only perfunctory attention (Blake has taken some trouble with their faces, using a fine pen to heighten the impression of patient uninterest conveyed by their languid bodies). Just to the left of these three young women a small boy looks up and to the right, oblivious to the Bard. He reminds us of a similar child on plate 2 of 'The Ecchoing Green.' Only a slightly older boy[10] directly behind the harp seems to be paying much attention to the Bard and his song.

The Ancient Bard is like Old John in plate 2 of 'The Ecchoing Green': a figure of authority whose influence is limited and dwindling. Our feelings towards him, though, are different from those aroused by Old John. Old John was *of* the homeward party he shepherded, not apart from it. Though a potential repressor, he was less a figure of Urizen than of what Grant calls 'Mr. Parental Spoilsport.'[11] The Ancient Bard, on the other hand, is a sterner and more serious figure. To neglect his guiding song, to give it only perfunctory attention, is to undermine a much more substantial dignity. This is what makes his depiction so poignant; so perfect a visual equivalent of the sad self-knowledge revealed in the last line: 'And wish to lead others when they should be led.' It is also what makes the design so richly ironic. The Bard depicts himself as cut off from those he would lead. Despite his position in the center of a gathering of innocents, we think of him as having stepped out of a different world, one he himself has taught us to distrust. The Ancient Bard, we realize, is allied with the very figures his audience has most reason to fear. In *Innocence*, the Piper was identified with shepherd, lamb, child, and Christ. In *Experience*, thanks to this final flash of redemptive self-knowledge, the Piper-turned-Bard admits his kinship to the several sorts of aged oppressors who precede him.[12] It is to these figures we must next turn, after the briefest of looks at Blake's practice elsewhere.

Much more often than not, Blake associates old men (who are invariably bearded) with law-giving, Jehovah-like, Urizenic tyrants. The only exceptions I know of in pre-1795 designs are in *All Religions Are One* (1788), where a bearded old man, associated with the Poetic Genius, appears above the title-page and again at the top of plate 4 (though even here one cannot be sure, since it could be argued that the youth of the figure on the frontispiece, under whom is etched 'The Voice of one crying in the Wilderness,' makes us distrust the age of the figures who follow);[13] early Job and Ezekiel engravings; and those copies of *Innocence* and *Songs* (though this too, I have suggested, is arguable) which include as innocent 'The Voice of the Ancient Bard.'

After 1795, only the 'Good Old Man' in plate 5 of Blake's illustrations to Blair's *The Grave* (1808); David, in the 1805 watercolor *David delivered out of many waters*; the Parson of the 1809 *Canterbury Tales* engraving; and an *Ezekiel* of 1805 qualify as positive figures (Job, of course, is only 'positive' at the end of Blake's *Illustrations*, his redemption pictured in a concluding plate much like that of 'The Voice of the Ancient Bard').[14] Even after accepting all remotely possible candidates (I have excluded figures like *Joseph of Arimathea* (two states: *c.* 1773, 1795) who, though bearded, is neither old nor enervated), the number of positive figures of old and bearded men remains small. For though Blake may have started out associating father figures with tenderness, love, and divine creativity, by late 1788 his attitude had already begun to change. The old men in the designs to *Tiriel*,[15] *Visions of the Daughters of Albion* (1793), *America* (1793), *Marriage* (1790–3), *Europe* (1794), and, of course, *Urizen* (1794) and *Song of Los* (1795), all embody the evils of a perverted, reason-bound society and vision.

As for *Experience* itself, there are four old men who precede the Ancient Bard in the designs: the Father God of 'The Little Vagabond,' the aged wanderer of 'London,' the self-tormenting tormentor of 'The Human Abstract,' and the mysterious 'deliverer' of 'To Tirzah.' All have white hair and long white beards. All are gowned in costumes that wholly obscure their bodies. All are bent over, either on their knees, or with backs curved by age and care. The colors of their costumes, though different, are none of them bright and cheery. The aged wanderer of 'London,' like the Ancient Bard, is gowned in dark blue, the color of the world 'out there' in the borders of innocent scenes in the designs to 'The Shepherd,' 'The Ecchoing Green,' 'The Lamb,' and 'The Blossom.'[16] The others wear pale grey or white. The innocent equivalents of these figures, their corresponding 'type,' are straight-backed children and youths: the shepherd, the little boy of 'The Lamb,' the jolly reveller of 'Laughing Song,' the Piper. Theirs are the divinely innocent virtues of energy, assertion, and open sexuality. They too, for all their youth, are protectors and guiding spirits. But they are also closely identified with those they care for (the shepherd is likened to lamb as well as ewe, the little boy in 'The Lamb' *is* a lamb, yet looks and acts like a shepherd). Both the aged elders of *Experience* and the shining youths of *Innocence* are associated with divinity, but the former are associated with God the Father and the latter with Christ.

The first of the old men in *Experience is* God the Father, a fact the significance of which most critics have chosen to ignore. His presence on the plate serves to reinforce our doubts about the little vagabond who invokes him. It also presents us with a visual amalgam of Earth's 'Starry Jealousy' and the Bard's 'Holy Word.' Not only is this God 'Cold and hoar' (white-gowned and white-bearded), but the youth he cradles ('weeping o'er') seems almost 'prison'd' in his embrace. The youth's naked body is strong, healthy, clearly defined, quite unlike the shapeless bundles of the poor at the bottom of the plate. His nakedness reminds us of Adam and Eve in the garden. Erdman, whose reading of the design is uncharacteristically reserved, calls the scene a repetition 'at a more desperate level (of) the father-like saviour's rescue of boy in forest in plate fourteen.'[17] The desperateness to which Erdman refers is in part a product of the impression created by the terrible constriction of the youth's body. Poverty and destitution enervate. This figure is energetic, which makes us speculate about the state from which he is being rescued. Might he not be hiding his head in shame rather than (or as well as) trust? Has he, perhaps, been indulging in the very sports the children of 'The Garden of Love' (on the previous plate in copy Z) have been deprived of? (They too, we note, are on their knees, like the Priest beside them.) Might his rescuer not be a type of the Holy Word who 'walk'd among the ancient trees' (note the scene's tree-trunk backdrop) in search of a 'lapsed Soul'? Such questions, of course, cannot be answered. Yet we ask them.

The aged wanderer of 'London' is much less formidable a figure. He's also a good deal more difficult to account for, in several ways. He and his guide illustrate no scene or episode in the poem, though his obvious misery allies him with those whose 'Marks of weakness marks of woe' are detailed throughout the poem. If anything we associate him with the speaker, though part of the power of the latter's description of his wanderings derives from our sense of his isolation. Establishing the identity of wanderer and guide is, moreover, only the first of the problems posed by this plate. Something also has to be said about the design's ultimate inadequacy – no matter how we interpret it – in the face of the poem it accompanies.

'London' the poem is immensely more powerful than 'London' the design. This disparity is so striking that the design's weakness detracts – or rather distracts us – from the poem's greatness. Only the design to 'The Tyger' is comparably disappointing, perhaps because it too has so much to do and to live up to. Yet the design to 'London' is by no means thoughtless or unsubtle. On the contrary, it is immensely complicated and illuminating – if, that is, one is alive to the larger narrative into which its central figure fits.

To understand the design we must look first to the poem's tone. 'London' is the most comprehensive as well as the most powerful of Blake's indictments of experienced society and its institutions. No other poem in *Experience* takes so wide and deep a view. Yet its speaker, like so many others in *Experience*, is himself a victim to the evils he so brilliantly exposes and analyzes.[18] The steady slowness and solemnity with which he details London's horrors is a measure not only of the poem's seriousness but of the toll his knowledge has taken on him. There is, for example, something deadened, despite the bitter irony of 'charter'd' about the opening stanza:

> I wander through each charter'd street,
> Near where the charter'd Thames does flow
> And mark in every face I meet
> Marks of weakness, marks of woe.

– something which reminds us of the anaesthetized matter-of-factness with which another knowing victim in *Songs*, the elder sweep in *Innocence*, begins his poem. The diction is also telling: the word 'mark,' for instance, both in 'mark in every face I meet,' and 'Marks of weakness, marks of woe,' tells us as much about the speaker as it does about the objects of his perception. For 'Marks' refers not only to what he sees – signs, scars, and symptoms – but to the way he sees, to his isolation or distance from individual suffering.[19] He can only guess at the full extent of the miseries of his fellows. Mere 'Marks' of weakness and woe replace the things themselves. To 'mark,' moreover, can suggest 'to note in passing' rather than 'to note with care.'

In stanzas 1 and 2 the speaker describes a world made up of disembodied 'faces,' 'cries,' 'voices,' 'sighs,' and 'curses.' These belong not to particular individuals but to 'every Man' and 'every Infant.' As the poem's denunciatory tone intensifies in stanzas 3 and 4 (the alliteration of strong consonants slows the lines, making them bitterer and more sonorous), victims of a particular 'type' are singled out. We move from 'every cry' to the cries of particular sweeps, soldiers, or harlots. This generalizing tendency of the speaker's is, of course, a symptom of experience, and though it lessens neither the truth nor the power of his protest, it contributes to our sense of his isolation from those whose oppression he so bitterly protests. It also helps us to distinguish between Blake's vision and that of his speaker. Blake views the forces of oppression through the speaker's eyes – in broad, though by no means unfeeling, social terms – but he also makes us see their effects on a single individual: the speaker himself. He manages to combine the indignant social analysis of a Jeremiah with the innocent visionary's reverence for minute particulars – a perspective the speaker, for all his extraordinary eloquence, falls short of.

This is one of the reasons I suspect him of being the Bard. That his ultimate vision seems darker and more pessimistic than the Bard's (think of 'Introduction' or the 'Lyca' poems) makes us doubt, though. What Hirsch calls 'Blake's revolutionary faith in a possible transformation of the human spirit'[20] may indeed fuel the poem's passionate irony and accusation, but the sheer intensity of the speaker's bitterness, along with the wholly implicit nature of his faith ('A Little Boy Lost' is as bitter as 'London,' but its reforming purpose – 'Are such things never done on Albion's shore' – are in question), makes us hesitate about identifying him with the Bard. Our doubts are partly dispelled, though, when we discover at the end of *Experience* that the Bard's appearance has changed over the course of the volume. Might the weary traveller of 'London' not be the Bard grown 'Ancient,' his earlier and more explicit optimism ('O Earth O Earth return!/Arise from out the dewy grass;/Night is worn') undermined by prolonged contact with the forces that hold Earth down? That the old man in the design to 'London' is almost identical in appearance (even their robes are similarly colored) to the white-bearded harper of 'The Voice of the Ancient Bard,' and that the poem is spoken by a character who strikes us as both Bard-like and 'Ancient,' in the sense of 'experienced' (contrast the open and commanding 'Hear the voice of the Bard!' with the deadened knowingness of the opening lines of 'London'), seems to suggest as much. Still, though, the speaker of 'London' is not yet the speaker of 'The Voice of the Ancient Bard,' if only because he lacks the latter's self-awareness. Rather we think of him as marking a middle stage in the Bard's spiritual progress. The youthful Bard of the experienced title-page grows into the lamed and embittered, though still powerful, old man of 'London,' a Bard who does not yet realize, as he will by the final plate, the dangers into which he has fallen.

If the old man in the design to 'London' is the Bard, who, then, is his youthful guide? Erdman associates him with what he calls the 'vagabond boy,'[21] in similarly-colored costume warming his hands by a fire to the right of stanzas 2 and 3. Both these figures, unlike the vagabond of the previous plate, are unmistakably child-like, and we have no reason to question their innocence. That the old man is led by a child sounds several sorts of grace notes: it reminds us that for all his faults – the ease with which he slips into experienced or Urizenic habits of mind, the confusion of prophetic and priestly or God-like authority (cf. his physical resemblance to the Father God of the previous plate) – the Bard is still guided by a vision of innocence; it connects that vision with a particular human child, one whose oppressed condition (suggested by his similarity to the lower figure) is individualized; and it anticipates the line 'And wish to lead others when they should be led' from 'The Voice of the Ancient Bard.' The light that illumines child and old man as they travel through the bleak, shadow-filled (midnight?) streets of the city, suggests divinity, but belongs to this world; as opposed to the supernatural light of the haloes of child and Bard (or Earth) on the frontispiece and title-page. The child is no longer totemized, nor is his movement restricted. He stands upright, reaching out his hand in the manner of the divinely human innocents of the earlier volume or the freer of the two youths on the *Age Teaching Youth* watercolor of *c.* 1785–90.[22] Blake has even taken the trouble to give him a smile in copy Z (in other copies he looks worried),[23] in contrast to the blank impassivity of the child led – or rather carried – by the Bard of the frontispiece. As in 'The Tyger,' the design counterpoints the poem's darkness. 'London lost,' writes Grant of this design, 'is a truth only of midnight streets: real but not final.'[24]

The old man in the 'London' design can also be taken as a figure of the city itself.[25] Those who thus interpret it note how 'the weakness and woe he symbolizes is also the weakness and woe he has caused,'[26] a reading which works perfectly well if we think of him as the fallen or flawed Bard. In the next plate, 'The Human Abstract,' a similar point is made, with reference to a similar figure.

> The Gods of the earth and sea,
> Sought thro' Nature to find this Tree
> But their search was all in vain;
> There grows one in the Human Brain.

The old man below this final stanza of 'The Human Abstract'

'illustrates' it, for the ropes (chains in other copies, reminding us of ' "the mind-forg'd manacles" of plate forty-six')[27] which hold him down, grow from out his 'Brain.' He is another of Blake's self-oppressed oppressors: not just tearful 'Cruelty' in stanzas 3 and 4, but the weeping 'Starry Jealousy' of 'Earth's Answer,' the trembling 'father white' of 'A Little Girl Lost,' Lyca's weeping mother. Though not himself the Bard, he is related to him, or rather to the experienced tendencies revealed in 'The Human Abstract' itself (and not just the first six lines), as was suggested earlier in this chapter. The delicate warning note struck in *Innocence* by the visual resemblance of Old John and the divinely human shepherds and children of 'The Lamb' and 'The Shepherd' grows more prominent in *Experience*. Though the Piper-turned-Bard is not yet (he will never be) wholly identified with an aged Urizenic oppressor, he has grown much closer to him, in both manner and guise.

The last of the old men we must discuss is found on the design to 'To Tirzah.' He too, I shall argue, is a figure of false divinity, a creation of what I have called the Bard's 'religion' of Innocence. 'To Tirzah,' though, raises special problems for anyone who approaches *Songs* as we have done – as, that is, the expression of a single, carefully organized, and ultimately coherent vision. In the first place, it is a late addition to *Songs*, etched sometime around 1804–5. Second, its speaker's views seem to coincide with those of Blake's late additions to *Vala*, composed at roughly the same time.[28] These views represent a shift in Blake's attitudes to nature, the body, and conventional Christianity, one which Morton Paley and others associate with his (and his age's) gradual loss of hope in the redemptive power of revolutionary energy.[29] They also seem, on the surface at least, to contradict not only the other plates of *Experience*, but those of *Innocence* as well.

The thematic conflict between 'To Tirzah' and both *Innocence* and *Experience* has been dealt with in one of three ways by the critics. Some, Holloway, for example, simply take it at face value, ignoring the effect it has on surrounding plates. Blake changed his views and wanted the change recorded: hence 'To Tirzah.'[30] Others, more concerned with *Songs* as a whole, argue that 'To Tirzah' represents a third stage of Blake's development after *Innocence* and *Experience*. Hirsch, for instance, makes much of its appearance in some copies at the end of *Experience*:

Blake's addition of 'To Tirzah' to the *Songs of Experience* is to be explained as an act of penitential self-correction. It is a repudiation, like the opening lines of *Milton* (probably composed at about the same time), of the false, vegetated tongue that had celebrated the natural world. ... It stands to *Experience* as *Experience* stands to *Innocence*. ... When Blake composed the poem and placed it at the end of *Songs*, he implied a sweeping repudiation of all the previous poems of *Experience*.[31]

Hirsch, though, says nothing of the fact that 'To Tirzah' ends *Songs* in only a few copies (E, I, O, and S), and that neither of the orders Blake seems to have thought most about (either that of copies T, U, W, X, Y, Z and AA, or of the list he himself transcribed)[32] end with it. Erdman, though, points out that in Z and the six other copies with the same order 'To Tirzah' is followed only by 'The Schoolboy' and 'The Voice of the Ancient Bard,' both of which, he believes, hint at apocalypse. Taken as a whole, he argues, the three concluding plates 'imply an apocalyptic metamorphosis at the end of a series of emblems, beyond Innocence and Experience.'[33] Like Hirsch, though, Erdman says nothing about the radical adjustments readers must make in order to accept this new and different state. Nor does he seem troubled by the abruptness with which it is introduced.

A third possible approach to the problems raised by 'To Tirzah' is that of Harold Bloom. Bloom, in his Blakean phase a true disciple of Frye, uses his knowledge of Blake's 'system' to account for the poem's seemingly straightforward references to the Atonement, Original Sin, and the body/soul dichotomy:

The Atonement set Blake free, not from the orthodox notion of original sin, but from the deceits of natural religion. Blake understands the Atonement as the triumph of the imaginative body over the natural body, a triumph *through* touch, an improvement in sensual enjoyment.[34]

How, though, are we to know this from 'To Tirzah' itself, or from the plates that surround it? 'Touch' is indeed omitted from the list of Tirzah-thwarted senses in stanzas 3 and 4, but this is hardly sufficient reason to think the poem's heaven anything other than that of beadle and priest, especially in view of stanza 2's wholly orthodox epitome of the myths of Fall and

Redemption. Even the inscription from I Corinthians 15:44 on the gown of the old man in the design – 'It is Raised a spiritual Body' – is as likely to suggest the conventional body/soul dichotomy as it is a more Blakean fusion. In its original context, it forms the second half of a wholly clear-cut division: 'It is sown a natural body; it is raised a spiritual body' – hardly a text to spark thoughts of the redemptive power of 'sensual enjoyment.'

The design poses similar problems. There are two ways of reading the scene below the text: Keynes thinks it is set on Earth, with the two women (mother-love and sex-love) representing different aspects of Tirzah's earthly influence, and the old man representing divine redemption (his vessel, according to Keynes, contains 'the water of life').[35] Erdman, on the other hand, sets the scene in a heavenly garden, calling all three figures 'spiritual comforters.'[36] Both approaches, though, ignore the appearance of the old man, whose unearthly whiteness – robe, face, hair, vessel identically bleached – identifies him as 'a spiritual body.' How can we possibly associate so spectral or sepulchral a figure (he reminds us of the marble effigies of the experienced title-page) with Bloom's 'improvement of sensual enjoyment' or Blake's own 'intellectual War' (the heavenly state into which the Zoas and their emanations are delivered at the end of *The Four Zoas* (139.9: E392)). How square it, moreover, with an episode of similar date, that of Urizen's reformation in Night Nine of *The Four Zoas*, in which

... he shook his snows from off his shoulders & arose
As on a Pyramid of mist his white robes scattering
The fleecy white renewd he shook his aged mantles off
Into the fires Then glorious bright Exulting in his joy
He sounding rose into the heavens in naked majesty
In radiant Youth. ...

(121.27–32: E367)

Of all the old men in *Experience*, though, none is so inhuman in his authority as this one on the 'Tirzah' plate, so orthodoxly 'religious' or 'spiritual.' Is this the state into which Blake wants us delivered? Bent, aged, bleached of color as of life?

Of course not, which is why Blake makes the aged, spiritual deliverer of 'To Tirzah' an epitome of earlier Father Gods, weeping tyrants, and false saviors. It is also why he places him in an experienced setting (both the apple tree, which seems almost to mold the old man's body, and the high-banked, empty expanse of green remind us of earlier experienced scenes, of plate 2 of 'The Little Black Boy,' for example, or of 'The Angel'), letting the curve of his body form one side of a womb-like enclosure – a parody 'Bossom' – from which the prostrate body of Man can find no exit. Even if we see him through Keynes's eyes, as a spiritual enemy of the two women on the left of the plate, he still belongs to an experienced vision of the world, one which expresses itself in black-white dichotomies of a sort Bloom and Hirsch would have us believe 'To Tirzah' transcends.

Blake took care about *Songs*, and about copy Z in particular. He would not have included 'To Tirzah' – and kept it there – if he felt that it contradicted the visionary purpose to which both *Innocence* and *Experience*, in their different ways, are dedicated. How could he ask us, after what we have been through and become over the course of the previous fifty-one plates, to embrace a divinity bleached of humanity, to sever body from soul, calling one fallen and the other pure? How could he plant the apple tree of Genesis in his paradise, or clothe the naked in gowns which hide the body's beauty? That he could not, has been the central argument of this book. That he might have, though – that the question is a real one, despite his greatness both as poet and painter – is something he himself realized.

It is the Piper-Bard, not Blake, who lives out Blake's temptation, who succumbs, even as does Los (his and Blake's *alter ego*), in the later prophetic books. 'To Tirzah' is the Bard's nadir, the familiar (to those who know the later epics) condensation of error before revelation – or rather self-revelation, there being no other kind for Blake the apostle of vision. This is the inevitable outcome of a prolonged and heroic exposure – in Earth's service – to a world of pain and suffering. Hirsch, Holloway, and Paley are not wrong to see 'To Tirzah' as an expression of profound revulsion from the life of this world. Where they *are* wrong is in associating that revulsion with the ultimate purpose of *Songs*. By including 'To Tirzah' in *Experience* Blake is warning us of the dangers prophets run – of the danger to which he himself might have succumbed. Nor has he left us unprepared for such a warning, having carefully introduced and developed it through a host of subtle discrepancies in *Experience* between matter and manner, youthful Piper-God and aged prophet-God. It is our ultimate, and yet at the same time, easiest test, for it reveals the Beast – Blake's spectrous self, the ancestor of Los's specter in the later epics – most clearly. We understand and we forgive, looking upon 'To Tirzah' as the Bard has learned, by the final plate, to look upon himself. Ours have become the eyes of innocent wisdom. We have learned the lessons of vision, tested them, and put them into practice. In the process, we have also realized Blake's ultimate purpose in writing *Songs*.

NOTES

Abbreviations for frequently cited references in the footnotes are:

Adams, *Shorter Poems*
  Hazard Adams, *William Blake: A Reading of the Shorter Poems* (Seattle: University of Washington Press, 1963).
Bateson, *Selected Poems*
  F. W. Bateson, ed., *Selected Poems of William Blake* (London: Heinemann, 1963).
Bentley, *Books*
  G. E. Bentley, Jr, *Blake Books: Annotated Catalogues of William Blake's Writings* (Oxford: The Clarendon Press, 1977).
Bentley, *Records*
  G. E. Bentley, Jr, *Blake Records* (Oxford: The Clarendon Press, 1969).
Bentley, *Writings*
  G. E. Bentley, Jr, *William Blake's Writings* (2 vols, Oxford: The Clarendon Press, 1978).
Bindman, *Artist*
  David Bindman, *Blake as an Artist* (Oxford: Phaidon, 1977).
Bloom, *Apocalypse*
  Harold Bloom, *Blake's Apocalypse: A Study in Poetic Argument* (Garden City, NY: Anchor Books, 1965).
Damon, *Philosophy*
  S. Foster Damon, *William Blake: His Philosophy and Symbols* (1929; rpt NY: Peter Smith, 1942).
Darton, *Children's Books*
  F. J. Harvey Darton, *Children's Books in England: Five Centuries of Social Life* (Cambridge University Press, 1958).
Erdman, *IB*
  David V. Erdman, *The Illuminated Blake* (Garden City, NY: Anchor, 1974).
Erdman, *Prophet*
  David V. Erdman, *Blake: Prophet Against Empire: A Poet's*

Notes

Interpretation of the History of His Own Times (1954; rpt Garden City, NY: Anchor Books, 1969).

Erdman, *VFD*
David V. Erdman and John E. Grant, ed, *Blake's Visionary Forms Dramatic* (Princeton University Press, 1970).

Frye, *Fearful Symmetry*
Northrop Frye, *Fearful Symmetry: A Study of William Blake* (1947; rpt Boston: Beacon Press, 1967).

Gillham, *Contrary States*
D. G. Gillham, *Blake's Contrary States: The 'Songs of Innocence and of Experience' as Dramatic Poems* (Cambridge University Press, 1966).

Gleckner, *Piper and Bard*
Robert F. Gleckner, *The Piper and the Bard: A Study of William Blake* (Detroit: Wayne State University Press, 1959).

Hirsch, *Introduction*
E. D. Hirsch, Jr, *Innocence and Experience: An Introduction to Blake* (New Haven: Yale University Press, 1964).

Holloway, *Lyric Poetry*
John Holloway, *Blake: The Lyric Poetry* (London: Edward Arnold, 1968).

Keynes, *Letters*
Geoffrey Keynes, ed., *The Letters of William Blake* (London: Rupert Hart-Davis, 1956).

Keynes, *Songs*
William Blake, *Songs of Innocence and of Experience*, introduction and commentary by Geoffrey Keynes (1967; rpt Oxford University Press, 1970).

Mellor, *HFD*
Ann Mellor, *Blake's Human Form Divine* (Berkeley: University of California Press, 1974).

Ostriker, *Vision and Verse*
Alice Ostriker, *Vision and Verse in William Blake* (New York: Oxford University Press, 1959).

Paley, *Keynes Festschrift*
Morton D. Paley and Michael Phillips, eds, *William Blake: Essays in Honour of Sir Geoffrey Keynes* (Oxford University Press, 1973).

Pinchbeck, *Children in Society*
Ivy Pinchbeck and Margaret Hewitt, *Children in English Society* (2 vols, London: Routledge & Kegan Paul, 1969).

Rosenblum, *Transformations*
Robert Rosenblum, *Transformations in Late Eighteenth Century Art* (Princeton University Press, 1974).

Rousseau, *Émile*
Jean-Jacques Rousseau, *Émile*, ed. W. T. Harris, tr. W. H. Payne (New York: D. Appleton and Co., 1911).

Stevenson, *Poems*
W. H. Stevenson, ed., *The Poems of William Blake* (1971; rpt London: Longman, 1972).
Stewart and McCann, *Innovators*
W. A. C. Stewart and W. P. McCann, *The Educational Innovators: 1750–1880* (London: Macmillan, 1967).
Stone, *Family*
Laurence Stone, *The Family, Sex, and Marriage in England 1500–1800* (London: Weidenfeld & Nicolson, 1977).
Wagenknecht, *Night*
David Wagenknecht, *Blake's Night: William Blake and the Idea of Pastoral* (Cambridge, Ma.: Harvard University Press, 1973).
Wicksteed, *Blake's Innocence*
Joseph H. Wicksteed, *Blake's Innocence and Experience: A Study of the Songs and Manuscripts 'Shewing the Two Contrary States of the Human Soul'* (London: J. M. Dent, 1928).
Wilson, *Life*
Mona Wilson, *The Life of William Blake* (1927; rpt Oxford University Press, 1971).

Introduction

1 W. H. Stevenson, *Oxford Street in Jerusalem: An Introduction to Blake's Major Poetry*, n.d., n.p., p. 2. Stevenson's study of the major poems, not yet published, is meant to complement his *The Poems of William Blake* (1971; rpt London: Longman, 1972).

2 *Selected Poems of William Blake*, ed. F. W. Bateson (London: Heinemann, 1963), p. ix.

3 'Blake,' in *The Sacred Wood* (1928; rpt London: Barnes & Noble, 1966), pp. 155, 152.

4 Robert F. Gleckner, *The Piper and the Bard: A Study of William Blake* (Detroit: Wayne State University Press, 1959), p. 34, his italics.

5 Wellek's comment, part of a criticism of Leavis's *Revaluation* (in *Scrutiny*, March 1937), and Leavis's reply, come from the latter's 'Literary Criticism and Philosophy,' in *The Common Pursuit* (Harmondsworth, Middlesex: Penguin, 1962), pp. 216, 217.

6 Appeals to 'the Public' are scattered throughout Blake's works: see David V. Erdman, *A Concordance to the Writings of William Blake* (2 vols, Ithaca: Cornell University Press, 1967), II, p. 1496, for a complete listing, but note especially those from 'A Prospectus to the Public,' 'The Descriptive Catalogue,' 'To The Public,' the opening plates of *Jerusalem*, and the letters.

7 My approach is similar to that of E. H. Gombrich in his discussion of the color red as a visual metaphor in painting. Gombrich grants his subject a 'life of its own' ('grounded on simple biological fact')

even as he insists that color values derive from tradition or cultural context:

> Red, being the colour of flames and of blood, offers itself as a metaphor for anything that is strident or violent. It is no accident, therefore, that it was selected as the code sign for 'stop' in our traffic code and as a label of revolutionary parties in politics. But though both these applications are grounded on simple biological facts, the colour red itself has no fixed 'meaning'. A future historian or anthropologist, for instance, who wanted to interpret the significance of the label 'red' in politics would get no guidance from his knowledge of our traffic code. Should the colour that denotes 'stop' not stand for the 'conservatives' and the green for the go-ahead progressives? And how should he interpret the red hat of the cardinal or the red cross? ('Visual Metaphors of Value in Art,' in *Meditations on a Hobby Horse and other Essays on the Theory of Art* (1963; rpt Oxford: Phaidon Press, 1978), p. 13.)

8 'On Poesy and Art,' *Biographia Literaria*, ed. J. G. Shawcross (London: Oxford University Press, 1907), II, p. 55.
9 Pierre Macherey, *A Theory of Literary Production*, trans. Geoffrey Wall (London: Routledge & Kegan Paul, 1978), p. 101: 'A true reading ... is a question of ... establishing that absence [*lacune*] around why a real complexity is knit.'
10 *The Uses of Division: Unity and Disharmony in Literature* (London: Chatto & Windus, 1976), p. 13.
11 See Morton D. Paley, *Energy and Imagination: A Study of the Development of Blake's Thought* (Oxford: The Clarendon Press, 1970), pp. 30–6, for what remains the most sophisticated study of Blake's 'dialectic' in *Songs* and elsewhere; also David Punter, 'Blake, Marxism and Dialectic,' in *Literature and History*, 6 (Autumn 1977), pp. 219–42.
12 In *Songs*, moreover, as Paley himself admits, in his study of 'The Little Girl Lost/Found' poems in *Experience*, the marriage is only implied: 'the theme of the harmonizing of the instinctual life ('their sleeping child/Among tygers wild') goes beyond Experience to a new state which *Songs of Experience* anticipates but does not otherwise describe' (*Energy*, p. 32).
13 See, for example, D. G. Gillham, *Blake's Contrary States: The 'Songs of Innocence and of Experience' as Dramatic Poems* (Cambridge University Press, 1966), p. 5:

> Blake has no message, or 'philosophy,' and would not be worth reading as a poet if he had. He offers something

better: a serious and responsible consideration of the ways in which human energy may manifest itself ... although he refers us to various dogmas in his description of the [contrary] states, Blake subscribes to no one of them, he presents no ultimate truths but leaves us to forge our own. He does attempt to awaken us to the responsibilities of becoming alive to the best truths of which we are capable, but the poet detaches himself from the task of saying what those truths should be.

14 David Bindman, *Blake as an Artist* (Oxford: Phaidon, 1977), pp. 59–61, discusses contemporary song books, medieval illuminated manuscripts, eighteenth-century devotional works, and prayer books as other possible models.
15 (Garden City, New York: Anchor Books, 1974), p. 14.

A note on copies

1 *IB*, p. 41. All in all, Blake tried thirty-four different arrangements for *Innocence* (twenty in separately issued copies of *Innocence*, fourteen in copies of the combined *Songs*), and eighteen for *Experience* (*Ibid.*, pp. 69–70, 95–6). G. E. Bentley, Jr, *Blake Books: Annotated Catalogues of William Blake's Writings* (Oxford: The Clarendon Press, 1977), p. 83, thinks the order was not fixed until later: 'by 1819 ... he settled on a fairly stable order.'
2 'An Interview with John Berryman,' *Harvard Advocate*, 103, no. 1 (Spring 1969), p. 5.
3 F. E. Hutchinson, ed., *The Works of George Herbert* (1941; rpt London: Oxford University Press, 1970), p. 58.
4 See Geoffrey Keynes and Edwin Wolf, eds, *William Blake's Illuminated Books: A Census* (New York: The Grolier Club, 1953), pp. vii–xii for a discussion of comparable techniques of relief etching in Blake's day. For a more detailed description of Illuminated Printing see Ruthven Todd's 'The Techniques of William Blake's Illuminated Printing,' and the selections from J. T. Smith, Gilchrist, Cumberland, Abraham Rees, and Robert Dossie in *The Visionary Hand: Essays for the Study of William Blake's Art and Aesthetics*, ed. Robert N. Essick (Los Angeles: Hennessey and Ingalls, 1973), pp. 7–44, and Raymond Lister, *Infernal Methods: A Study of William Blake's Art Techniques* (London: G. Bell, 1975), pp. 5–35.
5 Around 1795 Blake experimented with a new method of color printing, but he seems to have abandoned it for *Songs* after only a few attempts. See copies F, G, and H of the combined *Songs*

(Keynes and Wolf, *Census*, p. 52). (Single capital letters refer to copies of the combined *Songs*; capitals preceded by the abbreviation '*In.*' refer to copies of *Innocence* alone. The letters are those designated in the *Census*).

6 Keynes and Wolf, *Census*, p. xv. For the latest and most detailed discussion and description of copies see Bentley, *Books*, pp. 364–438.

7 On the difficulties Blake must have encountered in re-working the original copperplates see John Wright, 'Towards Recovering Blake's Relief-etching Process,' *Blake Newsletter*, 7, no. 26 (Fall 1973), pp. 32–9.

8 Keynes and Wolf, *Census*, p. xvi. The copies Keynes doubts are *In.*G, *In.*H, M and R.

9 *Ibid.*, p. 65.

10 *Ibid.*, p. 63.

11 *Ibid.*, p. xvi.

12 Erdman, *IB*, p. 16.

13 John E. Grant, 'Mothers and Methodology,' *Blake Newsletter*, 2, no. 6 (December 15, 1968), p. 50.

14 Those I have examined in the original are *In.*B, *In.*E, *In.*G, *In.*I, *In.*P, and A, B, C, E, H, M, N, O, R, U, V, W, Y, Z and AA of the combined *Songs*.

15 Letter to Thomas Robinson, October 18, 1790 in *Diaries, Reminiscences and Correspondence*, ed. Thomas Sadler (2 vols, Cambridge, Ma: Houghton, Mifflin, 1898), II, p. 372.

16 *Blake Records* (Oxford: The Clarendon Press, 1969), p. 323. *Records* contains Robinson's original 1811 essay on Blake from *The Vaterländisches Museum* as well as the relevant portions of the 1852 *Reminiscences*.

17 *The Life of William Blake* (1927; rpt London: Oxford University Press, 1971), p. 330.

18 Geoffrey Keynes, ed., *The Letters of William Blake* (London: Rupert Hart-Davis, 1956), p. 35.

19 Linnell claims that 'being really anxious to fathom if possible the amount of truth which might be in his most startling assertions, I generally met with a sufficiently rational explanation' (Bentley, *Records*, p. 8).

20 In fact, by 1825 Blake was probably closer to the spirit of *Innocence* (which also, I shall argue, means that of the combined *Songs*), than in any intervening period. One thinks of the innocent scenes in the *Job* engravings (1826), particularly the final plate, in which innocence is associated with vision, its seeming limitations (most keenly uncovered in the activist period of the Lambeth Books) forgotten; or the knowing (or darkened) innocence of the woodcuts for *Thornton's Virgil* (1821), so much, as we shall see, in keeping with the complex mood of innocent Songs like 'Night'

and 'The Ecchoing Green.' Even in periods when Blake was most likely to be at variance with what I take to be the original vision of *Songs* he seems still to have respected its larger themes, in the manner, for example, of the progressively more conservative and orthodox Wordsworth toning down but never repudiating *The Prelude*.

21 Quoted from the publisher's flyer to the 1955 edition of the Blake Trust facsimile of the combined *Songs*.

22 See John Grant's editorial footnote to Eben Bass's '*Songs of Innocence and of Experience*: The Thrust of Design,' in *Blake's Visionary Forms Dramatic*, eds David V. Erdman and John E. Grant (Princeton University Press, 1970), p. 197.

Chapter 1 Children's books, education, and vision

1 Letter quoted in G. E. Bentley, Jr, *William Blake: The Critical Heritage* (London: Routledge & Kegan Paul, 1975), pp. 22–4.

2 *Children's Books in England: Five Centuries of Social Life* (Cambridge University Press, 1958), p. 1. Much of the historical material in the following pages is drawn from Darton: also Cornelia Meigs, Anne Thaxter Eaton, Elizabeth Nesbitt, and Ruth Hall Viguers, *A Critical History of Children's Literature: A Survey of Children's Books in English from Earliest Times to the Present* (New York: Macmillan, 1953), Ivy Pinchbeck and Margaret Hewitt, *Children in English Society* (2 vols, London: Routledge & Kegan Paul, 1969), William Sloane, *Children's Books in England and America in the Seventeenth Century: A History and Checklist* (New York: Columbia University Press, 1955), Lawrence Stone, *The Family, Sex, and Marriage in England 1500–1800* (London: Weidenfeld & Nicolson, 1977), William Targ, ed., *Bibliophile in the Nursery* (1957; rpt Metuchen, NJ: Scarecrow Reprints, 1969), and Joyce Irene Whalley, *Cobwebs to Catch Flies: Illustrated Books from the Nursery and Schoolroom 1700–1900* (London: Paul Elek, 1974).

3 Most studies of the relation between *Innocence*, the combined *Songs*, and children's literature, concentrate on stylistic and thematic echoes from Bunyan, Watts, Barbauld, Doddridge, Smart, and the Wesleys: see, for example, John Holloway, *Blake: The Lyric Poetry* (London: Edward Arnold, 1968), pp. 32–53, for metrical and thematic parallels between eighteenth-century children's hymns and Blake's lyrics; E. D. Hirsch, Jr, *Innocence and Experience: An Introduction to Blake* (New Haven: Yale University Press, 1964), pp. 28–30, 37, 183, for Blake's debt to Mrs Barbauld; Vivian de Sola Pinto, 'William Blake, Isaac Watts, and Mrs Barbauld,' in *The Divine Vision: Studies in the Poetry*

and Art of William Blake, ed. Vivian de Sola Pinto (London: Gollancz, 1957), pp. 65–88, for the influence of Watts and Bunyan in particular; Jacob Bronowski, *William Blake: A Man Without a Mask* (London: Secker & Warburg, 1944), pp. 143 et passim, for Blake's relation to the Evangelical movement and its hymns; Frederick C. Gill, *The Romantic Movement and Methodism* (London: Epworth Press, 1937), pp. 146–59, Robert F. Gleckner, 'Blake and Wesley,' *Notes and Queries*, 3 (December 1956), pp. 522–4, and Martha W. England, 'Wesley's Hymns for Children and Blakes Songs,' in *Hymns Unbidden: Donne, Herbert, Blake, Emily Dickinson, and the Hymnographers*, eds Martha W. England and John Sparrow (New York: New York Public Library, 1966), pp. 44–63, for Blake's relation to Methodist hymnology. Heather Glen, in a review of Joyce Whalley's *Cobwebs to Catch Flies*, in *Cambridge Review*, 96, no. 226 (May 1975), pp. 132–5, writes interestingly of Blake's debt in *Songs* to William Ronksley's *The Child's Week's Work* (1712) and Dr J. Trusler's *Proverbs Exemplified and Illustrated by Pictures from Real Life* (1790).

4 Bentley, *Records*, p. 456. Smith's comments on Blake came from his biography, *Nollekens and his Times* (1828), excerpted by Bentley on pp. 455–76.

5 *Family*, p. 449. See also, Mona Wilson, *Life*, p. 2, who says that the Mathew set 'represented what was best in the cultured middle class which had grown up during the eighteenth century, intelligent, industrious, philanthropic, superbly didactic, pleased with themselves and their productions, but not wholly impervious to other influences.'

6 See the immensely influential *Letters on the Improvement of the Mind* (1773), with its detailed instructions for the education of young girls of quality.

7 See David V. Erdman, *Blake: Prophet Against Empire: A Poet's Interpretation of the History of His Own Times* (1954; rpt Garden City, NY: Anchor Books, 1969), pp. 93–4n. There were other such groups in Manchester and Liverpool, and clear links between all three cities and the radicals of London. See W. A. C. Stewart and W. P. McCann, *The Educational Innovators: 1750–1880* (London: Macmillan, 1967), p. 31.

8 *Prophet*, p. 98n, with Bogen's comment in the footnote.

9 Smith quoted by Bentley, *Records*, p. 457.

10 See Erdman, *Prophet*, pp. 153–8, for Blake's connections with Johnson and his circle.

11 See Bentley, *Records*, p. 46, for Blake's tenuous connections to Williams.

12 Chodowiecki's well-known *Farewell of Calas* (1767), a painting commemorating the martyrdom of Jean Calas, a sort of Protestant

Dreyfuss, prefigures the radical Davidian moralism of what Robert Rosenblum, in *Transformations in Late Eighteenth Century Art* (Princeton University Press, 1974), p. 74, calls 'the Neoclassical Historic,' a phenomenon about which we shall be talking in chapter 2.

13 In 1788, according to David Bland, R. Dutton may have commissioned Blake to contribute metal engravings to the fairy-tale *Little Thumb and the Ogre* (see *The Illustration of Books* (London: Faber & Faber, 1951), p. 96). No such listing is found in either Bentley, *Books*, or Hanns Hammelmann, *Book Illustrators in Eighteenth Century England*, ed. T. S. R. Boase (New Haven: Yale University Press, 1976). Later, in 1800, Johnson commissioned him to engrave a series of designs for *Gymnastics for Youth: or a Practical Guide to Healthful and Amusing Exercise for the use of schools. An essay towards the necessary improvement of Education, chiefly as it relates to the body; freely translated from the German.*

14 Fuseli gave his copy to the five-year-old daughter of a surgeon, according to Geoffrey Keynes's introduction to the Blake Trust facsimile, *William Blake's For Children: The Gates of Paradise* (2 vols, London: The Trianon Press, 1968), I, p. 3.

15 See Keynes, *Gates*, I, p. 41.

16 This, at least, is what Mona Wilson, *Life*, p. 43, thinks.

17 *Children's Books*, p. 112.

18 *Un*respectable juvenile literature could be found in chapbooks, late seventeenth- and eighteenth-century equivalents of the modern comic or the nineteenth-century Penny Dreadful. 'From 1700 to 1840,' writes Darton, 'the chapbook contained all the popular literature of four centuries in a reduced and degenerate form rudely adapted for use by children and poorly educated country folk' (*Children's Books*, p. 82). That respectable parents are unlikely to have approved of most chapbooks need not have prevented children from reading them (see the entry from Mrs Thrale's *Diary* quoted in Irma Strickland, ed., *The Voices of Children: 1700–1914* (Oxford: Basil Blackwell, 1973), p. 81). Literary figures as diverse and distinguished as Addison, Johnson, Wordsworth, Coleridge, Lamb, even Mrs Trimmer (none of whom came from particularly light-minded or inattentive families), all remembered stories and poems from the chapbooks of their youth. Blake's feel for the rhythms of ballad and folk song, and his frequent use of fairy, folk, and romance motifs (see John Adlard, *The Sports of Cruelty: Fairies, Folk-songs, Charms, and Other Country Matters in the Work of William Blake* (London: Cecil & Amelia Wolf, 1972), suggests that he did too.

19 *Institutes of the Christian Religion*, tr. John Allen (2 vols, London: T. Tegg & Sons, 1838), I, p. 8.

20 Quoted by Monica Kiefer, 'Mental Pabulum of Godly Children,' in Targ, ed., *Bibliophile*, p. 324.
21 J. Max Patrick, ed., *The Prose of John Milton* (Garden City, NY: Anchor Books, 1967), p. 230.
22 *Checklist*, pp. 131–231.
23 *Children's Books*, p. 53.
24 Quoted in J. H. Pafford, ed., *Isaac Watts, Divine Songs Attempted in Easy Language for the Use of Children* (London: Oxford University Press, 1971), p. 13.
25 Quoted in Pinchbeck, *Children in Society*, I, p. 266.
26 Quoted in Darton, *Children's Books*, p. 53. Bunyan's disapproval of 'fingle-fangles' was widely shared: in 1700 not a single shop in Britain, not even in London, specialized in children's toys (J. H. Plumb, 'The New World of Children in Eighteenth Century England,' *Past and Present*, no. 67 (May 1975), p. 66n).
27 Stone, *Family*, p. 68. The statistics that follow are taken from the same source, pp. 66–73.
28 *Ibid.*, p. 70.
29 Pinchbeck, *Children in Society*, I, p. 264.
30 *Idem.*
31 *England in the Eighteenth Century (1714–1815)* (1950; rpt Harmondsworth: Penguin, 1963), p. 14. Blake came from a lower middle-class family. His father, 'a modestly prosperous clothier' (Alexander Gilchrist, *Life of William Blake*, ed. Ruthven Todd (1863; rpt London: Dent, 1942), p. 1), seems never to have been tied to any one church or sect, though all the early biographers agree he was a Dissenter. That Blake and his brothers and sisters were brought up within the forms of the state religion suggests parental prudence rather than conformity. Within the home, his early religious and educational training was probably much like that of most bourgeois Non-Conformist children.
32 Quoted in Stone, *Family*, p. 467. See also E. P. Thompson, *The Making of the English Working Class* (Harmondsworth: Penguin, 1977), pp. 411–16 on the severity of Methodist educational principles and practice; also Plumb, *Eighteenth Century*, who stresses that Methodist attitudes towards education, like so many other aspects of the movement, were deeply influenced by the character and experience of Wesley himself. Wesley's own education had been scrupulously superintended by his mother, a woman who, though a member of the established Church, was wholly untouched by its latitudinarian spirit. Her avowed aim in educating her elder son was 'to break the child's will,' and Plumb writes of the unflagging energy with which she 'imposed the pattern of her belief upon her numerous children' (p. 91).
33 Plumb, *Eighteenth Century*, p. 94.

34 *Hymns Unbidden*, p. 58.
35 *Ibid.*, p. 57.
36 Quoted by Harry Escott in *Isaac Watts: Hymnographer* (London: Independent Press, 1962), p. 216. John Wesley's contribution to Methodist hymnology, it ought to be pointed out, was relatively small. Charles, though, wrote over 7,300 hymns.
37 Whereas the mainstream of the Methodist movement was drawn from what W. J. Warner, *The Wesleyan Movement in the Industrial Revolution* (London: Longmans, Green, 1930), p. 250, calls 'a single social stratum, located between unskilled labour and the middle class' (Whitefield's breakaway group, the so-called Calvinistic Methodists, or 'Lady Huntingdon's Connection,' was something of an exception), Anglican Evangelicism, a later though related movement, attracted many wealthy and influential followers from among the Anglican Church. See Warner Stark, *The Sociology of Religion: A Study of Christendom* (3 vols, London: Routledge & Kegan Paul, 1967), II, pp. 24ff., and Ford Brown, *Fathers of the Victorians: The Age of Wilberforce* (Cambridge University Press, 1961), pp. 82ff., for the relation between and inception of the two movements.
38 Quoted by Robert Isaac Wilberforce and Samuel Wilberforce in *The Life of William Wilberforce* (5 vols, London: John Murray, 1838), I, p. 84.
39 Quoted in Stone, *Family*, p. 469.
40 See *Children's Books*, pp. 158–80.
41 The purpose of this outing, according to Father Fairchild, was 'that [the children] may love one another with perfect and heavenly love' (quoted in Pinchbeck, *Children in Society*, I, p. 300).
42 Darton, *Children's Books*, p. 175.
43 That Mrs Trimmer was deeply affected by the Evangelical movement is seen in her publication in 1786 of *The Oeconomy of Charity*, a work based on the theories of Robert Raikes, an early Evangelical exponent of the charity school movement; her founding and helping to teach in the charity schools of her native Brentford; her membership in the 'Slavery Abolition Society' and 'The Society for the Suppression of Vice'; and the dispatching of her daughter Selina to be governess and moral missionary at Devonshire House, the heart of fashionable aristocracy. See Muriel Jaeger, *Before Victoria* (London: Chatto & Windus, 1956), pp. 57ff.
44 Darton, *Children's Books*, p. 162.
45 Quoted by Jaeger, *Before Victoria*, p. 109.
46 Quoted by Darton, *Children's Books*, p. 97, from the introduction to Mrs Sherwood's rewriting of Sarah Fielding's *The Governess, or Little Female Academy* (second edition, 1749).
47 Quoted by Plumb, *Eighteenth Century*, p. 94.

48 From the typescript of Stevenson's unpublished study entitled *Oxford Street in Jerusalem: An Introduction to Blake's Major Poetry*, n.d., n.p., p. 105.
49 James L. Axtell, ed., *The Educational Writings of John Locke: A Critical Edition with Introduction and Notes* (Cambridge University Press, 1968), p. 325. Locke devotes sections 1 to 32 to questions of physical health, and the next 100 to 'the general method of Educating a Young Gentleman.'
50 See S. Roscoe, *John Newbery and his Survivors* (Wormly, Herts.: Five Owls Press, 1973), pp. 1–33.
51 Locke, *Education*, p. 176.
52 *Ibid.*, p. 150.
53 *Ibid.*, p. 181.
54 *Ibid.*, p. 156.
55 *Ibid.*, p. 157.
56 *Ibid.*, p. 61.
57 *Ibid.*, p. 235.
58 *Ibid.*, p. 114.
59 'Ode: Intimations of Immortality from Recollections of Early Childhood,' ll. 130–2, in Ernest de Selincourt, ed., *Wordsworth: Poetical Works* (1904; rpt, London: Oxford University Press, 1969), p. 461.
60 Locke, *Education*, p. 158.
61 *Ibid.*, p. 145.
62 Or of Halifax in *Advice to a Daughter* (1688): 'You may begin early to make them love you that they may obey you. You are to have as strict a guard upon yourself amongst your children as if you were amongst your enemies' (*Complete Works*, ed. J. P. Kenyon (Harmondsworth: Penguin, 1969), p. 290).
63 Locke, *Education*, p. 172. The following passage from the Irish educational experimenter, David Mason, a sort of Newbery of the school room, provides a useful contrast with Locke:

> The rod only quenches the flame, which will break out afterwards with greater fury than before. Every tutor should endeavour to gain the affections and confidence of the children under his care, and make them sensible of the kindness and friendly concern for their welfare: and when punishment becomes necessary, should guard against passion, and convince them 'tis not their *persons* but their *faults* which he dislikes. The love of LIBERTY is as natural to children as to grown persons: the method, then, to make them easy under a state of discipline is to convince them that they are free; that they act from choice, not compulsion (quoted in Stewart and McCann, *Innovators*, p. 17).

64 Locke, *Education*, p. 183.

65 (1814; rpt, New York: New American Library, 1964), pp. 46–7.
66 Locke, *Education*, p. 143.
67 Hence Urizen's depiction in the prophetic books as both Reason and the God of Calvin. The Zoa who 'was Faith and Certainty, is changd to Doubt [i.e. strict rationalism]' (*FZ* 2.27.15: E311). He is 'Reason' in the guise of the world's and man's creator, the 'Jealous God' of strict Puritanism who planted the Garden with its fatal Tree, and authored the Ten Commandments.
68 *Lives of the English Poets*, intro. Arthur Waugh (2 vols, London: Oxford University Press, 1964), II, p. 360. Johnson's terms of praise are meant literally. In addition to his hymns for children and adults, Watts wrote on logic, astronomy, geography, theology, 'The Art of Reading and Writing English' (1721), charity, ontology, and a host of moral and theological issues. Johnson's praises remind us of the vocabulary of Mme Leprince de Beaomont, the 'Wise Governess' of the French children's book *Magasin des Enfants* (1757). Her aim in her tales was to inculcate 'the spirit of geometry' and to help establish 'the empire of reason' (quoted by Paul Hazard, *Books, Children, and Men*, tr. Marguerite Mitchell (1932; rpt Boston: The Horn Book Press, 1974), pp. 12–13).
69 In the first section of his *A Discourse on the Education of Children and Youth* (1763) Watts suggests that among the necessary religious lessons a child should be taught, one is 'that it is the Holy Spirit of God who must cure the evil temper of their own spirits, and make them Holy and fit to dwell with God in heaven' (*The Works of the Reverend and Learned Dr. Isaac Watts*, ed., Jennings and Doddridge (6 vols, London: J. Barfield, 1910), V, p. 359).
70 J. H. Pafford, ed., *Isaac watts, Divine Songs Attempted in Easy Language for the Use of Children* (London: Oxford University Press, 1951), p. 144.
71 *Ibid.*, pp. 145–7.
72 *Divine Vision*, p. 67.
73 *Works*, IV, p. 449.
74 To S. Foster Damon, *William Blake: His Philosophy and Symbols* (1924; rpt New York: Peter Smith, 1947), p. 269, 'for once Blake speaks in his own person.' To Harold Bloom, though, in *Blake's Apocalypse: A Study in Poetic Argument* (Garden City, NY: Anchor Books, 1965), pp. 38–9, 'The ambiguity of tone of Blake's Songs is never more evident than here, and yet never more difficult to evidence.' T. E. Connolly in 'The Real "Holy Thursday" of William Blake,' *Blake Studies*, VI (1975), pp. 179–87 has discovered that the procession described in 'Holy Thursday' never, in fact, took place on Ascension Day.
75 *Apocalypse*, p. 39.

76 M. Dorothy George, *London Life in the Eighteenth Century* (London: Kegan Paul, 1952), p. 254.

77 Basil Willey, *The Eighteenth Century Background: Studies in the Idea of Nature in the Thought of the Period* (London: Chatto & Windus, 1940), p. 65.

78 *The Guardian*, no. 105, July 11, 1713, in *Works*, ed. T. Tickell (6 vols, London: Vernor & Hood, 1804), IV, p. 39.

79 F. B. Kaye, ed., *The Fable of the Bees: Or Private Vices, Publick Benefits* (2 vols, London: Oxford University Press, 1925), I, p. 281–2.

80 'Irony in Blake's "Holy Thursday,"' *Modern Language Notes*, 71 (June 1956), p. 413. Gleckner was the first of Blake's readers to cite this parallel.

81 For more detailed treatment of the poem's Biblical echoes see Hirsch, *Introduction*, pp. 195–7.

82 Quoted in Bentley, *Records*, pp. 426–7.

83 Joseph H. Wicksteed, *Blake's Innocence and Experience: A Study of the Songs and Manuscripts 'Shewing the Two Contrary States of the Human Soul'* (London: J. M. Dent, 1928), p. 193. For the fulfillment of the speaker's fears in 'Holy Thursday' see the apocalyptic Night Nine of *Vala* or *The Four Zoas*: 'the children of six thousand years/Who died in infancy rage furious a mighty multitude rage furious/Naked and pale standing on the expecting air to be deliverd/Rend limb from limb the Warrior and the tyrant ...' (123.8–10: E377).

84 *Prophet*, pp. 119–22, stresses the importance of the Song's original setting in *Island* and the fact that Obtuse Angle is its singer. 'To deny the latent satire in the first song it is necessary to forget about Quid and the Cynic and accept Obtuse Angle as the self-portrait of Blake in 1784' (p. 122).

85 See Darton, *Children's Books*, pp. 182–204, and Pafford, ed., *Divine Songs*, pp. 326–30, for lists of Watts's imitators.

86 *Checklist*, p. 81.

87 A. P. Davis, *Isaac Watts: His Life and Works* (London: Independent Press, 1943), p. 77. Watts was the son of a well-to-do-clothier active in the Southampton Independent or Congregationalist Meeting. Though educated at an Anglican grammar school he decided against a place at university, enrolling instead in Thomas Rowe's Dissenting Academy at Newington Green. There, in addition to Rowe's mixture of doctrinal Calvinism, Cartesian physics, and Lockean 'mental science,' he gained important contacts, so that once he left the Academy he was able to secure a series of positions – as tutor, pastor, and resident scholar – in wealthy and distinguished Non-Conformist circles; what Donald Davie, with proper irony, calls 'the flesh-pots of the mercantile bourgeoisie' (*A Gathered Church: The Literature of*

the English Dissenting Interest, 1700–1930 (London: Routledge & Kegan Paul, 1978), p. 12).

88 'An Essay Towards the Encouragement of Charity Schools' (1728), quoted by Pafford, ed., *Divine Songs*, pp. 24–5.

89 Between the first English translation of *Émile* in 1762 and the turn of the century at least two hundred treatises on education were published in England which in some way were influenced by Rousseau (see Peter Coveney, *Poor Monkey: The Child in Literature* (London: Rockliff, 1957), p. 10; also A. A. Williams, 'The Impact of Rousseau on English Education,' *Researches and Studies*, University of Leeds, Institute of Education, no. 11 (January 1955), pp. 15–25). Godwin called *Émile* 'one of the principal reservoirs of philosophical truth as yet existing in the world' (*Enquiry Concerning Political Justice*, ed. Isaac Kraminick (Harmondsworth: Penguin, 1976), p. 497), though he goes on to qualify his praise; Wesley thought it 'the most empty, silly, injudicious thing that a self-conceited infidel wrote' (quoted in Stewart and McCann, *Innovators*, p. 33). Fuseli also wrote about *Émile*, in his *Remarks on Rousseau* (1767), and there is little question, given his loquaciousness, and the controversy Rousseau continued to spark, that Blake was privy to his opinions. Blake, of course, was a great admirer of Fuseli, and at no time more so than while at work on *Songs*: 'When Flaxman was taken to Italy,' wrote Blake in 1800, 'Fuseli was given to me for a season' (Letter to Flaxman, September 12, in Keynes, *Letters*, p. 47). That season began in 1787, a year or so at most before he began work on *Songs*.

90 See Stewart and McCann, *Innovators*, pp. 36–7.

91 The assumptions upon which it is founded, stated clearly in its opening pages, are first, that 'Everything is good as it comes from the hands of the Author of Nature; but everything degenerates in the hands of man' (Jean-Jacques Rousseau, *Émile*, ed. W. T. Harris, tr. W. H. Payne (New York: D. Appleton & Co., 1911), p. 1); second, that 'civilized man is born, lives and dies in a state of slavery. At his birth he is stitched in swaddling clothes; at his death he is nailed in his coffin; and as long as he preserves the human form he is fathered by our institutions' (p. 10); third, that the only way man can free himself is by returning to what Rousseau calls 'Nature' (defined for us by Basil Willey, *Background*, p. 206, as 'some earlier, simpler, and happier mode of existence'); and fourth, that children, because they are least tainted and corrupted by civilization, are types or models of the natural goodness and nobility we as civilized adults have lost. This last point is hardly new: the uncorrupted child belongs to a long but 'thin' (see Plumb, 'New World of Children,' p. 42) tradition of Hebrew and Christian thought, one whose antecedents include

the Cambridge Neo-Platonists (with their concept of the 'perfect pre-existent state'), Bacon, in 'Of Youth and Age,' the Vaughans, Traherne (who may have been influenced by Boehme), John Earle in his 'Character of a Child' in *Microcosmography* (1633), Aphra Behn and other dramatists and poets stimulated by the primitive cultures discovered by sixteenth- and seventeenth-century explorers, and Shaftesbury and Hutcheson, the eighteenth-century philosophers who argued that man's moral sense was innate, his behavior in nature benevolent. (See, for example, Coveney, *Poor Monkey*, pp. 1–14; Escott, *Hymnographer*, pp. 199–201; and, of course, Philippe Ariès, *Centuries of Childhood*, tr. Robert Baldrick (London: Jonathan Cape, 1962).) Ariès's argument that childhood was, in effect, 'invented' in this, what he calls 'the early modern period,' has been radically modified and complicated by Stone, *Family*, and Lloyd Demause, 'The Evolution of Childhood,' in *The History of Childhood*, ed. Lloyd Demause (London: Souvenir Press), pp. 1–25.

92 *Émile*, p. 57.
93 *Idem.*
94 *Ibid.*, p. 58.
95 *Ibid.*, pp. 11, 12.
96 *Ibid.*, p. 11.
97 *Prophet*, p. 123n. See page 35 of Blake's 1797 edition of the Illustrations to Young's *Night Thoughts*, for a particularly sinister version of numbering of this sort.
98 See the *Lectures on Education* (3 vols, London: John Bell, 1798), I, p. 112, where Williams deplores Rousseau's tendency 'to speak of everything with passion' and to rely on 'vague theories and hypotheses and visionary systems.'
99 *Émile*, pp. 83–4.
100 See, for example, his reaction to Locke's suggestion that children can be made truly liberal simply by restoring to them at once what they have just given away, or by causing them to give away money or goods of whose value they are ignorant: 'Proceed in such a way, says Locke, that they may be convinced by experience that he who is most liberal is always the best provided for. This is to make a child liberal in appearance but avaricious in fact. He adds that children will thus contract the habit of liberality. Yes, of a usurious liberality which gives an egg to gain an ox, but when it comes to giving in earnest, adieu to habit; when we cease to restore what they have given, they will soon cease to give. We must consider the habit of the soul rather than that of the hands. All the other virtues which we teach children resemble this. And it is in preaching to them these solid virtues that we wear away their young hearts in dreariness! Is not this a beautiful education!' (*Ibid.*, p. 67).

101 *Ibid.*, p. 44.
102 *Ibid.*, p. 156. See also his warning against the influence of nurses, with their foolish and fantastical superstitions (pp. 199–200).
103 If, for example, your children tell falsehoods, 'You will not preach against lying, nor punish them just because they have lied; but when they have lied you will heap upon them all the effects of falsehood, as not being believed when they have spoken the truth, and being accused of evil which they have not done and which they have denied' (*Ibid.*, p. 65). Similarly, if your child breaks the furniture in his room, 'be in no haste to give him more, but let him feel the disadvantage of its loss. If he breaks the windows of his room, let wind blow on him night and day, without caring for the cold he may take; for it is much better for him to have a cold than to be a fool' (*Ibid.*, pp. 63–4).
104 *Ibid.*, pp. 83–4.
105 *Ibid.*, p. xlii.
106 *Ibid.*, p. 60.
107 David Williams, for example, though in many respects a Rousseauphile, deplored the idea of letting children run about 'idly and at hazard' between the ages of 2 and 12, as Part II of *Émile* advises (see Stewart and McCann, *Innovators*, p. 39).
108 *Ibid.*, p. 245.
109 *Idem.* For the actual educational measures proposed at the New Church's first meeting in 1789 see R. Hindmarsh, *Rise and Progress of the New Jerusalem Church* (London: Hodson & Son, 1861), pp. 106–7: 'though the education of children in the principle of the New Jerusalem formed a part of the avowed design in convening a general conference, it was yet deemed of full importance that the first opportunity that offered of calling the attention of the Church to that subject, was eagerly embraced' (p. 106). See also J. Deans, 'Swedenborg on Education,' in *Encyclopedia and Dictionary of Education*, ed. F. Watson (4 vols, London: Sir I. Pitman & Sons, 1922), IV, pp. 1614–15.
110 Lavater's *Aphorisms on Man*, translated by Fuseli, was published by Johnson in 1789, with a frontispiece by Blake. The Annotations to Swedenborg are from Blake's copies of *The Wisdom of Angels, concerning Divine Love and Divine Wisdom* (1788) and *The Wisdom of Angels concerning the Divine Providence* (1790). Erdman, *Prophet*, p. 139, links Lavater and Swedenborg with 'The new humanism' of the 'pre-revolutionary spirit,' though neither were disciples of Rousseau.
111 Quoted in Erdman, *Prophet*, p. 178. For Erdman's conviction that Blake had read the *Remarks* see pp. 129, 177–8, 428.
112 His identity is discussed on the page 38 in the following chapter.
113 Bentley, *Records*, p. 566n.
114 *Émile*, pp. 45–6. This is like Henry Lord Holland on the

upbringing of his son, Charles James Fox: 'Let nothing be done to break his spirit. The world will do that business fast enough' (quoted in Stone, *Family*, p. 434).

115 Letter of August 23, 1799, in Keynes, *Letters*, p. 36.

116 To David Bindman, the Tracts 'though intensely serious ... resemble children's books of the most ephemeral kind' (*Artist*, p. 54). Their designs are filled, moreover, with instructional motifs: in *There is No Natural Religion*, series a, plate 3 depicts a sitting woman holding what Erdman calls a tablet (*IB*, p. 28), while a girl at her left (pupil ? daughter ?) holds a book; 'the word "Education" seems a relevant part of the text' (*Idem*); on plate 5, in a design reminiscent of the first plate of the innocent Song, 'Spring,' a mother holds a child out to see (or prevent from taking) a bird; on the next plate, a winged figure like that of the child on the innocent frontispiece instructs a man (note the child's upstretched arms) to look beyond sense experience; on plate 8 a naked boy, reminding us of the child in plate 5 (but free from its mother) reaches out to touch what looks like a swan or duck – goes beyond, that is, the restrictions of adult superintendence; in plate 9, the last of the series, the forces of restraint and constriction can be seen to have triumphed: a naked figure lies stretched out on the ground, reading or studying (the grass and a vine-entwined tree arch over and enclose the oblivious scholar, suggesting needless limitation). The designs, in sum, set the text's aphoristic abstractions about human nature, faith, and perception in a specific educational context; and they do so in the form of a children's book.

117 *Fearful Symmetry* (Boston: Beacon Press, 1967), p. 192.

118 *Introduction*, p. 28.

119 Quoted in Whalley, *Cobwebs*, pp. 41–1.

120 See Heather Glen, review of Joyce Irene Whalley, *Cobwebs to Catch Flies* (*Cambridge Review*, 96, no. 2226 (May 1975), pp. 132–5.

121 *Watts*, p. 26.

122 Meigs, *Critical History*, p. 62.

123 *Cobwebs*, p. 65.

124 Quoted in Thwaite, *Primer*, p. 25.

125 Quoted by Jaeger, *Before Victoria*, p. 108.

126 *Works*, V, 358.

Chapter 2   The designs

1 Letter to Dawson Turner, June 9, 1818, in Geoffrey Keynes, ed., *The Letters of William Blake* (London: Rupert Hart-Davis, 1956), p. 178.

2 See, also, the Second Prospectus to Blake's Chaucer Engraving,

E557: 'every Character and every Expression, every Lineament of Head Hand and Foot, every particular of Dress or Costume, where every Horse is appropriate to his Rider.'

3 Jean H. Hagstrum, *William Blake: Poet and Painter* (University of Chicago Press, 1964), p. 4.

4 Letter to Thomas Butts, July 6, 1803, in Keynes, *Letters*, p. 89.

5 Bentley, *Records*, pp. 251, 383, 454, 481.

6 *IB*, p. 16.

7 *Piper and Bard*, p. 96.

8 Kathleen Raine, *Blake and Tradition* (2 vols, Princeton University Press, 1968), I, p. 148.

9 See, for example, *Blake's Innocence*, pp. 115–22, or Gillham, *Contrary States*, pp. 139–47.

10 Blake was traditional in his association of southern or equatorial climates with the passions. In 'To Summer,' for example, in the early *Poetical Sketches*, the speaker brags that the youth of England 'are bolder than the southern swains.' And in the later symbolic books, while south is the direction (or location) of Urizen, this is only true for 'eternal times,' that is, before Albion's fall (see *FZ* 6.279: E319). In our fallen world of Generation or Experience, Luvah, the Zoa of the passions, has 'assumed the world of Urizen to the South' (*M* 19.19: E112).

11 See, for example, S. Foster Damon, *William Blake: His Philosophy and Symbols* (1924; rpt NY: Peter Smith, 1947), p. 279, or Raine, *Tradition*, I, pp. 128–39.

12 Perhaps she is seven years old for some of the same reasons that Lyca's parents are said to search seven days and nights. E. D. Hirsch, Jr, in *Innocence and Experience: An Introduction to Blake* (New Haven: Yale University Press, 1964), p. 225, thinks the number 'strongly suggest(s) providential control of events, as though everything happens at a divinely appointed time.' Glecker, *Piper and Bard*, p. 220, thinks the number seven suggests that 'a phase of life, of existence, of the soul is coming to an end. The creation as such has been completed, but life itself is yet to begin.'

13 In some copies, however, the dresses are colored differently; Erdman, *IB*, p. 77, cites *In*.F, A, B and Y, to which should be added *In*.I, E and M. Those in which they are the same are *In*.E (green), W (purple), L, N, O, S, T, X (pink).

14 William Blake, *Songs of Innocence and of Experience*, intro. and comment. Geoffrey Keynes (1967: rpt London: Oxford University Press, 1970), pl. 17.

15 Erdman, *IB*, p. 57.

16 *Apocalypse*, p. 40.

17 David Wagenknecht, *Blake's Night: William Blake and the Idea of Pastoral* (Cambridge, Ma.: Harvard University Press, 1973), p. 72.

18 *VFD*, p. 205.
19 See Homan Potterton, *A Guide to the National Gallery* (London: The National Gallery, 1978), pp. 34–5.
20 *Philosophy*, p. 272. Bindman conjectures an early Renaissance prototype for the design, though, on the grounds of what he calls its 'subtle' coloring (*Artist*, p. 59).
21 *Songs*, pl. 17.
22 *IB*, p. 58.
23 *Ibid.*, p. 16.
24 It looks almost as if it were color-printed, a technique Paley says Blake associated with 'seduction and deadly beauty' (*William Blake* (Oxford: Phaidon Press, 1978), p. 37).
25 Paley sees meaning in a comparable distortion in the famous 'Ancient of Days' design and title-page to *Europe*: 'Blake has made a deliberate change of emphasis here. His creator is the demiurge, and the grotesque left knee and impossibly elongated arm of this mighty form indicate Blake's ambivalence towards him' (*Ibid.*, p. 31). For the theoretical grounds for Blake's consistent refusal to employ techniques of three-dimensional illusionism see W. J. T. Mitchell, 'Blake's Composite Art,' *VFD*, pp. 57–81. Bindman, *Artist*, p. 22, and Rosenblum, *Transformations*, pp. 168–70, discuss Neoclassical sources and analogues for Blake's perspectival primitivism.
26 Wagenknecht, *Night*, p. 75.
27 Keynes, *Songs*, pl. 17.
28 *VFD*, p. 205.
29 See Wagenknecht, *Night*, p. 59. Similarly ambivalent feelings about female affection in general, not just maternal love, are found in the later epics, where weaving, a characteristic activity of fallen and unfallen females, can be protective and generative (germinating, as in a cocoon), as well as smothering.
30 See, for example, *In.*I., where the mother's neck, shoulders, and hair are exposed, or E, where the mother is thin, blond, and young, and the wash above the text is of pastel blues and pinks.
31 *Transformations*, p. 52.
32 Geoffrey Keynes, *Blake Studies* (London: Rupert Hart-Davis, 1949), p. 106.
33 Martin K. Nurmi, 'Fact and Symbol in "The Chimney Sweeper" of Blake's *Songs of Innocence*,' in *Blake: A Collection of Critical Essays*, ed. Northrop Frye (Englewood Cliffs, NJ: Prentice-Hall, 1966), p. 17.
34 See Bateson, ed., *Selected Poems*, p. 120. Jonas Hanway, in 1773, stated that the sweeps' bleeding knees and elbows were often treated with salt brine, to toughen the flesh, also that masters would light fires in the chimney grates 'to force reluctant climbers up and away from the flames' (see Pinchbeck, *Society*, II, p. 357).

35 For two quite different interpretations of 'duty' see Wicksteed, *Blake's Innocence*, p. 110: 'The "duty" is not, surely, the sweeping of chimneys but the dreaming of dreams'; and Gullham, *Contrary States*, p. 42: 'One's "duty" lies in doing what must be done, and it happens that this is, for him, an exercise of fellow-feeling.' For a detailed and in some ways complementary reading of the poem to my own, see Heather Glen, 'Blake's Criticism of Moral Thinking,' in *Interpreting Blake*, ed. Michael Phillips (Cambridge University Press, 1978), pp. 34–47.

36 *Blake's Innocence*, p. 109.

37 Nurmi, *Essays*, p. 18.

38 Hirsch, *Introduction*, pp. 184–5.

39 *Apocalypse*, p. 37.

40 Erdman, *IB*, p. 53, calls the figure 'Jesus himself ... the key and the angel, who would have wings, melt off as a metaphor for the swiftness of salvation for chimney sweeps (see Swedenborg's *Earths in the Universe*).'

41 Clear in the original and in the 1955 facsimile; barely visible in the 1967 edition.

42 Bentley, *Books*, p. 391, counts ' ? nine.'

43 Somewhat brighter and yellower in the original than in either facsimile.

44 Copy Z lacks the bright green vegetation found in other copies. The tree at the bottom right of the plate, and the few dull green sprigs of vegetation along the right margin hardly make the plate 'Alive,' as Erdman suggests (*IB*, p. 53).

45 *Prophet*, p. 196.

46 John E. Grant, 'Mothers and Methodology,' *Blake Newsletter*, vol. 2, no. 6 (December 15, 1968), p. 53.

47 See Keynes, *Songs*, pl. 42, and Erdman, *IB*, p. 84.

48 Wicksteed, *Blake's Innocence*, p. 193.

49 Erdman, *Prophet*, p. 196.

50 John E. Grant, 'The Art and Argument of "The Tyger",' *Discussions of William Blake*, ed. John E. Grant (Boston: D. C. Heath, 1961), p. 80.

51 *William Blake*, p. 70.

52 *Poet and Painter*, p. 86.

53 Quoted in Bentley, *Records*, p. 563n.

54 Keynes, *Songs*, pl. 14.

55 See Thomas E. Connolly and George R. Levine, 'Pictorial and Poetic Design in Two Songs of Innocence,' *PMLA*, LXXXII (May 1967), pp. 257–64.

56 Erdman, *IB*, p. 55.

57 'Mother of Invention, Father in Drag or Observations on the Methodology that Brought About these Deplorable Conditions and What Then is to be Done,' *Blake Newsletter*, vol. 2, no. 6, pp. 31–2.

58 *Artist*, p. 213n.
59 'Mother of Invention,' *Blake Newsletter*, p. 31–2.
60 *Songs*, pl. 14.
61 See, for example, Gleckner, *Piper and Bard*, pp. 98–9, who suggests that 'the attempt by "the little boy lost" to seize his "father" bodily is ... wrong.' The father the child sees is, in fact, 'the earthly law-giver of experience.' The child should be 'acting and being what he is, an "infant joy," a laughing bird, not usurping the rational powers of another realm.'
62 *Blake's Human Form Divine* (Berkeley: University of California Press, 1974), p. 65.
63 Bentley, *Records*, p. 19.
64 *A Concise History of English Painting* (New York: Praeger, 1964), p. 142.
65 *Poet and Painter*, p. 62.
66 *Artist*, p. 27.
67 *The Art of William Blake* (New York: Oxford University Press, 1959), p. 48.
68 *Ibid.*, p. 47.
69 *HFD*, p. 105.
70 *Poet and Painter*, p. 62.
71 Watteau, for example, or other illustrators of popular literary works, among whom Hagstrum includes Richard Westall, Angelica Kauffmann, Lady Diana Beauclerk, Cosway, Maria Flaxman, Romney, and Metz (*Idem.*).
72 Blunt, *Art*, p. 47.
73 There are, in fact, important differences between the pictorial styles of *Innocence* and *Experience*. Not only does *Experience* contain many more Graeco-Roman motifs or compositional forms than *Innocence*, but the style of engraving changes as well; see Keynes and Wolf, *Census*, p. 51: 'In the *Songs of Innocence* the larger surfaces of the etched plates have been generally lightened in effect by engraved lines, whereas in the *Songs of Experience* the heavy effect of these surfaces is unrelieved by subsequent engraving.'
74 Northrop Frye, *Fearful Symmetry* (Boston: Beacon Press, 1967), p. 4.
75 See Bindman, *Artist*, p. 59.
76 Erdman, *IB*, p. 56
77 *Idem.*
78 *Elizabethan Poetry* (Cambridge, Ma.: Harvard University Press, 1952), p. 31.
79 *Transformations*, pp. 20ff.
80 *Vision and Design* (New York: Peter Smith, 1947), p. 141.
81 For Fuseli, see Eudo C. Mason, ed. and intro., *The Mind of Henry Fuseli, Selections from his Writings* (London: Routledge &

Kegan Paul, 1951), p. 208: 'mixed expression is equally unfit for the sculptor, engraver, and printer; a little of many things is in art the destruction of the whole.' For Reynolds, see Discourse 15: 'An artist ... is not likely to be forever teasing the poor student with the beauties, of *mixed passions*, or to perplex him with an imaginary union of excellencies incompatible with one another' (*Discourses on Art*, ed. Robert R. Wark (New York: Collier Books, 1966), p. 235.

82 Excerpted in Lorenz Eitner, ed., *Neoclassicism and Romanticism: 1750–1850: Sources and Documents* (2 vols, London: Prentice-Hall International, 1971), I, p. 86.

83 From *Thoughts on the Imitation of Greek Works in Painting and Sculpture* (1755), excerpted in *Ibid.*, p. 11.

84 See Joseph Wicksteed, *Blake's Vision of the Book of Job* (London: J. M. Dent, 1910), pp. 13–28.

85 Morris Eaves, 'A Reading of Blake's *Marriage of Heaven and Hell*, plates 17–20: On and Under the Estate of the West,' *Blake Studies*, vol. 4, no. 2 (Spring 1972), pp. 81–116.

86 Rudolf Arnheim, *Art and Visual Perception* (Berkeley: University of California Press, 1954), p. 64.

87 *VFD*, p. 212.

88 *Introduction*, p. 193.

89 Erdman, *IB*, p. 59, suggests these figures may be Adam and Eve or Lazarus and the Woman taken in Adultery. In *In.P.*, the female is given a green dress.

90 The green gown of the facsimiles is, in fact, yellow in the original.

91 Erdman, *IB*, p. 59.

92 Blake may be making a similar point in the 1799 watercolor, *The Baptism of Christ*, in which everyone present looks either above or below the God who walks amongst them.

93 Similar dangers attend the application of psychological or psychoanalytic theories of form, by which I mean something more complex than speculation about the number and significance of the many womb-like shapes in *Innocence*. Adrian Stokes's distinction between 'carving' and 'modelling' traditions, in *The Invitation in Art* (London: Tavistock Publications, 1969), or Marion Milner's between the states of 'oneness' and 'twoness' in 'The Role of Illusion in Symbol Formation,' *New Directions in Psychoanalysis*, ed. Melanie Klein, Paula Heinemann, R. E. Money-Kyrle (London: Tavistock Publications, 1955), pp. 82–108 – both influential adaptations of the Kleinean 'paranoid-schizoid' and 'depressive' positions to the formal properties of art objects and their relations to the spectator – could (in fact, have, in Simon Stuart's *New Phoenix Wings* (London: Routledge & Kegan Paul, 1979)) shed interesting light on the overall purpose and meaning of Blake's work. But this is only to

be expected given the coincidence of an artist obsessed with unity and an aesthetic in which the affirmation and celebration of the whole object (what Richard Wollheim, in *Art and its Objects* (1968, rpt. Harmondsworth: Penguin, 1975), p. 145, calls 'the good inner figure') plays so prominent a role. Again, though, I am neither equipped to conduct such an analysis nor sanguine about the relevance of its findings to any but the most general of statements about Blake and *Songs*.

94 See Bindman, *Artist*, Blunt, *Art*, Hagstrum, *Poet and Painter*, Mitchell, *Blake's Composite Art*. Also Raine, *Tradition*, for esoteric, and Erdman, *Prophet*, for political analogues; and Collins Baker, 'The Sources of Blake's Pictorial Expression,' *Huntington Library Quarterly*, IV (1940–1), pp. 359–67; and Elaine M. Kauver, 'Blake's Botanical Imagery,' dissertation, Northwestern University, 1970.

95 See, for example, 'Infant Joy.'

96 Now lost, but probably related to three well-known and frequently reproduced works: a pen drawing in the Rosenwald collection, a watercolor for Butts, now at Pollok House, Glasgow, and another watercolor version, for the Countess of Egremont, still at Petworth House, Sussex. A preliminary version, belonging to Gregory Bateson, is now on loan to the Honolulu Academy of Arts.

97 Quoted by Jack Lindsay, *William Blake: His Life and Work* (London: Constable, 1978), p. 52.

98 The first to make such an attempt, at least among Blake's modern readers, was S. Foster Damon in *William Blake: His Philosophy and Symbols* (1924; rpt New York: Peter Smith, 1947). Its fullest treatment is still that of Raine, *Tradition*. Gombrich shares it, in 'Icones Symbolicae,' *Symbolic Images: Studies in the Art of the Renaissance* (1972; rpt Oxford: Phaidon Press, 1978), p. 187.

99 E. H. Gombrich, 'The Aims and Limits of Iconology,' *Symbolic Images*, p. 13.

100 See Mason, *Mind of Fuseli*, pp. 44, 56.

101 Basire's plates for Jacob Bryant's *A New System; or an Analysis of Ancient Mythology* (1774–6), on which Blake worked, are clear examples of the survival of the old Aristotelian or analogical emblem tradition in illustrative engraving; a tradition the Reynoldsian line opposed, or the end of which it symptomized (a point I owe to Helen McNeil).

102 Hagstrum, *Poet and Painter*, p. 14, briefly alludes to these poets' acknowledged debts to the icons of Ripa, antique statuary, and the paintings of the high Renaissance. See also Hagstrum's *The Sister Arts* (University of Chicago Press, 1958), and Robert J. Clements, *Picta Poesis: Literary and Humanistic Theory in Renaissance Emblem Books* (Rome: Edizioni di Storia e Letteratura, 1960). W. J. T. Mitchell's 'Blake's Composite Art,' in *VFD*, challenged

Hagstrum's account of Blake's debt to the *ut pictura poesis* tradition and prompted the latter's response in the same volume, 'Blake and the Sister Arts Tradition.' Mitchell reopens, or expands, the controversy in *Blake's Composite Art*, pp. 14–34.

103 For a modern, secular Neoplatonism see Frelhjof Schuon, quoted in Raine, *Tradition*, I, p. xxix: 'The science of symbols – not simply a knowledge of traditional symbols – proceeds from the qualitative significances of substances, forms, spatial directions, numbers, natural phenomena, positions, relationships, movements, colours and other properties or states of things; we are not dealing here with subjective appreciations, for the cosmic qualities are ordered both in relation to Being and according to a hierarchy which is more real than the individual.'

104 'Icones Symbolicae,' in *Symbolic Images*, p. 165.

105 Quoted by Janet A. Warner, 'Blake's Use of Gesture,' *VFD*, p. 174. Also Laurence Binyon, *The Drawings and Engravings of William Blake* (London: The Studio, 1922), p. 7, where again Binyon writes of Blake's having 'adopted from the outside a set of forms, attitudes and gestures which we see repeated again and again through his work.'

106 See, either Bo Lindberg, *William Blake's Illustrations to the Book of Job* (Abo, Finland: Abo Akademi, 1973), p. 115, or Janet Warner, 'Blake's Figures of Despair,' in Martin D. Paley and Michael Phillips, eds, *William Blake: Essays in Honour of Sir Geoffrey Keynes* (Oxford University Press, 1973), pp. 208–24.

Chapter 3 Entering 'Innocence'

1 *Blake's Humanism* (New York: Manchester University Press, 1968), p. 13.

2 From 'Characteristics' (1831), in *Critical and Miscellaneous Essays* (5 vols, London: Chapman & Hall, 1899), III, p. 20.

3 Erdman, *IB*, p. 43, says that the child floats 'On a cloud-blanket, tucked among tight-foliaged trees,' and that 'In various ways in different copies the cloud is strongly emphasized.' But in copy Z only the outline of the patch of sky suggests a cloud. The fold which appears beneath the child's waist in some copies (A, B, and I, for example) has been obscured or colored over here.

4 *Songs*, pl. 2.

5 *William Blake* (London: Thames & Hudson 1970), p. 51.

6 'The Presence of Cupid and Psyche,' *VFD*, p. 231.

7 Letter of February 12 (?), 1818 to C. A. Tulk, quoted in Bentley, *Records*, p. 252.

8 'In some copies the piper's garment extends below his leg muscles; in BZY it stops below the knees, with a tie BZ at his left

knee' (Erdman, *IB*, p. 43). In E, the piper's garment reaches mid-calf. M is another copy whose coloring makes the piper seem naked.

9 Damon, *Philosophy*, p. 271. See Keynes, *Songs*, pl. 3, and Bass, *VFD*, p. 213, for similar readings.

10 See George Ferguson, *Signs and Symbols in Christian Art* (New York: Oxford University Press, 1954), pp. 51–2.

11 Bass suggests that the children 'remind us of Adam and Eve before the Fall' (*VFD*, p. 198).

12 Satan as Serpent was frequently depicted curling around the trunk of the Tree of the Knowledge of Good and Evil. See J. B. Trapp, 'The Inconography of the Fall of Man,' *Approaches to Paradise Lost*, ed. C. A. Patrides (London: Edward Arnold, 1968), pp. 223–65. Note also the second plate of Blake's *The Ghost of Abel*, where a naked Adam and Eve stand under the Tree of Knowledge while Satan in serpent form twists vine-like round its trunk. For Blake's use of John 15:1, Christ as 'the true vine,' see page 94 of Night Nine of the illustrations to Young's *Night Thoughts*.

13 *Ibid.*, p. 224.

14 'Mariana,' lines 43–4, in Christopher Ricks, ed., *The Poems of Tennyson* (London: Longman, 1969), p. 189.

15 See, for example, Blake's watercolors *Age Teaching Youth* (*c.* 1785–90) and *An Allegory for the Bible* (*c.* 1784?); also plate 14 of *America* (1793), and the illustration on page 35 of the 1797 edition of Young's *Night Thoughts*.

16 *Philosophy*, p. 271.

17 *VFD*, p. 198.

18 Quoted in Lorenz Eitner, ed., *Neoclassicism and Romanticism: Sources and Documents, 1750–1850* (2 vols, London: Prentice Hall International, 1971).

19 Examples of natural costumes for children introduced in Blake's age (including the skeleton-suit) are to be found in P. Cunnington and A. Buck, *Children's Clothes in England* (London: Adam and Charles Black, 1965), pp. 122–77. Also C. Willet Cunnington and Phillis Cunnington, *Handbook of English Costume in the Eighteenth Century* (London: Faber & Faber, 1957), pp. 409–15.

20 *Émile*, p. 81.

21 Michael Ferber has suggested to me that the children are looking at a copy of *Innocence*, so that we are to think of the book as another form of the piper's music, like the word 'SONGS' which flowers above his head. (He also reminds me that 'books come from trees, ironically including the one before us.') But Blake is unlikely to have implicated his own work in the children's loss of innocence, despite his well-known penchant for ironic self-

reference. When first he etched the title-page he may well have thought more kindly of the mother, in which case the book could be a copy of *Innocence*. But even if we see it as the Piper's creation, we have still to account for the mother's unsettling appearance in Z.

22 Erdman, *IB*, p. 44.

23 See, for example, John Linell's 1821 lead-pencil drawing in Laurence Binyon, *The Drawings and Engravings of William Blake* (London: The Studio, 1922), p. 18.

24 *IB*, p. 44.

25 Gillham, *Contrary States*, p. 150.

26 Quoted in Eitner, *Neoclassicism and Romanticism*, I, p. 87.

27 *Blake's Innocence*, p. 81. For a similar interpretation see Hazard Adams, *William Blake: A Reading of the Shorter Poems* (Seattle: University of Washington Press, 1963), p. 21.

28 Quoted in Stewart and McCann, *Innovators*, p. 248.

29 John Holloway, *Lyric Poetry*, p. 28.

30 *Piper and Bard*, p. 85. See, also, p. 34 where Gleckner calls *Innocence* and *Experience* 'contributions to the formulation of a system upon which their *full* meaning largely depends.' Wicksteed, *Blake's Innocence*, p. 80; Holloway, *Lyric Poetry*, p. 62; Adams, *Shorter Lyrics*, p. 20; and Bateson, *Selected Poems*, p. 111, think the tears of line 8 joyful.

31 See Alice Ostriker, *Vision and Verse in William Blake* (New York: Oxford University Press, 1959), p. 45, for the influence of children's songs, nursery rhymes, and jingles on *Songs*.

32 Erdman, *IB*, p. 45. Bentley, *Books*, p. 387, is more cautious, referring only to a seated 'adult.'

33 *Philosophy*, p. 221. Bentley, *Idem*, speaks of a 'walking' figure.

34 Erdman, *IB*, p. 45.

35 Blunt, *Art*, p. 45.

36 Erdman, *IB*, p. 46.

37 Hirsch, *Introduction*, p. 174, believes that 'the scenes represent various stages of life from birth to old age. Thus, while the design does not illustrate the poem, it does introduce some of the main themes of *Innocence*: joy, sorrow, guardianship and the cycle of life.' Though this is a plausible reading, I wish that the 'stages' Hirsch talks of had been placed in some sort of sequence. There is little reason to believe that they move 'from birth to old age,' even in those copies in which the top left-hand loop depicts a child standing before an adult and the bottom left a mother looking 'lovingly' into a cradle. (Hirsch's readings are based on copies M and *In*.P.)

38 See, for example, the bottom half of 'The Little Boy Lost' plate, or the first plate of 'Night.'

39 Bunyan's *A Book for Boys and Girls* contains seventy-four poems

in seventeenth-century emblem form. Each poem was formally divided into description and comparison, and the moral was clearly set apart or detached. Each individual emblem is independent and self-contained. The 'detachable' character of individual 'Divine Songs' is suggested by their titles: 'Against Cursing,' for example, or 'Against Lying,' or 'Against Scoffing.'

40 Gilham, *Contrary States*, p. 226.

41 *Blake's Innocence*, p. 86.

42 *Introduction*, p. 43. Hazlitt, for example, would have thought the repetition too daring. Blake, he felt, 'had no sense of the ludicrous' (see Bentley, *Records*, p. 229).

43 See John Gross, *The Rise and Fall of the Man of Letters: English Literary Life since 1800* (Harmondsworth: Penguin, 1973), p. 14. An anonymous *Edinburgh Review* article (April 1834) on Cunningham's *Lives* refers in passing to 'Blake, the able, but, alas! insane author of some very striking and original designs [who] could scarcely be considered a painter' (quoted in Bentley, *Records*, p. 380). Gombrich notes a similar Jeffrey-like fear of childlikeness in the reactions of those who distrust comparably daring visual simplicities:

> We speak of a painting as 'pretty pretty,' to imply that such primitive gratification as it offers is not for the grown-up mind. We call it 'chocolate boxy' to describe its inartistic invitation to self-indulgence. Everywhere our reaction suggests that we have come to equate such indulgence with other childish gratifications we have learned to control. We find the 'cheap' work 'too sweet,' 'cloying,' 'pushy' ('Visual Metaphors of Value in Art,' in *Meditations on a Hobby Horse* (1963; rpt Oxford: Phaidon Press, 1978), pp. 20–1.

44 Adams, *Shorter Poems*, p. 294, cites the word 'for' as an example of Blake's 'awkwardness,' complaining that it 'tortures the syntax.'

45 Gleckner, *Piper and Bard*, pp. 89, 92, calls carefreeness of this sort 'irresponsible,' which only shows how far his own symbolic readings can stray. Aimless wandering and carefree play are virtues in *Innocence*. In 'A Dream,' Blake's parody of Bunyan's 'The Pismire' and Watts's 'The Ant or Emmet,' the road to salvation is lit by the sluggard, not by the industrious and prudent ant.

46 Though they resemble each other, they are not identical. Erdman, *IB*, p. 46, notes the shepherd's 'shorter hair, different neckline, tunic-like garment ending above the knees.'

47 For a pointed and uncharacteristic (because late) exception, no doubt influenced by the much earlier Newbery, see *Will Wander's*

Walk (London: J. Aldiss, 1806), on the title-page to which 'Says Will to his Sister/My Dog here proposes/To Take a nice Walk/ And just follow our noses' (reproduced in Stone, *Family*, pl. 22).

48 *Contrary States*, p. 226.
49 *Introduction*, p. 29.
50 *HFD*, p. 4.
51 *IB*, p. 46. Bentley, *Books*, p. 389 thinks it anticipated in the bottom-left vine-looped scene on the 'Introduction' plate.
52 See, for example, *In.*B, B, C, E, and I.
53 *IB*, p. 46.
54 'Sex Versus Loveliness,' in *Selected Essays* (1950; rpt Harmondsworth: Penguin, 1965), p. 17.
55 *William Blake: The Politics of Vision* (New York: Henry Holt, 1946), p. 117.
56 Ernest de Selincourt, ed., *Wordsworth: Poetical Works* (1904; rpt London: Oxford University Press, 1969), p. 155.
57 'Blake's Songs of Spring,' *Keynes Festschrift*, ed. Paley, p. 107.
58 *Introduction*, p. 40.
59 See, for example, *Ibid.*, p. 176, or Stanley Gardner, *Infinity on the Anvil: A Critical Study of Blake's Poetry* (Oxford: Basil Blackwell, 1954), pp. 24–5.
60 See Ostriker, *Vision and Verse*, p. 73.
61 Quoted in Bentley, *Records*, p. 315.
62 Only three other plates in copy Z, all of them in *Experience*, contain trees similar in appearance: 'Holy Thursday,' 'The Angel,' and 'The Poison Tree.' *In.* I and B are examples of copies which retain the original printed outlines of the spidery-branched trees on the first plate of 'The Ecchoing Green.'
63 *IB*, p. 47.
64 *Loves of the Plants* was published anonymously in 1789. Blake engraved five plates, after Fuseli, for the quarto editions of the completed *Botanic Garden* (1791–5).
65 *IB*, p. 47.
66 In the original printing this leaf is a triple-branched sprig of vegetation growing out of the word 'The' in the title.
67 In Z and a few other late copies a stream flows along the bottom of the plate. Erdman, *IB*, p. 48, suggests that 'the narrow stream of water that began under the Tree of Jesse continues here and in the next picture – the life's river or poetry of innocence, the "water clean" which the poet stains to make purple grapes – a condensation, Sevcik suggests, of the visionary cloud of plate 2.'
68 *Introduction*, p. 177.
69 *IB*, p. 48.
70 See Bass, *VFD*, p. 198.
71 *Introduction*, p. 177.
72 *Philosophy*, p. 272.

73 *Songs*, pl. 6.
74 W. H. Stevenson's note on this passage cites Song of Songs 2 : 13 as a possible source (*Poems*, p. 207).
75 Erdman, *IB*, p. 48.
76 *Newsletter*, vol. 2, no. 6, p. 52.
77 *Shorter Poems*, p. 236.
78 'The Lotus Eaters,' line 96 in Ricks, ed., *The Poems of Tennyson*, p. 433.
79 *Poor Monkey*, p. xiv.
80 *Night*, p. 81.
81 How close is Keats's 'the white dove/That on the window spreads his feathers light/And seems from purple cloud to wing its flight,' in 'Calidore,' ll. 43–5, in Miriam Allott, ed., *Keats: The Complete Poems* (London: Longman, 1970), p. 38.
82 *Night*, p. 81. Wagenknecht bases his interpretation of the plate on a supposed 'loverlike relationship between infant and lamb.' The stormy sky's 'suggestions of imminent release and cloudburst' constitute 'an esoteric reminder of the sexual constituency of the scene before us.' Wagenknecht might well have enlisted the help of Ernest Jones, for whom the qualities of doves makes them appropriate, and therefore frequent, phallic symbols (see 'The Madonna's Conception through the Ear,' *Essays in Applied Psychoanalysis* (2 vols, London: Hogarth Press, 1951), II, pp. 326ff.).
83 *IB*, p. 49.
84 *Shorter Poems*, p. 230.
85 Quoted in Pinchbeck, *Society*, II, p. 269.
86 Holloway, *Lyric Poetry*, p. 61.
87 *Blake's Innocence*, p. 92.
88 'The Aims and Limits of Iconology,' in *Symbolic Images*, p. 16.
89 This and the succeeding quote come from *Idem*.

Chapter 4   Innocence in maturity

1 *Fearful Symmetry*, p. 233.
2 *Apocalypse*, p. 402.
3 *Fearful Symmetry*, p. 45.
4 See Jack Lindsay, *William Blake: His Life and Work* (London: Constable, 1978), p. xiv.
5 Ostriker, *Vision and Verse*, p. 50.
6 Gillham,ary States, p. 185.
7 'On the Feeling of Immortality in Youth,' in *Lectures on the English Comic Writers and Fugitive Writings* (London: Dent, 1967), p. 314.
8 Douglas Bush, ed., *Milton: Poetical Works* (1966; rpt London: Oxford University Press, 1969), p. 67. For a somewhat more

explicit echo of the 'Nativity Ode' see the opening lines of *Europe*: 'The deep of winter came;/What time the secret child,/Descended thro' the orient gates of the eternal day' (3.1.3: E60).

9 Adams, *Shorter Poems*, p. 265, thinks that the 'shade' of the first line refers to the Tree of Life, so that 'Dove, angel and tree invoke, through their biblical connections, the figure of Jesus himself as an infant.'

10 *Night*, p.74.

11 *Apocalypse*, p. 40.

12 Hirsch, *Introduction*, p. 190.

13 *Vision and Verse*, p. 50.

14 Quoted in Pinchbeck, *Society*, II, pp. 274–5.

15 Gardner, *Infinity*, p. 26.

16 *Fugitive Writings*, p. 310.

17 *Introduction*, p. 32.

18 *Apocalypse*, p. 41.

19 Bateson, *Selected Poems*, p. 116, Adams, *Shorter Poems*, p. 254, and Hirsch, *Introduction*, pp. 199–200, believe that the poem's last two lines are spoken not by the nurse but by the poet. But there is no reason why the nurse cannot be speaking or thinking them to herself. And though it is true that Blake's punctuation was often erratic, does not the possessive 'Nurse's' of the title suggest that the nurse herself speaks throughout, like her experienced counterpart? Both Hirsch and Adams assume that the poem's opening lines are spoken by the nurse.

20 See, for example, the political cartoons of James Gillray. Erdman, *Prophet*, pp. 203–5, 218–19, clearly shows that Blake knew Gillray's work.

21 *IB*, p. 65.

22 *Idem*.

23 *Idem*.

24 *Idem*.

25 According to Morton D. Paley, *William Blake* (Oxford: Phaidon, 1978), p. 17, 'the idea of the Black Boy's superior tolerance for the beams of love is derived from Swedenborg's notion that the Africans were the remnant of the Most Ancient Church and therefore closer to God than the Europeans.' What the Blake of 'The Little Black Boy' thought of this doctrine (if indeed he knew it), and of Swedenborg in general, is impossible to tell. If he was an enthusiastic Swedenborgian in the first half of 1788, the probable year of his annotations to *The Wisdom of Angels Concerning Divine Love and Divine Wisdom* (see Bentley, *Writings*, II, p. 1744), by 1790, in the annotations to *The Wisdom of Angels Concerning Divine Providence*, he was sharply critical. In the *Song of Los* (1795), for example, Africa could, it is true, be seen as closest to Eternity (Los sings his song 'at the tables of Eternity./In

heart-formed Africa' (32.3: E65)), but it seems also to be the first to fall ('Adam shuddered! Noah faded! black grew the sunny African' (3.10: E66)).

26 See Jacob Adler, 'Symbol and Meaning in "The Little Black Boy," ' *Modern Language Notes*, LXXII (June 1957), pp. 412–15.

27 *Blake's Innocence*, p. 113:

He [Blake] knew, if any man did, the spiritual price of vision and the debt the visionary owes to those dimmer but steadier lights, men and women whose touch with earth enables them to protect the artist from the mortal consequences of his excess of light.

28 *Apocalypse*, p. 45.

29 For Bloom, *ibid.*, p. 43, 'bereav'd' 'has the force of "dispossessed" or "divested"; the myth of the Fall has entered the poem.'

30 *Ibid.*, p. 46.

31 'The LITTLE ENGLISH BOY at Christ's knee is uniformly Caucasian-Pink or once (*E*) Caucasian-Blue; the LEFT CHILD is generally Caucasian-Pink in early copies, ... but he is Negro-Grey or Negro-Brown in most late copies (F, L-O, Q, S *E*, *I-J*, *L*, *P*, *R-Y*)' (Bentley, *Books*, p. 391).

32 *IB*, p. 51.

33 In some copies, *In*.B, for example, his expression is non-committal.

34 Erdman, *IB*, p. 50, claims that 'The southern trees are of wilder shape than the village oak or elm.' But their appearance varies from copy to copy, and in Z the tree is not all that different in appearance from other sheltering trees in *Innocence*.

35 Erdman says of the little boy's gesture that 'We may understand him simply to be explaining what "black bodies" are like by pointing to "a shady grove" (15–16), but the gesture also suits the words "black as if bereav'd of light" (4)' (*Idem*.).

36 *Idem*.

37 Erdman points to 'the flourish of sheltering foliage that grows over the title word "Boy" [and] repeats again the willow's bending' (*Idem*.) – another unsettling note.

38 The willow's traditional associations are interesting but somewhat contradictory. Hugo Rahner, *Greek Myths and Christian Mysteries* (New York: Harper & Row, 1963), pp. 286–321, says that in Greek tradition they were associated with chastity, while in the Bible they are associated with a new life, fertility, contraception, eternal life and Behemoth.

39 See *Edward the Third* (*PS*: E28); *Four Zoas* 1.57: E265 and 7.31: E321; *Milton* 35.36: E526; and *Jerusalem* 17.32: E639.

40 *IB*, p. 51.
41 *Blake's Innocence*, pp. 11–113. For Wicksteed's theories of left and right, see *Blake's Vision of the Book of Job* (London: Dent, 1910), pp. 13–28.
42 *Introduction*, p. 181.
43 The Christ at the bottom of 'The Divine Image' flame-plant is but one of several ways of imagining the Savior.
44 Chief among the exceptions is *Christ and the Woman Taken in Adultery*, one of a series of at least ten watercolors painted for Thomas Butts in *c*. 1805. 'The gentleness of the depiction of Jesus,' writes Bindman of the series as a whole, 'is in marked contrast to his depiction elsewhere' (*Artist*, p. 143). Another exception occurs in a much earlier series: three pen and watercolor pictures of Joseph and his brethren, exhibited at the Royal Academy in 1785. In the first two of these, heroic Joseph is sitting, in the third his back is bent and his arms upstretched as he reveals his identity to his brethren. The evil brethren, it is worth noting, are bearded, while prophetic Joseph, youngest of the four, is clean-shaven. For a bearded but upright and energetic young Christ see *Night Thoughts*, no. 512, page 94 of Night Nine.
45 Bentley, *Books*, p. 391.
46 'My First Acquaintance with Poets,' in *The Collected Works of William Hazlitt*, ed. A. R. Waller and Arnold Glover (12 vols, London: J. M. Dent, 1904), XII, p. 262.
47 Arnold Hauser, *The Social History of Art* (2 vols, New York: Knopf, 1952), I, p. 146, tells us that in the second century the Neoplatonist Christian Clement of Alexandria interpreted the second commandment to extend to the depiction of Christ and that as late as the third century, Eusebius, the 'father of Church history,' condemned pictures of the Savior as idolatrous and contrary to Scripture. For a detailed study of the earliest Christian portraits see Part Two of André Grabar's *Christian Iconography: A Study of Its Origins* (London: Routledge & Kegan Paul, 1969), pp. 57–87.
48 *Ibid.*, p. 147.
49 'The Critical Path,' *Daedalus*, vol. 99, no. 2 (Spring 1970), pp. 282–3.
50 'Some Reflections Upon Religious Art,' *Art and Scholasticism: With Other Essays*, tr. J. F. Scanlan (New York: Scribners, 1933), p. 144.
51 *Lyric Poetry*, p. 29.
52 Erdman, *IB*, p. 66, and Irene Chayes, in 'The Presence of Cupid and Psyche,' *VFD*, p. 235, think it an anemone; Bass, *VFD*, p. 203, thinks it a parrot tulip. The flower is usually red or scarlet, though in *In*.A, *In*.G, D, E, F, I and X it is blue.
53 Hagstrum, *Poet and Painter*, p. 6.

54 Keynes, *Songs*, pl. 25, and Hagstrum, *Idem.*
55 Chayes, *VFD*, p. 232.
56 *Idem.*
57 *IB*, p. 66.
58 See Blake's reference to 'Apuleius's Golden Ass,' in *A Vision of the Last Judgement* (E546).
59 *VFD*, p. 235.
60 So too, though from a gruesomely pessimistic perspective, does the 'foetal skeleton' (Erdman, *IB*, p. 190) on plate 8 of *The Book of Urizen*, or the 1799 Butts tempera *The Virgin hushing John the Baptist*, the theme of which (Bindman, *Artist*, pp. 122–3),

> combines an intimate domestic scene with intimations of Christ's death in his sleeping posture, which reflects the *Eros funéraire* of the Psyche legend, explicitly referred to in the butterflies, one of which John brings in to show Christ while another flies off in the air. The butterfly which often accompanies the *Eros funéraire* signifies the belief in the return of the soul to the body when the temporary sleep of death has passed.

(Bindman reproduces the painting on plate 101 of *Artist*).
61 *IB*, p. 52.
62 *Night*, p. 59.
63 Erdman, *IB*, p. 52, thinks he is either 'writing on a book or a sheet of paper or reading a broadside.'
64 *Idem.*
65 Hirsch, *Introduction*, p. 197.
66 Ostriker, *Vision and Verse*, p. 74.
67 Wagenknecht, *Night*, p. 79.
68 Gillham, *Contrary States*, p. 240.
69 Alexander Gilchrist, *The Life of William Blake*, ed. Ruthven Todd (London: J. M. Dent, 1942), p. 6.
70 *Songs*, pl. 20.
71 *Idem.*
72 See Erdman, *IB*, p. 62, for quite a different interpretation.

Chapter 5 Entering 'Experience'

1 According to Hirsch, one of the earliest and most influential of post-Fryian anti-systematizers, Blake 'changed his interpretations of reality as radically as any figure in English letters': 'About God, Man, and Nature Blake fundamentally changed his mind not once but twice and he recorded these changes in his work not by unconscious implication but by deliberate choice' (*Introduction*, p. 6). By late 1789, after he had written the majority of the *Songs of Innocence*, Blake fell under the spell of

revolutionary naturalism: '*Experience*, for all its satirical bitterness, implies a far more hopeful and optimistic view of the natural world than *Innocence* does. ... *Innocence* places implicit trust in ultimate divine beneficence, but it invests very little hope or trust in the actual world ... with respect to natural life, *Innocence* is less illusioned and trustful than *Experience*' (p. 12). The second major change in Blake's ideas came in his 'later years, when he returned to some of his earlier beliefs and repudiated his temporary flirtation with the natural world' (pp. 12–13; see also pp. 106–65).

Ann Mellor, in *HFD*, and Morton Paley, in *Energy and Imagination*, also argue for change, Mellor adapting Paley's views on Blake's shift from 'innocence' to 'energy' to her theories of tectonic and atectonic forms: 'Between 1790 and 1795 ... Blake's poetic vision and philosophical principles came into conflict with his visual style. Philosophically he began to question the social and political implications of a commitment to self-sufficient religious vision. Since the closed vision had visually been associated with the framed compositions and bounding lines of Blake's early art, this also brought into question the nature and value of outline' (pp. xvi–xvii).

Erdman, on the other hand, though he approaches Blake's work historically, believes that *Innocence* grew out of much the same satiric spirit as *Experience*: 'The cultivation of innocence,' he writes, 'is itself a form of social criticism' (*Prophet*, p. 117). The difference between the two volumes is simply one of intensity, *Experience* deriving its 'peculiar anguish' from exceptionally bitter political restraints in the England of 1792–3; what Erdman calls the ' "grey-brow'd snows" ' of Antijacobin alarms and proclamations' (p. 272).

2 Damon, *Philosophy*, p. 284, seems to imply that the child is haloed in only one copy. Other copies, aside from Z, in which the child is haloed are Y, W, and AA. Some copies (C, for example) highlight the continuity between Piper and Bard by giving them similarly-colored costumes. Copy M, erratically colored, clothes the Bard (in what looks like buckskin), but uses flesh tones for what should be the Piper's costume. Copy W tips the child's wings and hair with glittering gold-leaf.

3 'Christ's Body,' *Keynes Festschrift*, p. 148.

4 Gillham's reading of this plate, in *Contrary States*, p. 150, is closest to my own. Erdman, *IB*, p. 71, who thinks both figures 'look directly at us,' ignores the blankness of their expressions. So too does Hirsch, *Introduction*, p. 102, who thinks the Bard 'looks straight ahead at the reader,' while the winged child 'seems to be enjoying a bouncy ride.'

5 See Erdman, *IB*, p. 71, and Keynes, *Songs*, pl. 29, neither of

whom is especially perturbed by the extreme age of the parents. Though the parents' death means 'loss of guidance' (Keynes) it also hints at new freedoms, especially given their patriarchal (or Urizenic) appearance.

6 Damon, *Philosophy*, p. 284.

7 *Keynes Festschrift*, p. 148.

8 Erdman, *IB*, p. 71.

9 *Idem*, and *Keynes Festschrift*, p. 148, and W. J. T. Mitchell, *Blake's Composite Art* (Princeton University Press, 1978), p. 7, where Mitchell reminds us that St Christopher was called 'reprobus' (reprobate or outcast) before his conversion.

10 *VFD*, pp. 325–6.

11 The process the Piper undergoes in his passage from innocence to experience is like that of the Ancient Poets' transformation in plate II of *Marriage*. In both cases imaginative exuberance is hardened into doctrine and dogma. See below, p. 138.

12 'Blake's Introduction to Experience,' *Blake: A Collection of Critical Essays*, ed. Northrop Frye (Englewood Cliffs, N.J.: Prentice-Hall, 1966), p. 25. Though in some works, notably *The Death of Abel* and the 1795 color print of *The Elohim Creating Adam*, Blake distinguishes between Elohim and Jehovah (the former representing negative, the latter positive aspects of the Father-God), elsewhere he uses 'Jehovah' pejoratively, as in *M* 13.24: E106: 'Jehovah was leprous; loud he call'd, stretching his hands to Eternity,/For then the Body of Death was perfected in hypocritic holiness, Around the Lamb.'

13 S. Foster Damon, *A Blake Dictionary: The Ideas and Symbols of William Blake* (New York: E. P. Dutton, 1971), p. 450.

14 *Contrary States*, p. 161.

15 *Revaluation* (New York: W. W. Norton, 1963), p. 142.

16 In addition to Wellek's initial reply to Leavis (discussed in the Introduction) see John Beer, *Humanism*, pp. 78–9: 'Blake himself would have made a clear distinction so far as the Druid associations of his poem are concerned ... the Druids of history would be nearer to the 'Starry Jealousy' of the next poem. ... Blake wished to *exclude* certain Druid associations from his invocation.' Here too, Leavis's response to Wellek (with which I agree) seems to suffice. For Blake's treatment of the Druids see Peter F. Fisher, 'Blake and the Druids,' *Blake: A Collection of Critical Essays*, ed. Northrop Frye (Englewood Cliffs, N.J.: Prentice-Hall, 1966), pp. 156–78. Also A. L. Owen, *The Famous Druids* (London: Oxford University Press, 1962), and Stuart Curran, 'The Key to All Mythologies,' *Shelley's Annus Mirabilis* (San Marino, Calif.: Huntington Library, 1975), pp. 33–94, for late eighteenth-century attitudes to the Druids.

17 *Selected Poems*, p. 113.

18 *Contrary States*, pp. 155–6.
19 See, for example, Adams, *Shorter Poems*, p. 26.
20 *Dictionary*, p. 25.
21 July 6, 1803, in Keynes, *Letters*, p. 68.
22 *Apocalypse*, p. 138. See also Thomas Frosch, *The Awakening of Albion* (Ithaca, NY: Cornell University Press, 1975), the central thesis of which, brilliantly argued, is that 'Blake is never willing in any way to renounce the here-and-now, or to surrender his conviction that the body will be risen in the world ... Blake is not interested in any God, paradise, or fulfillment which is not available to the immediate experience of the body ... when what we take to be ultimate reality is removed from the world of appearances, so too is paradise, which is the state of our complete involvement in that reality' (p. 26).
23 The only exception I have encountered is in copy E, where the child seems to be smiling.
24 See Bateson, *Selected Poems*, p. 114.
25 *Apocalypse*, p. 140. Frye, of course, places the Bard among the heroic, 'Reprobate' class ('Blake's Introduction to Experience,' *Blake: A Collection of Critical Essays* (Englewood Cliffs, NJ: Prentice-Hall, 1966), p. 31.)
26 'A View of the Present State of Ireland,' 1596, in *The Complete Works in Verse and Prose*, ed. Alexander B. Grosart (10 vols, London: Hazell, Watson & Viney, 1882–4), IX, p. 69.
27 For English interest in and portrayal of the Druids in the late eighteenth century see Fisher and Owen (previously cited in footnote 16).
28 *Fearful Symmetry*, p. 175.
29 Ed. Ernest de Selincourt, rev. Helen Darbishire (Oxford: The Clarendon Press, 1959), p. 75n.
30 See David V. Erdman, *A Concordance to the Writings of William Blake* (2 vols, Ithaca, NY: Cornell University Press, 1967) I, pp. 547–8.
31 *Dictionary*, p. 36.
32 *IB*, p. 380. For the Dante Illustrations see Albert S. Roe, *Blake's Illustrations to the Divine Comedy* (Princeton University Press, 1953).
33 We see him again, seated at his harp, on the title-page to another of Gray's poems, 'The Triumphs of Owen. A Fragment,' a work of exceeding violence and one we are to view as his creation. See Irene Taylor, *Blake's Illustrations to the Poems of Gray* (Princeton University Press, 1953), pp. 94–100.
34 'Edgar Allen Poe,' *D. H. Lawrence: Selected Literary Criticism*, ed. Anthony Beal (New York: Viking Press, 1966), p. 338.
35 *Keynes Festschrift*, pp. 83–4.
36 *Contrary States*, p. 129.

37 See Blake's ten watercolors of 1805 for Thomas Butts on the life of Moses, the unifying theme of which, according to Bindman, 'appears to be Moses' opposing roles of prophet and law-giver' (*Artist*, p. 143).

38 *Apocalypse*, p. 35.

39 Gillham, *Contrary States*, p. 75.

40 The proximity of 'Earth's Answer' and 'To Nobodaddy' (with its 'silent and invisible/Father of Jealousy' hiding himself 'in clouds,' 'darkness,' 'obscurity,' and 'all thy words and laws') in the *Notebook* is worth noting at this point. 'Earth's Answer' appears on page 109, and 'To Nobodaddy' on page 108. Erdman, in *The Notebook of William Blake: A Photographic and Typographic Facsimile* (Oxford: The Clarendon Press, 1973), p. 54, places them very close in order of composition.

41 *IB*, p. 72. In emblem 36 of the *Notebook*, ed. Erdman, p. N57, a similarly reclining, though clothed, figure is clearly male.

42 See Keynes, *Songs*, pl. 30, Bentley, *Books*, p. 397, and Grant, *VFD*, p. 350n.

43 *Selected Poems*, p. 113.

44 Hence the following well-known passage from the *Marriage*: 'The Cherub with his flaming sword is hereby commanded to leave his guard at tree of life, and when he does, the whole creation will be consumed, and appear infinite and holy whereas it now appears finite and corrupt. This will come to pass by an improvement of sensual enjoyment' (14: E38).

45 Damon, *Philosophy*, p. 239.

46 Beer, *Humanism*, p. 72.

47 Adams, *Shorter Poems*, p. 252.

48 *Contrary States*, pp. 220, 222.

49 The vacant or unseeing eyes of the cattle are like those of all animals when tending to the body's needs. Where the beast's eyes are closed, in copies M and W, for example, Blake is creating a similar impression in a different way.

50 Both quoted in Darton, *Children's Books*, p. 62.

51 Newbery's high-spirited good-humor (nowhere more succinctly characterized than in his motto to *The Twelfth Day Gift* (1767): 'Trade and Plumb-cake for ever, Huzza!') was everywhere at variance with the earnest, admonitory tone of more pious predecessors. He was the first 'respectable' children's bookseller to include chapbook material in his publications. 'Delectando monemus. Instruction with Delight,' was an apt motto for all his juvenile books, not just the famous *A Pretty Little Pocket Book* (1744).

52 At one point, perhaps as early as 1787, he may even have considered calling the combined *Songs* 'Ideas of Good and Evil,' the inscription which appears on page 4 (originally 14, facing the

first emblem drawing) of Blake's Notebook. 'This page,' writes Erdman, 'may represent Blake's earliest use of the Notebook ... the pencilled title, "Ideas of Good and Evil" (Msc 1), was inscribed as a title for the emblem scenes beginning on the facing pages; it was written ... in 1787' (*Notebook*, ed. Erdman, p. N14).

53 In the first place, Blake's use of the terms, and attitude towards them, changed over time, though he always retained the broader sense for which I am arguing. Bindman, in 'Blake's Gothicizing Imagination,' in Paley and Phillips, ed., *Keynes Festschrift*, pp. 29–49, and *Artist*, pp. 111ff, is particularly careful and clear about these shifts.

54 'Norm and Form,' in *Norm and Form: Studies in the Art of the Renaissance* (1966; rpt Oxford: Phaidon Press, 1978), p. 83.

55 *On German Architecture – D. M. Ervini a Steinbach* (1773), excerpted in Eitner, ed., *Neoclassicism and Romanticism*, I, p. 77. In those copies in which the vegetation stops half way across the plate (as in the original copies) Blake finds other ways to create his arch. In copy C, for example, the lower line of a patch of blue sky in the top left corner extends the arc of the curving foliage. In copies M and R, the foliage-arch has become the ledge of a cave – a cave from out of which we look (as in the frontispiece to *Visions*), and into which the Bard and the child are heading. For a strikingly similar example of contrasting frontispieces see 'Mirth' and 'Melancholy,' the opening designs to Blake's watercolor illustrations for *L'Allegro* and *Il Penseroso*.

56 As in the design to the experienced 'Nurse's Song,' there is no actual building here, just a bit of architectural backing. The formality of its style, though, suggests the interior of a church, rather than the outer wall of a cemetery or garden (Erdman's two other suggestions in *IB*, p. 71).

57 Perhaps the 'Couch of Death' Erdman talks of in *Prophet*, p. 79n: 'a frequent symbol in Blake's drawings: the human body lying lifeless as a copper-gilt effigy, pillowed, supine, the bedclothes like fluted marble.'

58 *IB*, p. 71.

59 *Songs*, pl. 29.

60 *IB*, p. 72.

61 *Transformations*, pp. 120–1.

62 *Artist*, p. 102.

63 Rosenblum, *Transformations*, pp. 65ff.

64 *Lyric Poetry*, pp. 66–7.

65 This is true for all copies of *Experience* I have seen. For an analogous motif, one in which creatures really do feed on one another, see plate 6 of *America*.

66 Erdman's phrase, from *IB*, p. 81.

67 See Janet A. Warner, 'Blake's Use of Gesture,' *VFD*, pp. 174–95, for a discussion of figures of this sort in Blake's work as a whole.
68 Erdman, *IB*, p. 82.
69 Gillham, *Contrary States*, p. 150.
70 *IB*, p. 73.
71 *Ibid.*, p. 16.
72 See, in addition to the title-page, plate 2 of 'The Little Girl Found,' 'The Angel,' and 'A Little Boy Lost.'
73 *Songs*, pl. 28. In his commentary to the Blake Trust facsimile of *There Is No Natural Religion* Keynes says ivy symbolizes the unpleasant qualities of material existence (2 vols, London: The Trianon Press, 1971), n.p. Here too, though, he gives no reason.
74 *IB*, p. 71. Though the decoration in some copies (E, I, N, W, and Y, for example) is tinted green, nowhere have I found a copy 'alive' (Erdman's phrase) with 'elaborate' foliage. Uncolored copies come closest to Erdman's description, since the original etched lines are allowed to show through.
75 The dead children of the 'Holy Thursday' design are no mere fantasy. Stone, *Family*, p. 70, refers to the spectacle of dead babies littering the streets of eighteenth-century England. On plate 9 of *Europe*, a similarly seductive beauty masks underlying malignancy: only gradually do we associate the design's graceful and energetic figures with mildews blighting ears of corn.
76 *Ibid.*, p. 75.
77 Bateson, *Selected Poems*, p. 112.

Chapter 6   False innocence

1 *The Collected Works*, ed. W. M. Rossetti (2 vols, London: Ellis & Scruton, 1886), I, p. 460.
2 Charles Dickens, *David Copperfield* (Harmondsworth: Penguin, 1966), p. 70.
3 W. H. Stevenson, ed., *Blake: The Complete Poems* (London: Longman, 1972), p. 219n.
4 *The Charity School Movement* (Cambridge University Press, 1938), p. 103.
5 *Contrary States*, p. 194. See also the Notebook fragment, 'An Answer to the parson,' immediately preceding the draft version of 'Holy Thursday': 'Why of the sheep do you not learn peace/ Because I don't want you to shear my fleece' (E461).
6 *Energy and Imagination*, p. 64.
7 *Introduction*, pp. 219, 220.
8 *Ibid.*, p. 221.
9 Though in the earlier 'To Spring,' from *Poetical Sketches*, the season is apostrophized as Christ-like redeemer, the redemption it

brings is wholly natural; and earth is to be its bride in the manner of the Song of Songs: 'O deck her forth with thy fair fingers; pour/Thy soft kisses on her bosom: and put/Thy golden crown upon her languish'd head,/Whose modest tresses were bound up for thee!' (13–16: E400).

10 Blake makes the point explicit in *Jerusalem*: 'You accumulate Particulars, and murder by analyzing, that you/May take the aggregate; and you call the aggregate Moral Law:/And you call that swelled and bloated Form; a Minute Particular./But general forms have their vitality in Particulars: and every/Particular is a Man; a Divine Member of the Divine Jesus' (4.91.26–30: E249).

11 Bloom, *Apocalypse*, p. 146. See also, for example, Damon, *Philosophy*, p. 279, or John E. Grant, 'Two Flowers in the Garden of Experience,' *William Blake: Essays for S. Foster Damon*, ed. Alvin H. Rosenfeld, (Providence, R. I.: Brown University Press, 1969), p. 342. Henceforth cited as *Damon Festschrift*.

12 *Lyric Poetry*, p. 24.

13 *Damon Festschrift*, p. 345.

14 *Introduction*, p. 257.

15 *Damon Festschrift*, p. 342.

16 *Lyric Poetry*, p. 24.

17 *IB*, p. 85. See also Grant, *Damon Festschrift*, p. 348: 'It is noteworthy ... that ... the Lilly is apparently never colored in vivid reds, oranges, or yellows, and is depicted as so lowly as to be almost "modest."'

18 Bloom, *Apocalypse*, pp. 148–9, Wagenknecht, *Night*, pp. 103–6, Hirsch, *Introduction*, pp. 255–6.

19 'The Complexities of Blake's "Sunflower": An Archetypal Speculation,' *Blake: A Collection of Critical Essays*, ed. Northrop Frye (Englewood Cliffs, NJ: Prentice-Hall, 1966), p. 63.

20 Erdman, *Notebook*, p. N114. Hirsch, *Introduction*, p. 226, mistakenly attributes these lines to a Swedenborgian 'Angel.' The Notebook clearly attributes them to a Devil.

21 *Contrary States*, p. 87.

22 *Lyric Poetry*, p. 65.

23 *Contrary States*, p. 87.

24 *Apocalypse*, p. 154.

25 *Introduction*, p. 278.

26 *Blake's Innocence*, p. 179.

27 'The Fly' is one of the most enigmatic of the Songs of Experience. Its many revisions in the Notebook betray 'greater uncertainty than the draft of any other poem by Blake' (Hirsch, *Introduction*, p. 236), and the critics are deeply divided about the design as well as the poem. My reading is closest to that of W. H. Stevenson,

Poems, p. 221n. I distrust the speaker, and think the ease with which he slides into generalizations about the fly he has killed a sign of callousness. 'Why bother?' seems to me the meaning of the poem's much-debated conclusion. The speaker accepts the world as one of blind and meaningless destruction. We are to think of him as a child already grown into experience but affecting innocence. His 'logic,' like that of the eponymous speaker of 'A Little Boy Lost,' is a product of his education. Hence the design's instructional theme, and its implied progression into casual violence. 'The Fly,' like 'A Dream' in *Innocence*, is in part concerned with the treatment of animals, a traditional theme in juvenile literature. For other, more complimentary treatments of the poem's enigmatic speaker see John E. Grant, 'Interpreting Blake's "The Fly," ' *Bulletin of the New York Public Library*, LXVII, 9 (November 1963), pp. 593–612, a response to and survey of the critical controversy surrounding Leo Kirschbaum's 'Blake's "The Fly," ' *Essays in Criticism*, XI (April 1961), pp. 154–62; also Jean H. Hagstrum, ' "The Fly," ' *Damon Festschrift*, pp. 368–82.

28 *Apocalypse*, p. 149.
29 *Contrary States*, p. 178.
30 *IB*, p. 86.
31 One of the few generalizations Erdman is prepared to make about the consistency of Blake's use of symbols concerns interlinear decoration: 'Small images of flames or flowers or birds, closely applied to particular words, are I believe uncomplicated in their message as notes of approval or warning' (*IB*, p. 20). The same is surely true of decorative thorns and roots.
32 *Contrary States*, p. 178.
33 *Ibid.*, p. 201.
34 *Idem.*
35 Dickens, *David Copperfield*, p. 64.
36 'The Schoolboy' was originally included in *Innocence*. It remained there in copies A–K, O, Q, R, and S of *Songs*, but was switched to *Experience* for copies L–N, P, T–Z, and AA. Copies O, Q, R, and S, though, seem to have been formed by the addition of *Experience* to an already extant copy of *Innocence* (see Bentley, *Books*, pp. 418–21.)
37 *Before Victoria* (London: Chatto and Windus, 1956), p. 111.
38 *The Age of Revolution: Europe 1789–1848* (London: Sphere Books, 1973), p. 300. See also Willey, *Background*, p. 208.
39 *Prophet*, p. 254.
40 *Original Stories from Real Life*, ed. E. V. Lucas (London: Dutton, 1922), p. iii.
41 Still, though, it is only by 'considering what he ought to do that we shall see what he ought to be' (*Émile*, p. 17).

42 'New Uncommercial Samples: Mr. Barlow,' in *All the Year Round*, No. 7, n.s., 16 January 1869, pp. 156–9, quoted in Stewart and McCann, *Innovators*, p. 27.
43 *The Prelude*, V, ll. 328–9, in *William Wordsworth The Prelude: A Parallel Text*, ed. J. C. Maxwell (Harmondsworth: Penguin, 1972), p. 187.
44 Pp. 33–4.
45 Thomas Day, *The History of Sandford and Merton: A Work Intended for the Use of Children* (3 vols, London: Stockdale, 1783) I, p. 12. Squire Merton's reply to Henry's extraordinary speech sets the book's plot in motion: 'Upon my word ... the little man is a great philosopher, and we should be much obliged to Mr. Barlow, if he would take on Tommy under his care.'
46 *Prelude*, V, ll. 313–14, p. 185.
47 See Muriel Jaeger, *Before Victoria*, pp. 105–17, for a discussion of Malkin and the model child.
48 See Wilson, *Life*, p. 218.
49 That the father's conscience was troubled is clear not only from his frequent protestations, but from the fact that four years earlier he had insisted upon an autopsy to disprove accusations that the child's death had been caused by brain disease, the result of force-fed overstudy.
50 Quoted in Benjamin Heath Malkin, *A Father's Memoirs of his Child* (London: Longmans, 1806), pp. 18–19, 36–8.
51 Young Malkin had read a number of the sort of books in which model children appeared: 'My dearest Mother,' he writes, 'I was four years old yesterday. I have got several new books; Mrs. Trimmer's *English Description; Mental Improvement* by Priscilla Wakefield and a Latin Grammar and English prints. I think I have got a great many besides the old ones that I had before' (*Ibid.*, p. 14).
52 *Before Victoria*, p. 107.
53 Eudo C. Mason, ed. and intro., *The Mind of Henry Fuseli. Selections from his Writings* (London: Routledge & Kegan Paul, 1951), p. 172.
54 Stewart and McCann, *Innovators*, p. 45.
55 *Harry and Lucy*, a collection of stories in the earlier *Practical Education* (1798), was one of ten parts of Edgeworth's *Early Lessons* (1801).
56 The earliest references to Rousseau, in *The French Revolution* (1791), are positive. But by 1795, in *The Song of Los*, Blake has begun to associate him, according to W. H. Stevenson, with Law and Reason (*Complete Poems*, p. 245n), though Erdman, *Prophet*, p. 258 n, would disagree.
57 Claire Tomalin, *The Life and Death of Mary Wollstonecraft* (New York: Harcourt, Brace Jovanovich, 1974), p. 33.

58 G. W. Gignilliat, *The Author of Sandford and Merton* (New York: Columbia University Studies in English and Comparative Literature, 1932), p. 83.

59 David V. Erdman, 'Coleridge, Wordsworth and the Wedgwood Fund,' *Bulletin of the New York Public Library* LX (Sept.–Oct. 1956), pp. 425–43, 487–507.

60 'Him, the author of the Songs of Innocence got on ill with and liked worse,' comments Alexander Gilchrist, *The Life of William Blake*, ed. Ruthven Todd (1863; rpt London: J. M. Dent 1942), p. 92.

61 Cornelia Meigs, Anne Thaxter Eaton, Elizabeth Nesbitt, and Ruth Hall Viguers, *A Critical History of Children's Books in English from Earliest Times to the Present* (New York: Macmillan, 1953), pp. 82–3. Meigs's view is supported by Dennis M. Welch, 'Blake's Response to Wollstonecraft's Original Stories,' in *Blake: An Illustrated Quarterly*, vol. 13 no. 6 (Summer 1979), p. 5. For a biographer who identifies Mary Wollstonecraft with Mrs Mason see Emily W. Sunstein, *A Different Face: The Life of Mary Wollstonecraft* (New York: Harper and Row, 1975), p. 165.

Chapter 7   The Bard redeemed

1 Orc, 'the terrible fiery boy' (*FZ* 5.62.25: E335) whose appearance in the prophetic books signals sexual as well as political and social revolution, has locks 'like the forests/Of wild beasts there the lion glares the tyger and wolf howl there' (*FZ* 5.61.25: E335).

2 *Introduction*, p. 222.

3 *Ibid.*, pp. 222–3.

4 Adams, *Shorter Poems*, p. 211.

5 *Ibid.*, p. 213.

6 *The Uses of Enchantment: The Meaning and Importance of Fairy Tales* (New York: Vintage, 1977), p. 8.

7 Erdman, *IB*, p. 92.

8 A similar point is made, in a somewhat different fashion, in Blake's series of designs to Milton's *L'Allegro* and *Il Penseroso*, the dates of which, 1816–20, correspond to those of Blake's fixing of the order and number of plates in Z and other late copies of *Songs*. Blake's designs to *L'Allegro* and *Il Penseroso* follow tradition to the extent that they imagine Milton himself embodying the poems' shifting moods. What is new is the story they tell: that of what I take to be their creator's spiritual fall and partial regeneration, in crucial respects similar to the story we have been tracing for the Piper–Bard. *L'Allegro* and *Il Penseroso* are, of course, early works, and Blake interprets them as Milton's

Innocence and *Experience*, with numerous pictorial echoes of the former series. At the end, Milton is depicted 'in his old Age' (Bentley, *Writings*, II, p. 1838), in a design as richly qualified as 'The Voice of the Ancient Bard.' The lines it illustrates strike a note of comparably elegaic promise:

> And may at last my weary age
> Find out the peaceful hermitage
> The hairy grown and mossy cell
> Where I may sit and rightly spell
> Of every star that heaven doth shew,
> And every herb that sips the dew,
> Till old experience do attain
> To something like prophetic strain (11.167–74).

The visual equivalent of Milton's soft but unbowed 'something like prophetic strain' is the image of blind Milton 'in his Mossy cell Contemplating the Constellations' (Bentley, *Writings*, II, p. 1838), heavily robed, seated not upright, underground, with long hair but no beard, and a huge volume, which must surely be the visionary but deeply flawed *Paradise Lost*, by his side. Aged Milton, in other words, is a picture of Blake as Blake saw himself in the 1820s, when he fixed the order of *Songs*: as the only partially redeemed 'Ancient Bard' of 1794, about to embark upon his major prophecies.

9 Other copies in which he wears blue are I, O, T, and AA.
10 Of indeterminate sex in most copies. Female in Y.
11 See note 62, chapter 3.
12 The Bard is by no means the only one of Blake's characters to change his appearance over the course of an Illuminated Book. Los, for instance, a figure much like the Piper–Bard, grows from young man to bearded oppressor (plate 21) in *The Book of Urizen*.
13 John the Baptist as 'just man' in the 'wilds' (*MHH* 2.16, 19: E33) is displaced by a false prophet associated with Law (note the mosaic tablet-like tombstone and book in plate 1), the false piety of 'the sneaking serpent' who 'walks in mild humility' (*MHH* 2.17–18: E33) (note the upturned gaze of the figure on plate 1), and unearthliness (note the cloud-couched figure on plate 4, up aloft, like Nobodaddy).
14 Hagstrum, *Poet and Painter*, pp. 127–8, would add several others to the list, as would Mellor, *HFD*, pp. 149ff.
15 Though Mellor, *HFD*, p. 141, would disagree.
16 Other copies in which both figures are garbed in blue are O, T, and AA. In E, P, and S, they both wear grey. In Y they both wear yellow.
17 *IB*, p. 87.

18 For a reading of 'London' that pays similarly close attention to the character of the speaker (and finds it equally disturbing), see Heather Glen, 'The Poet in Society: Blake and Wordsworth on London,' *Literature and History*, no. 3 (March 1976), pp. 2–28. E. P. Thompson, in 'Blake's London,' *Interpreting Blake*, ed. Michael Phillips (Cambridge University Press, 1978), pp. 5–39, Raymond Williams, *The Country and the City* (London: Oxford University Press, 1975), pp. 142–52, and Erdman, *Prophet*, pp. 276–9, show just how firmly rooted London is in contemporary social and political controversy.

19 Stan Smith, in 'Some Responses to Heather Glen's "The Poet in Society",' *Literature and History*, no. 4 (Autumn 1976), pp. 94–8, recalls the Mark of Cain (Genesis 4:35); Thompson, 'Blake's London,' p. 121, the 'mark of the beast' in Revelation.

20 *Introduction*, p. 263.

21 *IB*, p. 88.

22 See, also, the title-page to *America*, on which children and naked youths instruct bent and gown-shrouded adults in the ways, presumably, of liberty.

23 What his expression is is less important than that he has one.

24 *VFD*, p. 420n.

25 In plate 84 of *Jerusalem* we see the same old man being guided by a child towards an open door. Lines 11 to 12 – 'I see London blind and age-bent begging thro the Streets/Of Babylon, led by a child. His tears run down his beard' – identify him with the city. For an extended discussion of the relation of this plate to the 'London' design see Kenneth R. Johnston, 'Blake's Cities,' *VFD*, pp. 417–22.

26 Hirsch, *Introduction*, p. 265.

27 Erdman, *IB*, 29.

28 See Stevenson, *Complete Poems*, p. 590; also textual notes from E714, 722, 737–8, the last of which shows how hard it is to unravel the complexities of the *Vala* or *The Four Zoas* manuscript. The basic narrative of *Vala* was probably finished about 1800. Sometime around 1804, though, Blake added new material of a decidedly Christian character: a 'Council of God,' led by Jesus, the Divine Mercy, now resides in Eternity; a 'Divine Hand' directs many of the narrative's most crucial events; a Blakean version of the Atonement, in which Jesus takes the place of Luvah, Urizen's special enemy, helps lead to the Universal Man's (or Albion's) redemption. Bentley, *Writings*, I, pp. 681–2, conjectures a much earlier date, '? 1797,' for 'To Tirzah,' though he too locates many of the later Christian additions within 1803–5 (*Writings*, II, pp. 1722–5).

29 See footnote 1, chapter 5.

30 *Lyric Poetry*, pp. 69–70.

31 *Introduction*, p. 290.
32 See Blake's letter to Thomas Butts, *c.* 1818, in Keynes, *Letters*, pp. 179–81.
33 *IB*, p. 88.
34 *Apocalypse*, pp. 155–6.
35 *Songs*, pl. 52.
36 *IB*, p. 90.

INDEX

Paradise, 4–5, 25, 32, 150
For the Sexes: The Gates of Paradise, 25
Four Zoas, The, xix, 29, 48, 68, 93, 113, 130, 138, 141, 143, 188, 191, 201; *see also Vala*
Franklin, Benjamin, 23
Frontispiece (*Experience*), 131, 133–4, 136, 140–51, 153, 154, 156, 198
Frontispiece (*Innocence*), 61–4, 63, 70, 86, 115, 116, 131, 136, 147
Fry, Roger, 53
Frye, Northrop, xiii, xiv, 33, 51, 95, 116, 133, 134, 135, 137, 200
Fuseli, Henry, 29, 53, 58, 119

'Garden of Love, The,' 171, 172–4, 175, 177, 195
Gargantua (Rabelais), 25
Garrick, David, 2
Genesis, 133–4, 146, 186
Ghiberti, Lorenzo, 52
Giotto, 152
Gillham, D. G., 70, 76, 126, 133, 134, 140, 148, 163, 170, 173, 174
Gleckner, R. F., 19, 38, 72
Godwin, William, 3–4, 152, 183
Goethe, Johann Wolfgang von, 151
Gombrich, E. H., 58, 90, 150, 151
Gothic style, 150–1, 152–3
Grant, John E., 47, 49, 86, 132, 145, 166, 167, 192, 198
Grave, The, Blake's illustrations to, 193
Gray, Thomas, 58; Blake's illustrations to the *Poems*, 139

Hagstrum, Jean, 48, 51, 119, 131, 132
Hamilton, Gavin, 152

Hauser, Arnold, 116
Hazlitt, William, 98, 103–4, 115
Herbert, George, xviii–xix
Hirsch, E. D., 33, 54, 55, 76, 81, 84, 86, 104, 114, 163, 165, 166, 167, 170, 187, 197, 199–200, 202
History of England, 5
Hobbes, Thomas, 170
Hobsbawm, E. J., 178
Hogarth, William, 85
Holcroft, Thomas, 3
Holloway, John, 118, 153, 166, 167, 170, 199, 202
'Holy Thursday' (*Experience*), 114, 115, 153, 156, 162–6, 167, 190
'Holy Thursday' (*Innocence*), 3, 17–22, 25, 45, 51, 105, 123, 161, 162, 163, 176
Housman, A. E., xiii
'Human Abstract, The,' 168, 169, 175, 194, 198–9
hymns, 15–16
Hymns in Prose for Children (Barbauld), 2, 3, 46

iconography, 55–6, 57–9
Illuminated Blake, The (Erdman), xvii
'Infant Joy,' 51, 98, 102, 117–22, 129, 148
'Infant Sorrow,' 43, 121, 154
'Introduction' (*Experience*), xiv, xv, 132, 133, 136, 144, 149, 153, 155, 156, 157, 162, 165, 174, 194, 197
'Introduction' (*Innocence*), 33, 61, 62, 63, 69–75, 76, 83, 86, 132, 144, 160
Isaiah, 20, 136, 140
Island in the Moon, An, 2, 3, 33

Jaeger, Muriel, 177, 181
Janeway, James, 7, 8, 16, 35, 182
Jeffrey, Francis (Lord), 75